"*Awakening Joy for Kids* essentializes what's needed most in cultivating an authentic connection, offering a rare combination of heart practices with turnkey accessibility. This book is a sincere offering to parents and those of us honored to serve our youth."
— Vinny Ferraro, Mindful Schools and Against the Stream

"Chock full of easy and practical suggestions for finding joy—and peace!—as a teacher or parent, for helping children develop the skills they need for their own happiness. James Baraz is one the most important and inspirational happiness teachers alive today; if you have children or work with them, don't miss this terrific collaboration with master teacher Michele Lilyanna."
— Christine Carter, PhD, *Raising Happiness* and *The Sweet Spot*, Senior Fellow, Greater Good Science Center

"The lessons throughout *Awakening Joy for Kids* are timely as well as timeless. Knowing what brings true happiness, ease, and well-being is an important wisdom to be passed on to next generations. *Awakening Joy for Kids* has gifted parents and educators with a fun and accessible guide to teach our kids the social and emotion skills they need to live fuller, well-rounded lives."
— Kate Munding, Founder of Heart-Mind Education, creating mindfulness training for teachers

"*Awakening Joy for Kids* is the new go-to resource to help parents and teachers help children manage fears and worries and develop a deep inner wellspring of well-being. These lessons are fun, playful, practical, and easily adaptable for home and school. Well-organized and beautifully illustrated, *Awakening Joy for Kids* is kid-tested, reader friendly, and life-changing. Highly recommended."
— Linda Graham, MFT, *Bouncing Back*

"At once inspiring, practical, doable, and fun, *Awakening Joy for Kids* is for children and adults alike, making quality-of-life the highest priority. This book supports the development of the whole human being and is a much-needed addition to our curriculum for educating children in this world."
— Robert Gonzales, PhD, Co-Founder of the Nonviolent Training Institute, Past President of the Board of Directors of the Center for Nonviolent Communication

"Weaving together the discoveries of contemporary science with the real needs of children in classrooms and beyond, the authors have gifted adults everywhere a treasured resource. Central to the message is that all human beings have light, and we adults have a profoundly important role in ensuring we nurture an awakening of joy so that each child can grow and be all they were intended to be. I love this book!"

—Dr. Vanessa Lapointe, *Discipline Without Damage*

"Fresh. Friendly. Fantastic. Finally. In this era of testing and achievement, Michele and James give delightfully practical form and direction to educators, parents, and all of us humans who care about equipping our children (and ourselves) to lead joyful, resilient lives. Simple and profound, *Awakening Joy for Kids* is an inoculation against the maladies of fear and hopelessness that come when we lose track of our inherent playfulness, creativity, and wisdom. An easy, accessible reference that I will generously recommend."

—Ann McKnight, LMSW, ACSW, TEDx talk on Restorative Circles

## International Praise

"Grounded in ancient wisdom and robust contemporary science, *Awakening Joy for Kids* is a compendium of imaginative resources and practical activities that have clearly been tried and tested in homes and classrooms. Teachers, parents, and children themselves can have confidence that what is offered here has the power to transform individuals, families, and school communities."

—Chris Cullen, Co-Founder of the UK Mindfulness in Schools Project and University of Oxford Mindfulness Centre

"With the ever-increasing demands of daily life, we rarely just stop for a minute and be present in the 'here' and 'now'. *Awakening Joy for Kids* provides an easy to follow, step-by-step guide for bringing mindfulness to the lives of children and even adults. It encourages children to appreciate the small things in life and to cultivate the skills necessary to deal with everyday stressors. It fosters a sense of self-awareness, empowerment, and compassion; skills that form the core of emotionally intelligent, socially conscious children. Providing a synergy of real life experiences coupled with scientifically proven strategies, *Awakening Joy for Kids* is nothing short of amazing! A great resource for parents, teachers, and anyone looking to bring mindfulness practices into their lives."

—Amanda Fernandes, Caribbean Regional Director,
Project Happiness, Trinidad

"What a gem of a resource, offering an incredible weaving of contemplative wisdom and neuroscience into fun, easy-to-do, children-tested activities. These nourishing activities will equip our children with the much needed qualities of resilience, empathy, compassion and happiness."

—Diana Robertson, Pause, Breathe, Smile Facilitator,
New Zealand's national Mindfulness in Schools Program

"This book is a wonderful treasure trove for all adults who live or work with children! It will not only bring joy but also harmony, well-being, mindfulness, and compassion into families and help give them a solid ground to cope with the challenges of the life they will grow into."

—Lienhard Valentin, Founder/Director of Germany's
Growing with Children Program

"A treasure-trove of ideas to appeal to all styles of learner, this resource will help parents and teachers support children everywhere to 'enjoy being who they are and let their natural joy shine through'. In an environment of increased anxiety and mental unrest in children, this is a much-needed offering."

—Kellie Edwards, Psychologist, Mindfulness4Mothers
Radio and Blog, Australia

Awakening Joy for Kids

# AWAKENING JOY
## for KIDS

A hands-on guide for
grown-ups to nourish
themselves and raise
mindful, happy children

## JAMES BARAZ
## MICHELE LILYANNA
### FOREWORD BY TARA BRACH

PARALLAX
PRESS

Berkeley, California

Parallax Press
P.O. Box 7355
Berkeley, California 94707
parallax.org

Cover and text design by Gopa & Ted2, Inc.
Art and photography by Michele Lilyanna
Michele Lilyanna photo © Keith Shaw
James Baraz photo © Kathleen Harrison
Photos on pp. 1, 7, 17, 25, 26, 28, 51, 52, 53, 60, 79, 87, 89, 99, 101, 103,
113, 120, 123, 137, 147, 150, 156, 158, 163, 175, 184, 186, 198, 200, 201, 203,
205, 209, 222, 223, 230, 232, 235, 242, 244, 245, 250, 253, 258, 262, 263,
and 268 © Thinkstock
Photos on pp. 55, 111, 174, 202, 229 © Peter Francis
Photo on p. 67 © Keith Shaw

Authors' note: Most of the stories are conveyed as they actually
happened, but some stories or quotes are composites of different
people's experiences. Unless permission was specifically granted,
all names have been changed. Photos taken are taken with
permission and staged outside of school instructional hours.

Michele Lilyanna: www.happinessandjoylessons.com
James Baraz: www.awakeningjoy.info/teacher.html

ISBN: 978-1-941529-28-7

Library of Congress Cataloging-in-Publication Data
is available upon request

1 2 3 4 5 / 20 19 18 17 16

To my children, Adam and Tony, my grandchildren Jordan, Sydney, and Taylor and all the children of the world. May they be truly happy and share their love well! And to all teachers who love bringing out the best in their students. In doing so you contribute immeasurably in adding more goodness and joy to this world.
—James Baraz


To my sons, Kieran and Jaden, you make my heart shine bright. To children everywhere, thank you for the pure light you are and the  portals you open. May this offering nurture you and adults around the world.
—Michele Lilyanna

# Contents

# Foreword

"I'VE GOT TO TELL YOU what just happened with Sam!" My friend and fellow parent was so excited I could hear the enthusiasm through her voice on the phone. Her eleven-year-old son Sam had just burst into her home office declaring, "I didn't go ballistic, Mom!"

Breathless, he'd explained that his younger sister had once again trashed his treasured set of Magic cards, but this time instead of retaliating, he'd made another choice. "I remembered to take the five long deep breaths!" Sam declared triumphantly.

Sam's class at school had recently completed a mindfulness course in which they'd learned basic skills for regulating their emotions, responding to circumstances with resilience, and carefully communicating with awareness. Essentially, they'd been learning how to live a fulfilling life. The program was presented through a project called MINDS, Mindfulness in DC Schools, one of many springing up around the country.

Ever since that course began in school, Sam's mother had seen changes in her son. Sam had always seemed a somewhat anxious and self-conscious boy. Since the program, his mother said, he'd seemed more at ease. At the dinner table, he was now eager to share high points of his day. He was more playful with his sister. And he didn't "go ballistic" as often. "Mindfulness has helped him be more light-hearted," his mom told me.

As a parent and a teacher, I understand the significance of this kind of change in the children we love. This is why I am delighted to see the publication of James's and Michele's much-needed book, *Awakening Joy for Kids*. As parents and teachers themselves, both of them know how important and possible it is to nourish children's inherent creativity, compassion, and joy. This set of accessible exercises for children and adults to do together offers a way for both to bring alive the fullness of heart, mind, and spirit.

As an advisor to the MINDS program, I've heard many stories of children, parents, and teachers coming home to themselves through mindfulness practices. Parents and educators across the country are noticing the results:

positive change happens as children learn to find a refuge of inner quiet, to recognize and accept their feelings, release self-judgments, speak and listen from presence, take willing responsibility for their actions, and attune to the emotional state of others. Introducing our children to mindfulness is one of the most significant contributions we can make to our society and our world. Now *Awakening Joy for Kids* makes these powerful and enjoyable practices available for anyone.

Reading this book brought back to me some of the little mindfulness rituals my son and I developed when he was a child. At bedtimes and often before meals, we shared what we were grateful for that day. We did yoga together, and sent healing energy into tight or hurting places in our bodies. We spent a lot of time in the woods and by the ocean, learning "the law of nature."

One of our favorite practices—one that lasted well into Narayan's teen years—came from a story in one of Stephen Mitchell's books. An unhappy man traveled far to consult with a wise woman he had heard of to ask how he might find peace. The woman, Sono, gave him a mantra to say, no matter what was happening in his life: "Thank you for everything. I have no complaints whatsoever." A year later, after faithfully doing the practice, the man returned to report that he was still uneasy. What should he do? Sono said, "Say 'Thank you' for everything. I have no complaints whatsoever." As these stories go, the man immediately found happiness.

I taught that mantra to my son because he tended to be a bit of a complainer. I playfully dubbed him "King Kvetch." The mantra was a helpful clue to remind the King that things were pretty good overall, and I felt glad I could offer him this wise little technique. Then one day on the way to a dentist appointment together, we got caught in traffic and were clearly going to be late. I started complaining as my agitation mounted. Narayan elbowed me: "Hey Mom! Thank you for everything. I have no complaints whatsoever."

What we teach our children comes back to us, and when it's a practice of becoming present and opening our hearts, the benefits ripple beyond what we can imagine. Having a book like this when I was raising Narayan would have been a gift.

The Awakening Joy course and the *Awakening Joy* book for adults have transformed countless lives. I was thrilled when I heard this amazing program was being adapted so that it could be taught at home and in schools. The tone and style of this guidebook is just right—inviting, warm, clear and entirely practical.

The practices offered in *Awakening Joy for Kids* help parents, teachers, and kids to learn the pause that can make all the difference in a day, and in a lifetime. The practices and teachings in the book engage us in a shared journey with our families and our communities that contribute directly to the qualities of intimacy and love in our lives.

It gives me hope that this generation of children, like Sam, has increasing access to ways to awaken presence and compassion. I can't think of anything that has more potential to address the dis-ease of our culture and to contribute to the healing of our world. *Awakening Joy for Kids* is a rich current in this healing, and my hope is that this book will touch you and your family's life in a deep and enlivening way. Realizing the joy in being alive—our capacity for measureless love, creativity and wisdom—is the invitation of this book. All blessings as you walk this path!

—Tara Brach, author of
*Radical Acceptance* and *True Refuge*

# Introduction: Why Joy?

CAN JOY BE CULTIVATED? Would you like to teach your children practices to increase their well-being and enable them to meet inevitable stresses, with presence, self-compassion, and openness instead of fear and worry? Can adults and children simultaneously practice steps to become more resilient, compassionate human beings? When joy is awakened, does it mean one is always bright and bubbly, or can we be present to all emotions and still draw from a deep well of relaxing nourishment? Would you like to know that you are giving your children gifts that will last them a lifetime and change the very way they interact with the world?

As parents, teachers, and caregivers, if you have ever contemplated these questions, this book is for you. Our intention is for this guidebook to become a much loved, dog-eared, marked-up, living resource to awaken joy in your homes and classrooms.

**JAMES:** As a fifth-grade classroom teacher in Astoria, New York, in the seventies, my lesson plans were never going to win any awards for their brilliance. And I was sometimes criticized by my principal for not having the straightest lines when my class walked through the halls. But the kids enjoyed being there and still reach out forty years later to let me know how special it was to be in my class.

I had one rule that I stated clearly on the first day of school. The excited kids—and they *were* excited to be in the cool, longhaired teacher's class—were told that kindness was the key. If we treated each other with respect we'd have a great year together. And we usually did. When I met Michele and she shared her lesson ideas with me, I knew I had met a master teacher who embodied the principles of *Awakening Joy*. She was sparked with enthusiasm and her joy was seriously contagious. Over the years we have shared ideas and had so many that we decided to write *Awakening Joy For Kids*, a combination of wisdom practices and practical teachings for parents, teachers, and children.

Michele and I agree that classes need a spirit that goes beyond imparting a curriculum of information to be absorbed. First and foremost, we want the students to experience being part of a safe environment where they can relax, be fully themselves and delight in being together.

So often we are concerned with our children's success—whether grades or accomplishments—at the expense of their simply enjoying being who they are and letting their natural joy shine through.

*Awakening Joy for Kids* was written with this in mind. It is a guidebook for parents, caregivers, and teachers to help bring out the innate aliveness and joy that children naturally possess, combining contemplative wisdom with light-hearted, kid-tested activities. Between us, we have more than sixty years' experience teaching children and adults of all ages.

In 2003 I began teaching *Awakening Joy*, a popular online course designed to awaken our natural capacity for well-being, at times having 2,000 people going through the material together. The book based on the course, *Awakening Joy: 10 Steps to Happiness,* was first published in 2010. Through the book, the online course, and workshops led by me and my wife, Jane, in the US, Canada, Europe, Australia, and New Zealand, thousands have been inspired around the world to actively bring more joy into their lives.

## Nurture Yourself and Your Children Too

JAMES AND MICHELE: This book is for grownups and the kids they spend time with, whether at home or in school. Each theme has an introductory section with the principles and practices taken from the *Awakening Joy* course specifically for adults. These are followed by lessons that have been tested in the classroom or home, geared toward children. We suggest the grownups discover firsthand the benefit of the practices along with offering them to their kids. Why not have a happy teacher or parent share from his or her own direct understanding the principles and practices of well-being? That way it will be a genuine shared experience. Of course, the adult doesn't have to master the material before sharing it.

A main principle of the course is that it should be a nourishing experience with no pressure or guilt in not doing it the "right way." Do it in any way that is fun for you.

The first part of each chapter of this book gives practices for adults to integrate into their lives. Then, there are practices to help parents, caregivers, grandparents, and teachers guide children to become more compassionate, connected, and happy human beings. Once, as grownups, we can more easily access joy, we can cultivate well-being while we learn along with our children.

As you're more in touch with your own well-being you will model happiness for the children around you. In cultivating more joy in yourself and your children, you will also be bringing more happiness into the world around you.

## What Does It Mean to "Awaken Joy"?

Some people have trouble with the word joy. It seems too over-the-top bubbly and cheerful. We use joy to describe all the healthy states of mind that bring us ease of well-being: contentment, peace, happiness, calm, delight, and open-heartedness, to name a few. Whatever word fits your temperament and means those things to you works here.

The practices here are designed to strengthen our connections to ourselves and each other so that we can live happier and more successful lives. The lessons help develop self-knowledge, resilience, empathy, compassion, persistence, love, and caring. Children can learn how to value and understand their own thoughts and feelings as well as those of others. Grown-ups can learn how to strengthen, relax, and open their own minds as well as those of the next generation. These lessons provide a solid groundwork to encourage children to become authors of their own lives. Each lesson comes with a complete resource list of books that compliment and deepen each practice.

## Our Joy Is Connected to the Health of Our Planet

Cultivating personal joy benefits those around us and produces a ripple effect of bringing more consciousness and well-being to the planet. Our global family is growing increasingly connected; each tiny choice we make has a distinct imprint that echoes out across the Earth.

Caregivers of children have one of the most important jobs on the planet. Ask parents, relatives, caretakers, counselors, or teachers what their greatest wish is for the children they care for, and they most often say it is for their happiness. Sure, health, abundance, success, and a huge list of other dreams are mentioned, but in our experience, people report that happiness comes up first and most often. For many, happiness seems to be a dream cloud, something elusive that only a lucky few can possess if all the stars are aligned.

Change is inevitable in life, as well as pain, pleasure, and all the ups and downs of being human. But the skills that cultivate happiness can be practiced and taught, creating neural pathways in the brain. We can wire the brain and our emotional being toward happiness, and in doing so with our children they can become more resilient in the face of an ever-changing world. The University of California Greater Good Science Center publishes cutting-edge research on well-being. Their extensive research shows that increased mindfulness—a key component of *Awakening Joy*—positively affects all areas of our lives, including intelligence, energy, creativity, productivity, and resilience, while decreasing depression and anxiety. In addition, studies have shown that increased happiness lowers your blood pressure, strengthens your immune system, lessens pain of chronic disease, combats stress and disease, and lengthens your life. All this research confirms something almost everyone can agree on: we feel good when we're happy.

## How to Use This Book

The practices in this guidebook are built around ten steps that parallel the steps in *Awakening Joy: 10 Steps to Happiness* by James Baraz and Shoshana Alexander. This book stands complete on its own or can be read in combination with *Awakening Joy*. Each chapter in our book has an introduction and adult lesson so you can practice, at a deeper level, right along with your child. For teachers, we have paired the children's lessons with curriculum content areas so you can rest in knowing you are enhancing your learning outcomes with supportive lessons. We have also included a guide at the back of the book, to instruct you on how to seamlessly integrate these practices into your teaching day while honoring your current educational curriculum.

We often hear educators, parents, and caregivers say they just need something quick and easy that makes a difference. We've created each of these activities with that in mind so there is no significant planning or preparation necessary for any lesson. At the beginning of each lesson, targeted strengths we are aiming to build are highlighted so you can choose your activity to enhance specific social emotional areas.

There is also a guide for the age appropriateness of the practices, although every lesson can be modified to serve a wide range of children. Although the primary audience is elementary and pre-school age children, parents and teachers of middle school and high school children may adapt the lessons in more age-appropriate ways.

At the end of each lesson is a list of both adult and children's resources. To create ease for you, this book can be opened to any page and a simple, meaningful lesson will be available. Pick and choose one a day or one a week. Each activity builds the muscles of a joyful heart and helps children self-regulate and learn to cultivate their own happiness. You can then take each step and adapt or expand it in your own way. The practices are endless.

These activities are a guide to help create a new way of being in your body, nurturing yourself and the children around you in equal measure. You know your own rhythms and those of the children you care for and you are the best person to decide when to access what practice. Regardless of the activity, make sure your child is relaxed and at ease so that this process is fun. This is not meant to be work. If something doesn't feel right, drop it or try again another day or another way. Most of all, enjoy the process. There is no failing with this material. Practice and play with your child and be the change yourself.

One thing to keep in mind: New parents, grandparents and teachers often have an idea of "how things are going to be" and that our own children will always reflect our "good parenting." But good parenting or not, once kids come into the mix, they bring their own chemistry, personality, desires, and challenges to the equation. There is no guaranteed magical outcome and some children may resist participation strongly.

Be gentle on yourself when offering this material, let go of outcomes and know that you are planting seeds of well-being. These seeds are an offering and an invitation; ultimately it is up to the child to accept that invitation to whatever degree they choose. In our experience, we may not know until much later on that the seeds of awareness have sprouted. Do what you can and most of all nourish yourself. By awakening joy within yourself you will embody just what you're hoping to nurture in your child. This will create an inviting energetic field, increasing the likelihood that your child will join you.

## Michele's Story

MICHELE: I have been teaching many of these social and emotional skills in the classroom for twenty-five years, but was not aware of the growing body of science in neuroplasticity that could show how the changes take place in the brain. In the past fifteen years I have been studying and gathering information to support the very practices I had already been doing for years, practices designed to support the creation of happier human beings in the world. In order to test these ideas, I set about creating a curriculum based on these lessons, using many themes from my past daily teaching practice. I wanted to see if theory-based lessons matched my own experience.

In my years as a classroom teacher I have taught over a thousand children. Children with all kinds of needs pass through my doors and these lessons can be used with all of them. Moreover they've proved successful in even the most difficult situations.

"You seem so together." "Your classroom is like a love bubble." "I am so relieved to hear you struggle too." I have heard these statements more than once in my teaching career.

I was an anxious and very sensitive child. My first memory is of attending kindergarten in the late 1960s. I had never been apart from my mother for a whole day. We didn't have a car and lived in the suburbs, so attending a preschool program wasn't even an option. The idea of my mum, my anchor, walking away and leaving me was terrifying, as it is for many children.

I cried so loudly when I saw my mum and brother's heads passing by the exit window that the teacher went out and brought them back because she couldn't stand the sobbing noise I was making. She allowed my younger brother to stay for the morning. After that, I was on my own. I had to cope. The motto was, "Chin up and get on with it."

My mum and teacher didn't know any other way to help traverse the bridge from anxiety to calm in a compassionate, self-empowering way. Luckily we do now. We are now understanding neuroplasticity and ways to regulate the emotions beyond what we ever believed possible.

## How These Practices Were Developed

When I first started teaching decades ago, like most teachers, I followed the prescribed curriculum to the letter. I had been taught that spelling lasted twenty minutes, followed by writing and then math. Chop, chop. Behavior issues were something I dealt with at recess and before or after school. I was absolutely worn out trying to teach this way. I really felt I couldn't continue. I even went back to university, after receiving a scholarship for excellence in teaching, to look for another career. I realized my being mostly an introvert, loving nature, and valuing deep meaningful connection, did not fit into managing a classroom with up to thirty children, many of whom were complete extroverts.

My professor at the career department said, "Do what you love, do your passion and teach...." So I shifted to teaching part-time and dove into art lessons. I taught art after school and found I had a lot of freedom. From art classes, girls' groups to build self-esteem started. The girls were tense, scared, and frustrated. I brought in art and began doing yoga and using mindfulness techniques with them. The girls loved it. At one point I had thirty out of

thirty seventh-grade girls sign up for the after-school course. As I found things that worked, I was also maintaining my own practice of yoga, self-discovery, mindfulness, nonviolent communication, and brain-based learning. I started to bring these lessons into the classroom. In those days, people were wary of even the word "yoga," but I was also in a more "alternative" community, so when parents walked by and the class was in the tree position, they would smile. Year after year I did more and more yoga with the kids. Now twenty-five years later, I have students coming back to tell me that it changed their lives. I recently taught a parenting workshop with several of my students, now parents, soaking up the strategies to practice in their own homes.

The bonus of bringing these practices into my home and classroom for me was more than survival as a teacher. I could have a quiet mindful moment and take the kids on a mind journey from which they would come back relaxed. I had no idea then about brain-based research, as this was not well known at the time.

When mindfulness training became more mainstream, I was thrilled. I discovered brain-based research, but I found many of the programs too prescribed. Children love the lessons I am now teaching using the ten steps of *Awakening Joy* as a framework. It really is very simple and there is a huge amount of room for creativity and autonomy within the practices. I am in awe as my students open their hearts and embrace the practices that we do. They are the most real, honest, supportive group of people that I know. They give me constant feedback on my lessons and on life in the classroom itself.

The adults to whom I was teaching mindfulness were putting down the prescriptive guidebooks and asking for a quick easy lesson. They also wanted storybooks and resources to further guide them.

There are huge limitations in my day. The curriculum is increasing, and demands are huge, but honestly, these moments of mindfulness are absolute lifesavers. As the years go on, we build the muscles of awareness and our days become easier. Do I still have incredibly challenging days after which I leave the classroom exhausted and depleted? Days when I wonder if public school teaching makes any sense at all? Days when kids are unruly and I act unskillfully? Yes, of course! It is at these times I give myself the utmost care and self-compassion, chat with a friend, eat chocolate, and go in to try again the next day. As my own personal teachers have told me, the lessons build the muscle and then the compassionate consciousness arrives. To me, it is grace that allows this.

As a mother I also know that I have less and less effect on my children as they grow older. The key time—although any time to bring these practices in can help—is when your child is young. As parents we know the brain develops through interactions with its environment beginning at conception, and continues changing through adulthood. The activities we engage in help to wire the brain's circuitry. Since the brain grows most actively in early life, that is when we have the best potential to hardwire happiness into our brains.

As parents and guardians, it's natural to want to control the future and make it as rosy as possible for our children. Has this ever worked for you? Probably not, but giving your child rich skills to use in the face of crisis and anxiety can. The practices we offer will simply intertwine with your day.

By practicing these skills early on with your child, you are building emotional resilience, self-regulation, and well-being before they even enter the school system. Parents and guardians with children already in the school system or those who are homeschooling can enhance emotional well-being in colossal ways.

## My Wish

My greatest wish is for children for them to have skills to regulate their own anxiety and to have ways of moving themselves into well-being. It is through our educated parents and families that we will learn these crucial skills before entering into the school system.

Every year children and parents coming into my classroom have more and more anxiety issues. Counseling time is limited and parents don't know how to help the children they so love. When your child arrives at school, I want their teachers, principal, and support staff to have the keys to support them even when there might be an oceanful of needs but limited resources. I want teachers to have the skills to offer calm and centering practices while building a loving classroom community. I want teachers and students to realize how challenging it is to live five days a week amongst a group of twenty-five or more people and be present to their joys, pain, growth, and difficulties with a level of presence and open-heartedness that allows for individuals to be authentic and alive. I want us to celebrate meeting these challenges with as much skill as possible and to learn from unskillful actions while forgiving ourselves when we fall short. I want families to develop strength in these mindfulness practices and for children to embody an energy that comes from a loving place. I want each child's needs to matter. I want teachers to matter and for them to have vital energy at the end of the day. Pretty big wish, isn't it? But I believe it is possible.

While some of the children in your classrooms will naturally acclimatize to the hustle and bustle of school, some will cringe, some will thrive, some will develop coping skills, and some will curl up and retreat, crippled. To this day, I personally don't find having twenty-five to thirty people in a classroom easy. The introverts are seeking corners and the extroverts are gathering into groups to interact. I am watching, teaching, and trying to orchestrate a place for all to be themselves, to honor their own needs as well as those of their classmates, and *learn*.

I am lucky to live in a rural community with access to the great outdoors. We are constantly putting on our jackets and heading out to the forest, ocean, and garden to reconnect with ourselves. Inside we practice quiet mindfulness activities as well as rambunctious group activities. We try to care for the whole group. What an amazing feat this task is.

When children turn eighteen, they can leave school and choose to spend their days in ways that allow their nature to thrive. During the twelve years of school I want children to have tools to flourish in any environment.

## James's Story

JAMES: As a schoolteacher in New York City schools for ten years in the sixties and seventies, I always tried to make my classrooms fun. Besides the curriculum, I would bring in the guitar, go on cool trips, and try to create as enjoyable an atmosphere as I could. When I personally began to learn mindfulness techniques I found that sharing them in accessible ways with my children created a much more centered classroom for myself and all the kids. However, I still had quite a ways to go to discover true well-being inside. That was a process that took many more years—long after I left the classroom in 1979.

I first discovered mindfulness meditation in 1974 and knew that I'd found a path to true well-being. I was certain it would help me discover the elusive inner peace I so longed for. For the next ten years I devoted myself to studying mindfulness, particularly through intensive silent retreats of up to three months at a time. This was such a transformative process that I became a mindfulness teacher myself, eventually helping cofound Spirit Rock Meditation Center in northern California, now considered one of the most respected mindfulness retreat centers in the world.

However, as can happen, along the way I became very serious about my meditation practice—DEAD serious, with emphasis on the *dead*—and lost my joy. When I saw what had happened, I wanted to understand how the teachings could specifically focus not only on calm and inner peace, but also on true happiness and joy. Out of that intention came the *Awakening Joy* principles, course, and book, which I've had the privilege of sharing all these years.

Since that time, I've been blessed to work with and teach others the powerful practices that I've outlined in *Awakening Joy*. I've shared the course principles with thousands of people over the years and can say with utmost confidence that, when practiced with a clear intention, patience, and a positive attitude, they work.

## Our Natural State Is Joy

As babies, we come into this world with a natural joy. A baby who's been fed, diapered, rested, often squeals with delight at life on receiving some loving attention. We were all that baby at one time. And an adult in an MRI machine who is free of physical or mental stress exhibits a brain that is conscious, calm, creative, caring, and content. We don't have to look for well-being outside of ourselves. It's right inside us waiting to be remembered, accessed, and awakened. And we can help our children get in touch with that joy by teaching them simple practices and encouraging them to live from that place more and more.

Every one of us wants to be happy. Even those who like being grumpy act that way because they think it makes them feel better! The wish for happiness comes from the most basic movement of heart that wants greater well-being. Everything we do or say is based on a motivation deep within to either bring relief or improve our internal state. Even the misguided actions that lead to more suffering come from an attempt to increase our feeling of well-being.

The problem is we often don't realize which things lead to genuine happiness and which things lead to suffering.

## The Three Principles of *Awakening Joy*

The steps in *Awakening Joy* and in *Awakening Joy for Kids* are based on three underlying principles. Everything we do is motivated by the wish to feel better or feel less bad. Most of us can relate to being caught in habits that don't serve us or are even self-destructive. But we do them anyway because in the short term they make us feel good in some way. The *Awakening Joy* Three Principles are:

1. Understand where true happiness lies.
2. Take in the good.
3. Practice makes perfect.

### *The First Principle: Understand Where True Happiness Lies*

The first important principle is understanding where true happiness lies and what conditions support it. Think of times when you're feeling true well-being. I don't mean the quick hit of pleasure when you're eating a jelly donut. I'm talking about things like dancing, snuggling with your pet, having fun with your kids, or being outside in nature on a gorgeous day.

When you examine true states of healthy well-being like these, they are accompanied by a feeling of expansiveness that can be experienced in the body as well as the mind. These are directly in contrast to states of distress such as anger, worry, fear, or sadness that are accompanied by contraction or agitation in the body as well as the mind. Even wanting something might seem like a positive experience but looking at it carefully, there's a feeling of incompleteness that is really unpleasant. So what we're doing in awakening joy is first identifying and then cultivating ten different expansive states that are fundamental to true well-being.

### *The Second Principle: Take in the Good*

The second principle is a reminder to notice that these states of true well-being have a quality of uplift or gladness such as aliveness, openness, ease, relaxation, or lightness. The mind also feels invigorated and light as well. As good as these feel, we all too often miss the sweet delight of these pleasant moments. We might know we feel good but we don't take the time to feel what feeling good actually feels like. Instead we're lost in our head thinking about the past or planning the next thing to do. In fact, we're wired up to look for danger and what can go wrong. As neuroscientist Dr. Rick Hanson says, our brains are like Teflon for positive experiences and Velcro for negative ones.

By taking a few moments to truly savor the feeling of well-being, our awareness is registering the experience in a very profound way. Awareness acts like both a spotlight and a vacuum for the brain. When we're present for the uplifting experience, it's both brought to the forefront of our consciousness and registering deeply in our brain's neural pathways.

### The Third Principle: Practice Makes Perfect

As we practice letting our moments of well-being register, we begin a profound shift: instead of being stuck in the ruts of our mind, we start creating happiness grooves. This theory that repetition affects the likelihood of subsequent firing was first proposed by neuroscientist Donald Hebb in his book *The Organization of Behavior* published in 1949. Siegrid Lowel later put it into the famous neuroscience axiom: "Neurons that fire together, wire together." Hanson suggests taking 10–15 seconds to really let it sink in when you're experiencing a joyful moment and to try doing that six times in a day. (Can you handle 60–90 seconds of well-being in a day?) If you practice doing this over a two-week period, you will likely notice a significant increase in well-being.

This is because you are not only registering those feelings of well-being, but you're also getting into the habit of looking for them. We begin to "prime the brain," as Dr. Dan Siegel says, to be on the lookout for those moments. Another way of understanding this is what is referred to as the brain's "confirmation bias." That is, your brain will selectively notice what it's looking for. Why not be on the lookout for joy?

## The Ten Steps of *Awakening Joy*

With these three underlying principles, the process of *Awakening Joy* includes cultivating ten different healthy states of well-being, being present when they arise so that over time the brain becomes more and more inclined toward happiness. Although each state can be cultivated on its own, there is a logic to the particular sequence as it's presented that builds over time.

First, we start with intention to be happy, which means deciding to allow more happiness in our lives. This is Step One, the most important decision we can make. It sets in motion the whole process of inclining the mind and heart toward true well-being. Next, we learn the power of mindfulness, which is what I call the basic tool of a joyful life. As we become more present in our life we naturally develop the third state, a grateful heart.

Appreciating all the good in our lives helps us open to the inevitable difficulties that arise. Learning to be with our challenges in a skillful way is the Fourth Step in this process. The Fifth Step understands the power of integrity, not doing harm and knowing the joy of being aligned with our highest values. The Sixth Step naturally follows, the joy of letting go, learning to restrain ourselves from impulsive behavior that we will later regret.

As we act with wisdom and kindness we can experience for ourselves the Seventh Step, learning to love ourselves. We know and do what is good for us because we feel deserving of true happiness. This supports us to experience the Eighth Step, enjoying a healthy connection with others. As our connection and caring increase we enjoy the Ninth Step, expressing our compassion when we see others around us having a hard time. Finally, the Tenth Step is the joy of simply being, where we learn to truly relax and embrace what's happening right now even when it's not exciting or fun. We can learn to find joy in the ordinary moments of life and know that they are worthy of our attention.

### Create Your Nourishment List

Instead of just leaving the arising of joy to chance, it's helpful to remember what awakens it in you. To a large degree our experience of joy is supported by how much we actually nourish our spirits. Nourishing our spirits is usually connected with engaging in healthy activities and experiences. If we're too busy to nourish our spirits, we're too busy. Try this exercise to help you create your "Nourishment List," adapted from *How We Choose to Be Happy* by Rick Foster and Greg Hicks:

✳ Take four minutes to write down everything that brings you joy. The list can include the simplest thing, like watching a sunset; or something exotic, like hang-gliding; or anything in between (walking your dog, listening to music, etc.).
✳ Check all the items you do regularly in your life.
✳ Now circle the things that are realistic to include in your life these days.
✳ At least twice a week, choose to engage in one of the items as a support for awakening joy. Remember to be present for the feeling of well-being whenever it arises.

## Try This

### Is Joy the Right Word for You?

Take a few moments to reflect on how you respond to the word "joy." Notice if there is any resistance you have to the word.

If the word "joy" is a stretch or a turn-off, is there another word that resonates more for you, that authentically expresses what you are hoping to cultivate through this course such as well-being, contentment, delight, happiness, aliveness?

Substitute that word whenever you see or hear "joy." You might use a variety of words to describe these open states.

### Notice When You're Happy

To deepen our happiness, a key practice is noticing a joyful state when it's here. When we feel grateful or happy or calm or compassionate, it registers more deeply if we are present right in the middle of the experience. These moments are easy to miss unless we have our radar out for them.

### Pay Attention to When You're Feeling Good

Notice with interest how it feels in your body and mind so you can directly experience it. This is different from vaguely knowing, "I feel good." Rather, you are exploring with curiosity the landscape of well-being by exploring what it's like to feel good.

When you're in the middle of an enjoyable moment, whether it's walking, listening to music, or watching a sunset, don't miss it! Be present for these uplifting joyful experiences.

This will be an ongoing practice to awaken joy. With each theme we will introduce different healthy qualities. The key will be remembering and reminding your child to be aware of feeling any moments of well-being.

# Set Your Intention

1

## James: Practices for Grown-Ups

OUR FIRST THEME and practice is to set an intention of happiness for yourself. Even though we all want to be happy, many of us don't put this at the center of our lives. We might think: "When I go on my vacation then I'll be happy," or "When I'm with my friend I'll be happy," or "When I retire I'll be happy." Why postpone your happiness? Why not make it a priority right now?

According to neuroscientist Dan Siegel, when you get in touch with your intention to develop more well-being and joy, your brain is primed to look for opportunities that will support it. For instance, Jerry, an *Awakening Joy* course participant from Canada, was a very serious, dedicated musician. But he was finding that he was beginning to miss the joy that originally led him to play. He decided to set his intention to once again find the joy in his work. He described practicing the violin and working very hard on some new material. After an intense period of concentration, he remembered his intention to enjoy himself while playing. "I noticed a sudden impulse to move back to play some simpler material I had not returned to in awhile. I found myself almost dancing as I played and rediscovered the joy of this endeavor."

Barbara, a San Francisco Bay Area mother of two who had enrolled in the *Awakening Joy* course, was working with her intention to do chores from a more enjoyable frame of mind instead of her typical grumpiness. She experimented with bringing a new attitude to doing her finances and paying the bills, an activity she had always disliked. She said, "This time, I consciously set my intention to be open to joy doing finances, and I realized that I really enjoyed some aspects of it. I felt great after I got finished and was 'caught up!' I very much appreciated this experience."

### Putting Happiness at the Center of Your Life

Sometimes people have a hard time with the idea of putting their well-being and happiness at the center of their life. But the truth is if you're happy, everyone around you will benefit. You'll be more patient, more understanding, and more fun. It will set an excellent example for your children.

Setting an intention is *not* wishing or hoping something will happen. You are simply inclining your mind toward a particular vision. Then you make a heartfelt decision to do what you can to bring it about—in this case, the natural impulse of the heart toward making greater well-being a reality. The clearer you and your child are about opening to joy (or happiness or well-being), the more you empower your vision.

Intention is different from a goal or expectation. When you set an intention you let go of your timetable or your inner report card that measures whether you've passed or failed.

### Try This

Imagine what it would look and feel like if you put your well-being and happiness at the center of your life?"

Let yourself imagine how your life would be if you stayed connected to this intention for the next six months. What would it be like two or three years from now if you kept developing that attitude?

If this seems like a good thing to give yourself, decide right now to do your part to make it happen, and let life support you.

Take a few moments to put your intention into words. Write them down and refer to them regularly as a way to remind yourself what you want to create.

Notice if any resistance comes up for you. If it does, don't judge yourself. It's simply good information to be aware of old thought patterns getting in the way of your true well-being. Remember that if you open to greater well-being, everyone in your life will benefit.

### Widening Your Intention

Your intention can go even beyond your own happiness. Widening your intention so that your well-being benefits others as well will motivate you even more. For example, think of how your children or other loved ones will benefit from your developing more love and kindness in your life.

✳ How will developing happiness and well-being within myself benefit my child (or the children in my life)? How will it affect others in my home (or school)?

✳ Imagine having strengthened your own happiness and joy as a gift to everyone else in your life. What will this look like in your relationships with them? How will this affect them in *their* other relationships?

If this seems like a good idea, take a few moments to align your intention to be happy with the thought of benefiting others. The more encompassing your vision of happiness, the greater is the potential for joy.

## Michele: Intention Setting with Children

Children are often told what to do and when to do it. They don't think about setting their own intention or path. When I first started teaching, I set the path for all the students. Now, after many years I encourage them to set personal intentions throughout the day. Each person sets individual intentions, and we also set group intentions as a class. Setting an intention is akin to putting the rudder on a boat to guide it in stormy weather. It is also like using a map when going on a road trip. With either tool, you can change direction when you feel the need, but you are on the lookout for a clear pathway to get you where you want to go.

Here is a story of a young student in my classroom that demonstrates the usefulness and power of setting intention as a daily practice.

Journal

Nothing good ever happens. No one plays with me. ☺

Keith, a boy of eight, had a very difficult time socially. Every day there was an issue on the playground or a tussle in the classroom. He would go home and say, "Nothing good happens—ever." As you can well imagine, his parents were very worried. They would wait for his daily report on how bad things were and become agitated and scared. They came in after school to share their frustrations and concerns with me. Keith's parents wondered if they should pull him out of school and teach him at home, but both of them worked, so this option was not viable.

Along with other daily mindfulness practices, each day I encouraged Keith to write in his journal one small thing that was good or brought him joy. Slowly his story changed. Bit by bit, he acknowledged moments of joy and they started to build into something greater that he could write about in his journal. One day he filled a whole page. I also had him set an intention for his day to look out for the good things, such as when another child asked him to play or asked him to be a partner in an activity. Lo and behold, when he paid attention, he saw that he was asked to partner with others and small things did go his way. When class-sharing time came, he was able to voice a special moment and smile. He expressed that everything wasn't bad and he had shared good moments with peers in the room. The other children shared that they had fun with him too. I saw him light up when he heard this mutual joy expressed. At the end of the year, he decided to stay at the school, as he had friends to play with at recess.

I also worked with the parents and suggested that instead of looking for a report of the bad things, they might ask him what was one good thing that happened. This reinforced and helped their son remember that there were good moments in the day. I can't say every day became easy for him or that all his struggles were gone, but he began to notice good things happening and he learned to set intentions to look for the positive rather than the negative.

This chapter offers you a variety of ways to set intention with yourself and your family. For teachers, the lessons easily translate into morning classroom practices. We invite you dive in and try these practices while noticing the difference that finding the "good" makes in your days.

# Lesson 1: Setting Intention

## Inclining the Mind toward Joy

Having an intention is not wishing or hoping something will happen. And it's different from a goal or expectation. When you set an intention you let go of your timetable or report card that measures whether you've passed or failed. You are simply inclining your mind toward a particular vision. Then you make a heartfelt decision to do what you can to bring it about.—*James*

**Builds strengths of:**
- Self-awareness
- Self empowerment
- Clear vision
- Priming our brain and gearing our neural system

**Materials**
- Pencils
- Paper

**Ages**
- Preschool to adult

**School Curriculum Connections**
- Oral language
- Written language
- Listening skills
- Reading
- Social and emotional learning

One of my favorite practices is setting intention. I do it myself every day and offer my students the opportunity to practice this skill each time we meet. There is abundant research to support that just imagining an activity has an impact on neural structures. One Harvard Medical School study of music students found that subjects asked to imagine playing a five-finger piano exercise over the course of a week showed significant improvement, which was also evidenced by accompanying positive neural changes in the brain region associated with the activity (*Awakening Joy*, p. 9). Hanson points out that you can prime your brain to look for the good or the bad, so why not point yourself in the direction of well-being?

## *Practicing at Home*

How can you set intention in a sweet, effective way at home? With your child, go pour a cup of tea, put your feet up, and relax together. No time for that? Set intention on the way to school or daycare.

1. Sit with your child and put your hand on your own heart. Encourage your child to do the same with their own heart.
2. Can you feel the beat of your heart?
3. Ask each other, "What are you feeling?"
4. Ask, "What is your heart's deepest desire in this moment?"
5. Ask, "If you could bring some activities to fill this desire, what would they be?"

(You may wish to have some cards on which you have drawn pictures so younger children can simply pick a card. These picture symbols might include images of love, fun, safety, quiet, success, and connection.)

Share these ideas with others. You can light a candle, sit in a special spot to do this and make it more of a ritual, or just go around the breakfast table or share in the car on the way to school.

Share with your child that we don't always get our desire and are not attached to outcomes, but setting intention allows us to look for the good and to notice when these moments arise. We are priming the brain to look and notice.

Sometimes when a child comes home and we ask them how their day went, they may say, "Bad!" or, "Nothing good happened at all." If we can prime the senses and the brain in advance to look for the good, when your child comes home they might be able to not only acknowledge the struggles but also start to build on their successes.

By connecting at the end of the day and talking about how intentions unfolded or what the children noticed in their day, slowly children start to see that there are good moments, which may be the simplest things, such as snuggles from their dog or a hello from a friend, that can bring them joy. Our job is to point our compass in that direction and witness the moments.

> I am Tessa. I am Full
> of creativity. I need to
> express myself: Paint
> Draw, Art!

## *Practicing at School*

After a mindfulness session at the beginning of the day, I ask the children what they would like to bring into their day and to set intention around what would bring them a feeling of well-being. To get them started, I form a circle with the students and ask them to state, in one or two words, how they are feeling and what they are yearning for. Many will say they are tired and yearning for rest. Some say they are sad and yearning for a quiet day. Of course there are some who say they are flying high and just want to celebrate. Saying their needs aloud allows for the whole scope and breadth of the human experience to arise and be heard. When the students see that others like themselves experience the ebbs and flows of life, they can relax and just be with their feelings.

After the intentions are said aloud, the students go to their desks where they write one sentence of intention on a strip of sticky notepaper. Sometimes a student says, "My intention is to play video games." I look under that statement and ask what need the video game fulfills. The student might say, "Competition" or "Relaxation." I guide them to see that the video game is just a strategy to meet their need and there are many ways to meet the same need. I keep pointing them toward recognizing the need.[1]

After writing their need down, they hold their papers up to their foreheads and move into the middle of the room.

Circulating, each student reads aloud another's paper and says, "You are _____ and you are inviting _____ into your life today. I see you and honor your intention." The other partner then thanks them and says the same to them about what the intention is on their forehead.

After the students circulate, the intention is firmly embedded in every student's consciousness and is supported by the entire group. Finally, they stick their intentions to their desks and throughout the day look for evidence of them unfolding.

## Co-creating Our Day

One of our favorite parts of setting intention in the classroom is co-creating our day on the board. After sharing our intentions, we write up the needs that we hope to meet during the day. I say that not all needs will be met, but we will acknowledge the need and do our best to fit it in. Needs for play, rest, sharing, creative time, and outside time are usually part of the list and I can easily work them into the structure of the day. Children feel empowered and happy that their needs are being honored by the whole class. I, as the teacher, feel grateful for being able to hear and honor the group rather than impose a day plan upon them. I am still able to cover the academic curriculum while nurturing the social-emotional curriculum at the same time.

Throughout the day, I may ask them to stop and share with the group if their intention is unfolding. There is no push to have it unfold but there is just an acknowledgment of the intention.

> One day when I was at school I mentioned I had a headache and
> yearned for well-being. I told the children that instead of looking for
> the moments when my head hurt, I would look for the moments

1. For more information on vocabulary to do with needs, see Marshall B. Rosenberg's *Nonviolent Communication: A Language of Life*, (Encinitas, CA: Puddledancer Press, 2003.)

I felt good. Sharing the intention with the group was so powerful. At points in the day I rang a bell and we each checked in with our intention. I was amazed to find I had many moments when I felt good instead of focusing on my sickness. The children smiled at me and I felt the empowerment of the whole group. At the same time each child was holding their own intentions and sharing them throughout the day with the group. It brought us incredibly close together.—Teacher

Finally, at the end of the day children can write in their journals how they had a need honored or how they helped someone else with a need or joy. If their need or joy didn't fit in, they can reassess at the end of the day and look for ways to bring it into their evening plans.

Setting clear intention inclines our minds to look for the positive and appreciate joy unfolding.

> *Intentions create an integrated state of priming, a gearing up of our neural system to be in the mode of that specific intention: we can be readying to receive, to sense, to focus, to behave in a certain manner.*
> —Daniel J. Siegel

## Resources

### ADULT BOOKS

Lapointe, Vaness. *Discipline without Damage: How to Get Your Kids to Behave Without Messing Them Up*. Vancouver, BC: Tree Life Media, 2016.

Marshall B. Rosenberg. *Nonviolent Communication: A Language of Life*. Encinitas, CA: Puddledancer Press, 2003.

Shauna Shapiro and Chris White. *Mindful Discipline: A Loving Approach to Setting Limits and Raising an Emotionally Intelligent Child*. Oakland, CA: New Harbinger Publications, 2014.

CHILDREN'S BOOKS

Cheri J. Meiners. *Dream On!: A Book about* Possibilities. Illustrated by Elizabeth Allen. Golden Valley, MN: Free Spirit Publishing, 2015.

Tam Veilleux and Russ Cox. *Molly Kite's Big Dream*. Rancho Mirage, CA: Enchanted Forest Press, 2011.

 # Lesson 2: Drop by Drop

The more you are motivated by kindness and the desire to act from the goodness of your heart, the greater the possibility of awakening joy. —*James*

## Build your and your children's strengths:
- Self-awareness
- Awareness of others
- Well-being/balance
- Family vision or goal setting

## Materials
- Pen
- Paper
- Good intentions

## Ages
- Preschool to adult

## School Curriculum Connections
- Oral language
- Written language
- Listening skills
- Reading
- Fine arts
- Social and emotional learning

## Home and School Practice

We have so many needs to take care of: our own needs and the needs of our family members, as well as the needs of everyone we come into contact with outside the home. We can become so disconnected from valuing each other's needs that agitation can grow and grow. When it all gets too overwhelming, someone ends up yelling, "You don't care about what matters to me!"

The simple daily practice of setting intention not only allows us to know what our intentions and needs are, but also allows us to know what matters to our loved ones. This activity is a two-part process. Part one is for each family member to put on his or her own oxygen mask. It helps people access what matters to them as individuals.

Part two of this activity shines the spotlight on what brings joy to your beloved family members. For my partner, it is being alone playing a word game, while for me it is having time to paint or draw. My son Jaden would have time to build something, while my older son, Kieran, would have time to skateboard. I have to admit sometimes I am surprised at what a family member needs on any particular day, as needs are always changing.

By working together as a family, this activity provides a strategy to make life more wonderful for ourselves and each other.

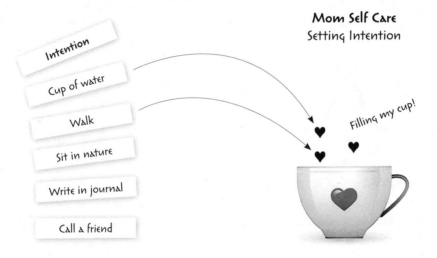

**Mom Self Care**
Setting Intention

Intention

Cup of water

Walk

Sit in nature

Write in journal

Call a friend

Filling my cup!

## Part One

The image above shows my daily intentions written on small pieces of paper on the left hand side at the beginning of this practice. On the right hand side is an empty cup. As I honor one of my intentions and enact it, I can move it over to the right hand side of the paper. This helps me keep track of my intentions for the day.

Be gentle with yourself. You may not get to all of your intentions and they may change throughout the day. The idea is to bring awareness to your needs.

Take a look and see what you might write and then follow the directions that follow to create your own intention board.

## Create Your Own List

Start by creating a list of what healthy, fun, and connecting activities are important to bring into your life today.

## Embark on This Together

If you are working on a big list as a family, you can brainstorm all kinds of things that would make life more wonderful. You can help younger children by reminding them of things they enjoy. The family list might look something like this.

| | | | |
|---|---|---|---|
| Cup of water | Build a puzzle | Share a story | Make bed |
| Stretch | Hold hands | Listen to me | Call Grandpa |
| Walk | Draw | Skateboard | Little massage |
| Meditate | Tidy two things | Water garden | Plant a seed |
| Good meal | Cuddle Mom | Clean up together | Ride bikes |
| Sit in nature | Read Aloud | Make playdough | Snuggle |
| Random acts of kindness | Go swimming | Read together | |
| Play with me | Feed Dog | Brush teeth | |

Cut the ideas into individual slips of paper. These slips can be easily moved around on your intention sheet.

## If You Want to Get Fancy

If you want to make this board more permanent, you could write the ideas with markers on stones or on Popsicle sticks. Glue small magnets on the back. These items can be moved back and forth on the fridge or a magnetic board. The children will find joy in moving the magnets or papers from side to side. They will also tell you when intentions have not received attention! If day after day you find you have moved very few papers over to the filled side of your cup, you may need to reevaluate how you spend your time. Is there a way you can get up a little earlier to have a walk or sit in nature?

## Meet Me at the End of the Day

As a family you might like to meet at the end of the day and see if you were able to move a few of your intentions across the board. Talk about how you felt when you were able to incorporate these self-nourishing practices. Talk about when you were not able to meet your intentions and how that felt. It is all part of the process. There is no beating yourself up for doing or not doing. This is meant to be joyful, not a to-do list.

## Making a Request of Another Family Member

You may also place a request on a family member's paper. Marshall B. Rosenberg, a teacher of mine, states,

It is very important to remember this request is a gift that is given. It has no strings attached or demands. It is a way for the person making the request to show what they would enjoy having in their life and for the other family member to have an opportunity to gift this person if they would find it joyful.

So to incorporate this added step of gifting others, you could have family members place a request for attention.

## Oh Honey, I Need a Little Loving

My husband wanted a cuddle and to hold hands while my son wanted to build a puzzle and have me listen to him for five minutes without saying anything. They placed their little slips of paper on my chart. Then I knew what might bring an added sense of joy to their day. I didn't always get to it but I set my own intention to gift them when I had the time and space. It made me happy to fill their requests when they were given to me without demand. This takes practice as so many of our requests are actually demands.—Parent

## Valuing Needs

Feel in your heart the wonder of filling someone else's cup and the satisfaction of caring for your own wonderful self.

## Remember the Benefits

- [ ] This practice allows us to see and feel what is important to our own well-being.
- [ ] It acts as an indicator of how we might be getting out of balance.
- [ ] It helps us tap into the needs and intentions of our family.
- [ ] It allows our children to make requests of our time and for us to make requests of theirs.
- [ ] This practice teaches us that we are mutually valuing each other, and everyone's needs matter.

## Resources

### ADULT BOOKS

Sura Hart, and Victoria Kindle Hodson. *Respectful Parents, Respectful Kids: 7 Keys to Turn Family Conflict into Cooperation*. Encinitas, CA: Puddledancer Press, 2006.

———. *The Compassionate Classroom: Relationship Based Teaching and Learning*. Encinitas, CA: Puddledancer Press, 2004.

Inbal Kashtan. *Parenting from Your Heart: Sharing the Gifts of Compassion, Connection, and Choice (Nonviolent Communication Guides)*. Encinitas, CA: Puddledancer Press, 2004.

Marshall B. Rosenberg. *Nonviolent Communication: A Language of Life*. Encinitas, CA: Puddledancer Press, 2003.

### CHILDREN'S BOOKS

J.P. Allen and Marci Winters. *Giraffe Juice: The Magic of Making Life Wonderful*. Illustrated by Tamara Laporte. Charleston, SC: CreateSpace Independent Publishing Platform, 2010.

Mercer Mayer. *I Was So Mad (Little Critter) (Look-Look)*. New York: Random House Books for Young Readers, 2000.

Jean Morrison and Christine King. *Kids GROK* (these are feelings and needs cards). Self Published, 2011.

Mo Willems. *The Pigeon Has Feelings, Too!* New York: Disney-Hyperion, 2005.

# Lesson 3: The Shredder—Start with the Negative and Move to the Positive

Are you ready to bring more joy into your life? If you are, take whatever time you need right now to make the heartfelt decision to do so. Be willing to be open and receive the feelings of well-being you are inviting.—*James*

**Builds strengths of:**
- Self-awareness
- Ability to acknowledge and let go of difficulties
- An awareness of how to set intention

**Materials**
- Paper
- Scissors
- Pen
- Shredder if handy

**Ages**
- Preschool to adult

**School Curriculum Connections**
- Oral language
- Written language
- Listening skills
- Reading
- Physical education
- Social and emotional learning

### Home and School Practice

Setting intention takes practice. This activity allows children to dig deeply into what bothers them throughout their days and helps them create a clear focus on what qualities they would like to bring into their daily awareness. Parents and teachers can do this along with the children, as many have found deep insights for themselves when delving into this practice.

Starting with the negative, or what we don't want in our lives, gives children a way to enter the positive. For many children and adults alike, negative thoughts and feelings are at the surface, blocking our way to the positive.

## Start

Settle in and do a five-minute mindfulness breathing practice to bring yourself and your child into the body and quiet the mind.

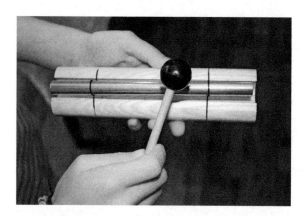

In this activity, ask your child to divide a blank piece of paper into two by folding it in half. On one side have them write, "What I don't want in my life," and on the other, "What I do want." If you have young children, you can write for them while they speak or they can draw pictures to show the images. You can do the activity with them and share your inner knowledge afterward.

Children need to know they can share anything, and while you may not be able to fix or change the things, you can listen without judgment. The more you build this trust, the more willingly they will share the deep burdens that they feel.

At this point when I am working with children, I share with them some of the things I have written that I do not want in my life. Sharing and being vulnerable in front of the children opens the doorway for them to be open.

I might write, for example:

I don't want

* Sadness
* Tightness in my stomach

* To be judged
* To overeat

I then ask them to write as many things as they would like on the "don't want" side. Many, many children write that they do not want to have fighting in their house, poor grades, too many activities, etc.

When everyone has exhausted this—some write much more than others—I ask them to draw a line to connect each "don't want" to each "do want." I might do one on the board that looks like this:

### Don't Want to Do Want:

Don't want sadness→want joy and ease

Don't want tightness in my stomach→want relaxation and acceptance

Don't want to be judged→want to be accepted

Don't want to overeat→want to eat mindfully

I then ask them for examples that they might have that they are stuck on. This question has two purposes. First, it shows them how to translate the negative of what we do not want into what we do want. This is a skill I come back to time and time again. Second, it brings in a sense of vulnerability to the group and allows others to know that we can all feel the same and it is okay.

Finally, I ask them to cut their papers in two. They keep the "do wants" in a very special place. I ask them to refer to this list whenever possible.

With great ceremony I tell them I have something to take away their "don't wants" ... it literally eats them. I go to the office and bring down the paper shredder. Each student walks to the shredder and says aloud, "I let go of these things in my life I don't want and open to what I do want." Physically shredding the list is such a relief.

In the past, when we were allowed to build fires on the school grounds, I have taken the shredded bits and had the class burn them in a circle to surrender them to the universe. If you don't have access to a firepit, you might like to take the kids outside and have them dance, yell and jump around, physically letting go of their "don't wants."

### Resources

#### ADULT BOOKS

James Baraz and Shoshana Alexander. *Awakening Joy: 10 Steps to Happiness*, Berkeley, CA: Parallax Press, 2012.

Rick Hanson with Richard Mendius. *Buddha's Brain: The Practical Neuroscience of Happiness, Love, and Wisdom*. Oakland, CA: New Harbinger Publications, 2009.

#### CHILDREN'S BOOKS

Chris Haughton. *Shhh! We Have a Plan*. Somerville, MA: Candlewick Press 2014.

Cheri J. Meiners. *When I Feel Afraid*. Golden Valley, MN: Free Spirit Publishing, 2003.

Cheri J. Meiners, M.Ed. and Elizabeth Allen. *Bounce Back!: A Book about Resilience*. Golden Valley, MN: Free Spirit Publishing, 2003.

Watty Piper. *The Little Engine That Could*. New York: Grosset & Dunlap, 2012.

# Mindfulness Matters

# 2

### James: Practices for Grown-Ups

MINDFULNESS IS THE underpinning for all the other practices in this book. We are now in the middle of a "Mindfulness Revolution"; it is appearing on the cover of *TIME* magazine, in best-selling books, and being taught in schools, businesses, hospitals, prisons, and senior centers.

As a father, grandfather, and former schoolteacher, I can attest to the positive benefits of mindfulness. Mindfulness is simply being aware of what is happening right now without wishing it were different, enjoying the pleasant without holding on when it changes (which it will), and being with the unpleasant without fearing it will always be this way (which it won't). With greater mindfulness, we become less reactive, more interested and more attuned to what's really going on inside of the young person. When a child feels understood, he or she is able to trust and feel safe around us.

Although mindfulness is sometimes associated with quietly sitting in a meditative manner, that is only one method to develop it. There are countless ways to be mindful since we are simply bringing a kind, interested awareness to any activity we're engaged in. Michele has developed some simple, effective exercises for the classroom and home that have been used with great success. I think you'll find that your child or children will enjoy and benefit from them.

## Mindfulness as Appreciation Practice

Mindfulness is really the art of appreciating the moment just as it is. You're not merely waiting for pleasant moods in order to be open to well-being. You can be present for whatever is happening. Instead of leaning forward into the future, looking back at the past or being lost in fantasies of what you long for or fear, when you're mindful you are brought into the immediacy of the moment. You can appreciate whatever your experience is as a sacred moment of life worthy of your attention.

By valuing mindfulness, you are simply encouraging your child's natural sense of wonder. In the process you will begin to slow down enough to see the world through the eyes of a child as you become more present for your life. If you want to fully enjoy life, developing an attitude of mindful appreciation is a prerequisite. With mindfulness we expand our usual tunnel vision to notice what is good or interesting around us. Instead of being wary of what can go wrong, we can look for what can uplift us right here, right now.

Here's a mindfulness exercise of appreciating the moment:

✳ For the next two minutes, notice everything in your actual experience to appreciate in this moment, for instance: "I'm able to hear sounds," "My body is breathing and keeping me alive."

✳ Notice how it feels to turn your attention to appreciating what's happening in your experience right now.

Whether you're a child or an adult, mindfulness is central to awakening joy for two reasons. First, it has the unique quality of developing many other healthy mind states such as generosity, kindness, and clarity, while weakening painful mind states such as anger, greed, and confusion.

Second, mindfulness actually amplifies states of well-being. When you are in an uplifting state and feeling good there is an accompanying gladness of heart. Being present for that gladness or expansive feeling when it arises is one of the main principles of the course. Bringing mindful attention directly to this feeling increases the gladness. So mindfulness is the tool we use to notice these states and deepen their impact.

## Four Properties of Mindfulness

There are four characteristics intrinsic to mindfulness:

1. We recognize what our actual experience is. If we're sad, we're sad. If we're tired, it's okay to be tired. If we're peaceful, we're peaceful. Mindfulness calls it like it is without embellishing our experience, making it more dramatic and intense or pretending it's not as difficult as it is. We are completely honest with ourselves about what is happening.

2. Mindfulness means being here in the present moment instead of in the past or future or lost in fantasy, which is where we often find ourselves.

3. As we pay attention, we begin to see for ourselves that the present moment is constantly changing. No matter how bad our experience is right now, it will change. And no matter how good it is, it will also change. Over time, when things get rough, knowing they will pass gives us more courage to be with them and learn from the experience. And when things are terrific, we don't get surprised or shocked

when they pass away. With practice we can learn to enjoy the roller-coaster ride of life, rather than thinking we will arrive at some fixed destination.

4. Finally, with mindful presence we are not lost in judgments of how we think our experience should be. You don't have to set up a pass-fail test for life. Thoughts filled with judgment and expectation lead to a lot of suffering. Things are the way they are. When you can't do anything to change the facts, you can either wish they were different and feel frustrated or accept your situation and respond as wisely as you can.

The serenity prayer describes the power of not getting lost in judgment: "God grant me the serenity to accept things I cannot change, courage to change the things I can, and wisdom to know the difference." Mindfulness cultivates both serenity to be with things as they are and wisdom to see things clearly. Don't be bothered by or try to get rid of judging thoughts. The judgments will probably still be there, but the secret is to not judge yourself for having them.

### Interrupting Negative Thinking

Our minds want to make sense of the world in order to feel safe or to get our needs met. But often we get confused in our attempt to sort things out: *What if things don't work out? What if the worst happens? What do I need to do to avoid disaster?* Joy is nowhere to be found when we're lost in worry and confusion. Mindfulness interrupts confused and negative thinking by bringing your attention back to what's actually happening right now. Coming into the present moment is a refuge from our negative thinking. As one Awakening Joy participant wrote:

> *When I found myself going down the rabbit hole of thinking about something in the past and feeling very badly about myself, I realized that if I focus on the current moment in my life (being on a beautiful walk) that I am actually quite happy in the moment.*

You have a choice where to focus your attention. With practice you can remember to ground yourself in your breath or body and short-circuit the negative pattern. Right now as you're reading this, turn your attention to the fact that you're sitting here and breathing. Take a few mindful breaths. Notice how available it is to you to come back to yourself and relax in the present moment.

## The Neuroscience of Mindfulness

Neuroscience expert Rick Hanson gives impressive evidence of how mindfulness affects the brain. Brain research confirms the power of mindfulness to affect and change our level of well-being and happiness. It activates positive neuronal circuits and strengthens their circuitry throughout the brain, particularly in the left frontal lobe, producing numerous beneficial effects.

Mindfulness triggers brain wave patterns associated with relaxed alertness. It increases serotonin levels, activating positive emotions. Mindfulness strengthens awareness of our internal state, which increases empathy. It counters the "fight or flight" part of the brain to help us relax, and it strengthens the immune system, improves cardiovascular health, and dampens chronic pain.

## Some Daily Life Mindfulness Exercises

There are many ways to incorporate mindfulness into your daily life whether your moments are pleasant or not. Make a game of trying to be mindful in common activities like the following:

1. When the phone rings, use it as a reminder to take a few mindful breaths before answering.
2. Do the same as your computer is booting up.
3. When you find yourself waiting in line at a store or at the movies, or when you're stuck in traffic, instead of feeling frustrated, use the time as a mini-mindfulness period. Remember that you're alive, be aware of the feelings in your body, and take a few mindful breaths.
4. Before you eat, stop and reflect on how the food got to be in front of you. This can help connect you with the web of life. Give thanks for the food and taste the first bite mindfully.
5. Take a regular chore or routine—washing the dishes, making the bed, taking out the garbage—as a mindfulness practice period. Again, make it a game to see how mindful you can be. (I've used shaving for many years.)
6. See if you can take a mindful walk around your neighborhood. No need to do anything special. In fact, just walk and know that you're walking. Feel your feet on the ground with each step.
7. Whenever you think of it, stop and take three mindful breaths and feel your body's sensations. You might set your computer or watch to ring every half hour or hour to remind you to do this.
8. This one might be revolutionary: instead of multi-tasking, try *uni-tasking*. That is, try doing one thing at a time. It's much easier to be present when you do.

## *Practicing Mindfulness Meditation*

Taking five to fifteen minutes (or more) a day to practice mindfulness meditation is one of the best ways to strengthen mindfulness. When we do this, moments of mindfulness are more likely to occur throughout the rest of the day. This is like planting seeds of awareness that sprout in their own time. If formal meditation seems daunting, then just have a quiet cup of tea and simply be aware of your experience as best you can. Here are some simple suggestions you may enjoy following. If your child is curious, you may try adapting them with her or him and "play the awareness game."

1. Sit in a posture that allows you to be comfortable and relatively still but not so relaxed that you fall asleep. You want to be both alert and at ease. Mindfulness meditation practice typically begins with focusing on the breath, but then the attention is turned to whatever else is happening in the body and mind.

2. Begin with paying attention to your breath. How do you know you're breathing? Where in your body do you feel it most clearly? You might notice the breath coming into your nostrils and passing out again. You might instead feel the rising and falling of your abdomen. Or you might simply be aware of your whole body sitting and breathing. Each time your mind wanders, gently return to the breath. Paying attention to breathing helps focus and calm your mind so that it can more easily stay present in the moment.

3. In addition to the breath, you can be mindful of other experiences inside you as they call your attention—various sensations in your body, your moods, your thoughts as they come and go. One moment you might notice a breath, the next you're aware of an itching in your back or arm, then a sound, then a thought, then the breath again. The key to being mindful is remaining aware of any of these experiences as they arise, without getting lost in the story or thoughts connected with any of them.

Most people find that soon after they begin to pay attention to their breath or to some sensation in their body, without even knowing it, they're gone, lost in their thoughts. This is not bad. It's just the way it is. The eye sees. The ear hears. The mind thinks. Thoughts are not the enemy, and the mind can be trained.

How we respond when we realize the mind has been wandering is critical to the process of developing mindfulness. If you get lost in a thought, patiently bring your attention back to the moment, remembering that you're sitting and breathing. It's important to do this with kindness, because reacting with frustration or annoyance only strengthens those qualities. You're in the process of training your mind, and just like training a puppy, patient repetition works better than punishment. Rather than feeling aggravated because you've been lost in your thoughts, you can appreciate that you've woken up from the dream.

Each time you return your attention with patience and kindness to the moment, you strengthen those qualities as well as your ability to remain present. Over time you will find negative patterns naturally unwinding and wholesome attitudes increasing.

It's important to realize that mindfulness requires great patience. The mind easily slips into thoughts about past or future. Don't judge yourself if that happens. Feel good about any moment you happen to be present while meditating as well as other times in your day.

## Michele: Mindfulness Practice with Children

Four years ago at the University of British Columbia, I attended a weekend workshop facilitated by James and his wife, Jane. During the weekend, I found a way into mindfulness that met with my playful side. I had been sitting on and off for years but James's ten steps to awakening joy had me thinking about how I could bring the practices more fully into my life and my classroom. Up to that point I believed that practice had to be a serious matter. But by incorporating joy into my practice, I began to enjoy practicing some form of mindfulness daily and have witnessed a new level of presence in

my life. I am now much more compassionate with myself as I gently shepherd myself in the present moment.

Prior to this I had taught various mindfulness practices in the classroom for over twenty years. Through that time, I came to see that even the simplest of breathing practices and relaxation could have profound effects. My now-adult sons have witnessed and participated as I have cultivated my own practice over many decades. They still roll their eyes at times, but more and more the practices that seemed "weird" at first are now a part of daily life. Every single night, at the dinner table, we take time to hold hands and share our gratitude for the best moments that happened in the day. I want to reassure you that the practices in this book can be integrated joyfully and seamlessly into your day. You won't be yanking your child to the cushion and having them sit for hours while you attend to your breath! As both a parent and teacher, I want to be cultivating mindful awareness with my actions and teaching my children how to embody these qualities too.

Mindful parenting, as defined by Mindfulness-Based Stress Reduction founder Jon Kabat-Zinn, consists of "paying attention to your child and your parenting in a particular way: intentionally, here and now, and non-judgmentally."

Mindfulness can improve well-being, and reduce worries, anxiety, distress, reactivity, and poor behavior choices. It can also improve sleep and self-esteem, as well as bring about greater calmness, empathy, relaxation, self-regulation, and awareness.

## One of the Simplest Descriptions of Mindfulness

Mindfulness is simply paying attention to your life, here and now, with kindness and curiosity. There are many ways into mindfulness. Take a first step.

You can teach children to notice or watch what comes into their minds and then teach them how to anchor their awareness back to their breath and body. An anchor can be anything that brings us back to the moment. I love the lesson on "Puppy Breathing" in this chapter, as children deeply connect to the love and anchor of a pet.

## Inviting Mindfulness into Your Home

If you give yourself permission to explore how to bring more mindfulness into the home, it can shift the idea from a single act or moment of mindfulness to actually living mindfully throughout your day.

This chapter gives you the tools to set up a simple home practice and offers you lessons that have made a huge impact on my teaching and family life. I work part-time as a teacher, and on some of my days off I substitute-teach students I have had before. Every time I come in, they beg me to do a progressive relaxation or mind journey. We quickly clear the desks and chairs and prepare to relax. Students say these are simply the quietest and deepest moments with the self they have ever had. Some of the children I taught in primary school are now big seventh graders and they still want to lie on the floor and relax.

There are many practices you can do together with your child. In fact, it would be very difficult to teach your child or students mindfulness if you are not practicing yourself. You wouldn't have someone teach your child dance if you they did not have skills in dance. You don't have to go off to a cave or retreat and be a long-term meditator. These are fun activities that you can do together with your child(ren). Hopefully, you can cultivate your own practice too!

Children as young as two or three can begin paying attention to their breath, thoughts, emotions, and senses. There are many strategies and techniques that can supplement your family practices. Just teaching children to stop and breathe can be enough. It can have a profound effect on their well-being. Below is a story of how a child who learns mindfulness can remember the practices years later and find peace. Even if it appears that nothing is happening while you build a practice, have trust. We all feel discouraged at times, but know these practices *will* make a difference.

## Mike

A twelve-year-old boy named Mike, a charismatic leader in the class, was haunted with nightmares. He had never told anyone about his terrible anxiety until he shared with me while we were chatting in the library one day. On that day I was substituting in the grade seven class. He came to school and told me that he had barely slept. His eyes looked glassy and he was white as a sheet. I asked if he would like to do a relaxation exercise with the class. He readily agreed. As we sank down into our mats, I gently guided all the class through the various parts of the body, deeply relaxing each part. Head to toe we went into every organ, bone, and muscle, relaxing and thanking each part for serving us. The practice also included imagining a safe place inside and relaxing. The place of safety may be in a meadow, at the ocean or cuddling a pet. With a class of thirty seventh-grade students, you would think it would be chaos, but the class became so quiet you could hear a pin drop. Although some students kept their eyes open, they were relaxed and quiet, while others were snoring softly and deeply, off in Never-Never Land. At the end of the session, Mike pulled me aside and shared that he had not felt that relaxed in over a year. He felt he had a place to go inside when he was scared. He even thanked me and asked when I might be substituting again. I told him he could use the techniques himself and let him know he could come and chat whenever he liked. I saw him many times that year and checked in with him. He said the relaxation had helped greatly and he used it regularly.

All of this relaxation took place within forty-five minutes. If this can happen for one child in such a short time span, imagine the gifts you are giving your own child with continual practices. I invite you to read through the lessons and choose a practice that fits into your busy days. As they say, if you don't have time to do ten minutes of practice, you probably need to do thirty minutes! Enjoy mindfulness on a daily basis.

# Lesson 1: A Breathing Practice

## Stress-Free Ways to Begin

Mindfulness is simply being aware of what is happening right now without wishing it were different; enjoying the pleasant without holding on when it changes (which it will); being with the unpleasant without fearing it will always be this way (which it won't).—*James*

### Building Strengths of:
- Mindfulness
- Perseverance
- Self-connection
- Well-being
- Training the mind

### Materials
- None

### Ages
- Preschool to adult

### School Curriculum Connections
- Oral language
- Written language
- Listening skills
- Physical education
- Fine arts
- Social and emotional learning

## *Home and School Practice*

### Beginning with Children

Beginning a mindfulness practice at an early age reaps many benefits. It helps children develop concentration and self-awareness. It reduces vulnerability to anxiety and enables children to recover more quickly from unpleasant experiences. Developing the part of the brain (prefrontal cortex) responsible for important skills such as impulse control, abstract reasoning, long-term planning, and working memory, mindfulness training may also make it easier for children to access their inner calm.

### *An Invitation*

Nonetheless, practice must start with an invitation. Demanding that your child sit with you (or on their own) will only create resistance. This is the work of invitation and introduction, not demand and authority.

### *Simple Ways*

Here are some simple ways to invite your child to enter the practices of mindfulness.

### Lead by Doing Yourself: Monkey see monkey do!
### And repeat, repeat, repeat

One minute here, one minute there, and then begin to extend the times. Set an example by doing the practices yourself. When the moment feels right, invite your child in or ask them to let you know when they might like to practice. I find that as the children practice more and more, they will come to me and say they need some time to settle.

### Set the Space: Create a Peace Corner or Mindfulness Room

Creating a beautiful space, even a corner of a room or a table reminds us to sit. You can add little bits of nature, like leaves, flowers, and rocks to the table and a few cushions or chairs to begin. It does not have to be elaborate in any way. My children have always loved to decorate the mindfulness corner. They are on the prowl for nature's gifts to bring to the altar. We also had a little candle that we would light together and blow out at the end of a sit. When we blew it out we would send our good wishes out to the world on the twirls of smoke.

## Set the Time

I always have some kind of timer and a bell to signal the beginning and the end of a session. The children love to ring it and we use it only as a tool to signal the mindfulness sessions, not as an instrument to be played. In this way it keeps its sacred nature.

## How to Sit

Children can start by sitting on your lap or by themselves.

When my children were as young as two, they would come and sit on my lap while I was doing a meditation. They knew this was Mummy's special time and that I was not available to them in the way I usually was. In retrospect I see it was an incredibly healthy way to set boundaries and let my boys know I had needs too. I must admit they did not always give me quiet and space, but after a while they came to know mum would be doing this every day and it was important to her. To give yourself a period of silence, you might set out a little tub of quiet toys they can play with while you are sitting. If I felt I needed more time on the cushion, I also had time when the boys were asleep to meditate and truly relax into myself.

As the boys got older, they would come and sit beside me and breathe or simply relax close by. They loved to set intention by holding hands and look-ing deep into my eyes, so we did this practice at the end of each session before starting our day.

## What to Sit On?

You can use any comfortable cushions, stools, or chairs. If you sew, what fun it is to sew a cushion together. You can pick special fabric and stuff it with cot-ton or buckwheat hulls. Beware, making a buckwheat hull cushion is a much larger project than I ever imagined. We had hulls everywhere!

See: https://www.youtube.com/watch?v=AZsSg7zUo9c

## At the End of the Session

Invite your children to share one word or more about how the session was, and value their experiences simply by being present to what they share. You can share too. Be careful not to judge the session as good or bad, successful or anything. Just see and hear what arises and share only if you are inclined.

## Journals and Drawing

You may want to have journals and drawing materials close by so children can write or express in pictures anything they wish. I like to have a tub of old magazines available so the kids can cut out pictures and create collages. Again there is no demand with this activity, but the resources are there if they are needed.

## Do a Guided Mindfulness Practice Together

There are many guided mindfulness practices available on the web. You can play one while you both sit. I have included in this chapter one "Magical Cave" visualization you can read aloud. Feel free to read it directly off the page until you feel confident leading your own relaxation practice. Once you feel comfortable with the guided meditations, you might like to make some up with characters and stories that inspire you. I have had many parents share that after a mindfulness practice at school, children as young as six years old go home and want to guide their parents. Some say that their parents really, really need this and ask, "Can Ms. Lilyanna do mindfulness with my Mom and Dad too?"

## A Few Playful Practices

**Bathtub breathing:** Water is a natural relaxant; adding essential oils such as lavender and chamomile to a hot bath creates an inviting envelope of scented steam. This sets the stage for mindful breathing. Fill the tub so the water just reaches the tummy when your child is lying down. As they breathe in, they can watch the water softly cover their tummy and as they breathe out, the water recedes so the skin is back to being touched by the bathroom air. You can softly count the in- and out-breaths as your child deeply relaxes in the tub. Breathing in … 1, 2, 3, 4; hold, 1, 2; breathing out 1, 2, 3, 4, and 5. Relax … and repeat. I guarantee both of you will be much more relaxed after a session in the tub.

Older children can do this on their own. My own boys would light candles and set up their favorite aromatherapy oils for their baths and emerge an hour later calm, wrinkled, and ready for bed.

**Stuffy breathing:** This connects a child to their breath in a simple way. Take their favorite stuffed toy and have them lie on their back with the little fellow resting on top of their tummy. Have your child notice the stuffy going up and down with the breath. There is no need to force the breath. Gradually, they can begin to notice subtler and subtler movements of the tummy.

**Body weather:** If you were the weather right now, what would you be? Cloudy, foggy, rainbows and sunshine—or is there a storm on the horizon? Have your child describe their inner weather.

Checking in often with the body builds a valuable connection from heart to head. Children learn that emotions come and go just as weather passes and changes throughout the day. For parents it is a window into the emotional state of a child, especially when a little one does not have the words to describe the whole picture of what is going on inside. Just have them notice their body weather and acknowledge that is how they are feeling without trying to change it.

**Head, heart, body check-in:** What is your head saying? What is your heart saying? What is your body saying? Try this right now and connect in with yourself.

Emotions that are freely experienced and expressed without judgment or attachment tend to flow fluidly. People who have good emotional health are aware of their thoughts, feelings, and behaviors. By turning inside, your child will begin to recognize their emotions and understand why they are having them. Sorting out the causes of sadness, stress, and anxiety in life can help manage emotional health. Your child will feel empowered as they learn what triggers various emotional states and how they can then use the tools of *Awakening Joy* to help navigate their emotions.

## Other Ways to Integrate Mindfulness into the Day
Can you remember a favorite moment as a child?

People often recall moments when they were deeply relaxed and "watching the world go by." Children describe the feeling as spacious, peaceful, smooth, restful, and light. We'll elaborate on this more in chapter 10.

In this day and age, with electronics and the quick pace of daily life, parents and children don't often have the opportunities to just slow down. I know as a teacher and a parent I feel I have to cram so much into the day to just stay on top of things.

What reminds me to slow down is listening to the top weekend "bests" children share on Monday mornings. The slow moments we have on weekends and after school really are savored by our children.

At school we sit every Monday in a circle and celebrate our greatest moments of the weekend. Children are encouraged not to share television or electronics stories at this time.s

---

They share ideas like:

- ✳ I got to lie on my back and float in the ocean.
- ✳ I read a book all day.
- ✳ I love snuggling.
- ✳ I just hung out.
- ✳ I drew for hours.
- ✳ I watched a cloud.

- ✳ I played with all my Legos.
- ✳ I played with my cat.
- ✳ My brother and I played in the forest.
- ✳ I jumped off a cliff.
- ✳ I rode my bike to the store.
- ✳ I played a game with my Dad.

---

After they share, I have them open themselves to the feeling of well-being in their bodies. I also really want them to wire in positive neural pathways. As Dr. Rick Hanson states, "Let the memories sink in and create neural pathways in the brain."

So sit with your child or students and do something slow, unplanned, and restful. Savor these happy moments and recall them often. You are building neuro-circuitry for awakening joy.

## Stop and Listen

When was the last time you really stopped and listened to the sounds around you? Children love mindful listening practices. It may sound easy, but it requires concentration. Try stopping everything and opening your attention to your ears and listening for the sounds arising and falling. The sounds will rise and fall like instruments in an orchestra.

Try not to label or hang onto a sound but simply let it pass by. You can set a timer and try to concentrate for five minutes.

The other day I had sixty children sitting in a very loud, busy classroom. I had them stop and tune into the sound of the clock ticking. This is a sound we rarely hear in our day. Time slowed down and the clock became loud. Other hallway noises passed by and they returned their attention to the tick of the clock. Here are some comments from students after the exercise.

"My ears felt huge. It is like everything was right there."

"I didn't even know the clock ticked. It was the first time I heard it."

"I felt all tingly like I had super hearing. I heard things I never heard before."

"I like it. I relaxed but I felt really tired after."

## It May Look Strange

It may look odd to others, but stick by your intentions to practice.

One day my whole class was lying on their backs at the front entrance to the school doing a listening meditation. I thought we were pretty much alone until a truckload of maintenance workers pulled up. I felt a sense of tightness in my stomach, imagining what they were thinking looking over the rails of the school fence seeing a teacher and twenty-five little ones lying on their backs with their eyes closed for over ten minutes. Was the teacher sleeping or slacking off? What was school coming to?

The most amazing thing was that the sound of the truck, wheels, tools, and scraping all became part of our practice. The children stuck by their meditation in the midst of chaos. They said it was really cool to hear the symphony of sounds. Later in the day, in the staffroom, one of the maintenance workers asked what we had been doing and said he wished he could have been doing it too!

The offerings in this book are practices that children can cultivate and grow with, which can help balance their inner and outer worlds while they create habits that sustain them for life. They offer a taste of peace and well-being that will not be forgotten.

# Lesson 2: Mindfulness through the Eyes of a Child

## Allowing Your Child's Natural Curiosity to Lead the Way

With mindful presence we're not lost in judgments of how we think our experience should be. You don't have to set up a pass-fail test for life. Things are the way they are. When you can't do anything to change the facts, you can either wish they were different and feel frustrated or accept your situation and respond as wisely as you can.

### *Twelve Little Practices to Enrich Mindfulness*

You can copy this lesson with ten little practices and keep it in your pocket or beside your bed. It will be ready to use to build mindfulness moment by moment!

### Building Strengths of:
- Mindfulness
- Perseverance
- Companionship
- Connection
- Social and emotional well-being
- Training the mind to enhance well-being

### Materials
- An open mind
- Time

### Ages
- Preschool to adult

### School Curriculum Connections
- Oral language
- Written language
- Listening skills
- Reading
- Social studies
- Science
- Physical education
- Fine arts
- Social and emotional learning

For me, awareness of the possibility of joy in the ordinary events of life has been a big discovery. I once considered my life to be relatively bland and uneventful. It was even hard for me to remember what had happened during the day, since it was almost by definition "unimportant." But I now think this is more a matter of perception than fact. Seeing the wonder in what is rather than looking for something wonderful and disregarding the rest is a significant development.
—Awakening Joy course participant.

## Home and School Practice

James reminds adults to take the time to notice what is around them in the world as a mindfulness practice. Children do this naturally until they begin to get so busy that they let it go. Parents and teachers, often in a rush to get from A to B, forget to slow down and really see!

After a while children quit asking us to look deeply and also forget to look themselves. This natural curiosity can die.

In this offering, I am going to share with you ten little mindfulness practices. Do you remember doing any of these playful activities? Can you bring them back into your lives again just for fun?

To enrich these practices and create an awareness of what a calm and receptive mind and body feel like, ask your child to take a moment to notice their breathing patterns. Also ask them to describe what they are feeling as they are engaging in these relaxing activities. Make this questioning casual. There is no goal in mind. Just simply notice the mind and body states as they pass through our being.

### Bonus

We all love a bonus, so I have underlined some character strengths that may be found and talked about in each activity.

### Ant Roads

Ever watch an ant traveling and carrying a load? They are such an incredible inspiration and they never stop moving. Children love to lie on their bellies and watch the *perseverance* ants have in carrying out a task.

Get down low with your child and relax into the patterns and pathways they create. It is mesmerizing. Talk about the strengths of *persistence* and *working together* as a group to achieve a goal.

### Clouds

What could be better than lying on your back, side by side, simply watching clouds go by? The attention is totally captured in the movement of the sky. Talk about strengths of *change* and *adaptability*. All things change, moment to moment. I often talk to children about the mind as a sky, clear blue, when we sink down deep with drifting thoughts and emotions passing by. Notice the passing clouds and sink into the blue.

### Water Running Down a Hill

Children are absolute magnets to water and dirt. Capture this natural curiosity and playfulness with building little dams and pathways. Quietly watching water flow downhill and creating diversions to change patterns is a way to talk about the fact we have *choice* in the way we *face obstacles*. Water will always run and we can go with the flow or get blocked up.

### Bugs in the Garden

My little ones love watching bugs. They are always coming into class and yanking on my hand to take me to see a tiny creature in the school garden. Take time to watch a bug or butterfly. Sink into the sheer experience of *being present* to the life around you. My son Kieran had a pet slug for many days. We watched its slow movements and slime trails for ages.

### Colors of the Leaves

Leaves are an incredible focal point for the mind. The act of watching leaves, not only their ever-changing, exquisite colors, but also the movements of these jewels in the wind is an exceptional mindfulness practice. One of the best books to read about leaves is *The Fall of Freddy the Leaf* by Leo Buscaglia. Children love this book and adults cry. As Freddie experiences the changing seasons along with his companion leaves, he learns about the delicate balance between life and death. After reading this book to my grade-three students, I found them running around the maple trees trying to catch Freddy the Leaf and bring him back in to the classroom to talk to him one more time!

### Rain Down a Window

Where I live, the rain pours down for six or more months of the year. Children are often inside, yearning to go out and play. Watching rivulets run down the windows is a quiet, *mindful practice* on a rainy day. A raindrop splats and runs for five or ten seconds. Try to clear the mind and simply be present to the pathways of the water.

### Snow Falling onto Black Paper

Waiting in anticipation for a flake to fall and catching it on black paper is a quiet mindfulness practice. If you don't have paper, stick out your tongue and feel the ice crystals melt as they hit the warmth. Your senses of *touch and taste* are greatly heightened during this practice.

### A Tiny Section of the World

Zero in on a tiny section of the planet by taping four straws or chopsticks together into a square and laying it on the ground. Then you can either take a magnifying glass or simply look at what is in the square. The longer you look, the more you see. You can also quietly draw the tiny world on paper allowing the section to reveal itself line by line.

### Looking for a Color

This is a great game to play on a walk, at the park, or even in the living room. Get the mind to focus on one simple thing. This builds strengths of *concentration*. Choose a color and see how it reveals itself. I have given out colored paint chips and had students search for the hue outdoors. It is amazing what they find.

## I Spy with My Little Eye

Of course *I Spy* is such fun to play during long car rides. You can change the object of the search from colors to looking for something beginning with a certain letter of the alphabet. Playing this game strengthens *mindful concentration.*

As your child does more and more of these practices, they may be more inclined to start a five- or ten-minute breathing practice of their own. As James says, mindfulness takes practice, and we must teach our mind to become more focused and present. The above activities will invite both you and your child into a relaxed state that may or may not include a breathing practice as well.

## School

Teachers can do any of these short practices during classroom breaks, as a way to get the students' attention or simply to calm the minds of both the teacher and the children. You may be amazed at what great classroom management tools these are. Your students will be calmer, more focused, and ready to learn. You could have a list of the practices on the board for the children to pick when the time comes.

They might even come to you and say, "I think we need to do a practice." I know my students do this all the time and then we pick from the list or create a new activity. I get requests like, "Ms. L, it is too noisy for me. I need people to settle down." "Some kids seem pretty nuts today. Can we do a practice? "I had a really stressful weekend. Can we start with a mind journey?" "I don't think the new boy knows about mindfulness. He is all over the place. Can we help him?"

You could also send a list of the activities home with the children, knowing you are introducing, building, and reinforcing the mindfulness practices at home. What could be better?

## Resources

### ADULT BOOKS

Barbara Brannen. *The Gift of Play: Why Adult Women Stop Playing and How To Start Again.* Bloomington, IN: iUniverse, 2004.

Thich Nhat Hanh. *Planting Seeds: Practicing Mindfulness with Children.* Illustrated by Wietske Vriezen. Berkeley, CA: Parallax Press, 2011.

Daniel J. Siegel and Tina Payne Bryson. *The Whole-Brain Child: 12 Revolutionary Strategies to Nurture Your Child's Developing Mind*. New York: Bantam, 2012.

Judy H. Wright. *Playful Parenting—Fun Games & Activities For Families (77 Ways to Parent)*. Missoula, MT: Artichoke Press, 2012.

## Children's Books

Leo Lionni. *Let's Play*. New York: Knopf Books for Young Readers, 2003.

Maud Roegiers *Take the Time: Mindfulness for Kids*. Washington, DC: Magination Press, 2010.

Whitney Stewart. *Meditation Is an Open Sky: Mindfulness for Kids*. Illustrated by Sally Rippi. Park Ridge, IL: Albert Whitman & Company, 2015.

Mo Willems. *Can I Play Too? (An Elephant and Piggie Book)*. New York: Disney-Hyperion, 2010.

 # Lesson 3: Puppy Training

You can deepen the happiness grooves in your brain. When you're feeling good, doing something enjoyable, are in the middle of a kind act, are not feeling negative, or are in touch with the blessings in your life—pay attention to how it feels in your body as well as your mind. DON'T MISS IT!—*James*

## Building Strengths of:
- Mindful concentration
- Social and emotional well-being
- Empathy
- Loving-kindness
- Self regulation

## Materials
- An open mind
- Time

## Ages
- Preschool to adult

## School Curriculum Connections
- Oral language
- Listening skills
- Social and emotional learning

## Home and School Practice

My little dog, Teddy Bear, has made many guest appearances in my classrooms over the past two years. I first brought him into the room out of desperation and necessity. My family had gotten him from his breeder on Saturday and school started on Monday. My students willingly jumped in and built him a temporary kennel out of cardboard and tape. I thought we would use it for a few weeks until we could work out our family dog-care schedule. Well, the weeks turned into months and months into years and Teddy continues to make many guest appearances in the classroom. He has become the source of more empathy, love, and well-being than you can imagine.

Teddy is hypoallergenic and very socialized. When he comes in for special visits, he is free to move around the classroom and the children accept him as a very important member of our room. Many times when a child has been hurt or upset, they ask for "Teddy time." Children with the most anxiety or extreme behavioral outbursts will calm down when Teddy sits close by. Students who have reading challenges will read to Teddy, as he is a loving presence that does not judge their stumbles or the difficulties they have with the text.

### Introducing a Puppy Mindfulness Practice

That being said, I wanted to introduce a "peaceful puppy practice" after participating with James in a puppy meditation originated by Jack Kornfield. I thought it would be perfect for my students with my own added twist. The power of this mindfulness practice is that children naturally love their animals and have observed them very closely many times. They can lie for hours watching their cat or dog breathe. The children's nervous systems calm when close to a beloved pet and their body is already primed and ready to relax.

Jack Kornfield shares in his book *A Path with Heart,*

> *In this way, meditation is very much like training a puppy. You put the puppy down and say, "Stay." Does the puppy listen? It gets up and it runs away. You sit the puppy back down again. "Stay." And the puppy runs away over and over again. Sometimes the puppy jumps up, runs over, and pees in the corner or makes some other mess. Our minds are much the same as the puppy, only they create even bigger messes. In training the mind, or the puppy, we have to start over and over again.*
>
> *When you undertake a spiritual discipline, frustration comes with the territory. Nothing in our culture or our schooling has taught us to steady and calm our attention. One psychologist has called us a society of attention spastics. Finding it difficult to concentrate, many people respond by forcing their attention on their breath or mantra or prayer with tense irritation and self-judgment, or worse. Is this the way you would train a puppy? Does it really help to beat it? Concentration is never a matter of force or coercion. You simply pick up the puppy again and return to reconnect with the here and now.*

## Tested in the Classroom—A Winner in Your Home

During mindfulness sessions I have the children lie down on the floor in the room wherever they wish.

I ask them to slowly relax and tune into their breathing.

I then ask them to imagine Teddy Bear or a pet coming into the room.

I remind them that when they have wild or frenetic energy, Teddy gets amped up too.

I ask them to simply relax enough so that Teddy would come onto their laps.

They imagine the small hairs on his neck and the soft breathing of his belly as he calms down.

I tell them that like their minds, Teddy will wander off, and when they notice the puppy off their laps, to gently bring him back with lots of love and compassion.

Finally, I say that Teddy might turn into a pet they know, an animal they love, or a forest creature, and encourage them to just bring the softness of their concentration to that animal while they watch its breathing.

*I love puppy mindfulness. I miss my animals in the day. I can see the hairs on Teddy's back in my mind and I feel calmer.—Student*

## Add in a Bit of Loving-kindness

I also want to add in a little practice of "loving-kindness." I invite my children to feel a deep sense of love for themselves for just doing this practice. Then they can open their hearts to their animal and breathe into that feeling of love.

One time we did this for a few breaths and then I had them bring to mind someone that they just knew but did not have strong feelings for either way and send that person good wishes.

With the last moments of the mindfulness session I knew they were ready, as we had been practicing for many months, to bring to mind someone that they felt they had blocked their feelings toward or that they had a hard time liking. I asked them to imagine this person relaxed and happy and to see if they could possibly send them good wishes.

This entire process took only fifteen minutes.

After fifteen minutes, these are the results.

So out of the mouths of seven-year-olds, please read and know how meaningful these moments are to the children.

✳ "I felt my heart getting bigger."

✳ "I felt like I could feel Teddy and he felt really soft. I felt as if he was licking me. I felt really relaxed and all my worries went away. I also thought of my dog that we gave away and my dog made friends with Teddy in my mind. I thought of my cat named Dollar and I could feel him. It made me so happy. I could feel his soft fur and hard whiskers."

✳ "I felt like I was floating."

✳ "Today I felt like I just wanted to relax. I wanted to just go to sleep. I felt Teddy on my lap. I think this was probably the best mindfulness. I love mindfulness when everyone in the class is relaxed. I could see my dog like he was here. I really hope I have a really good day today. In my body I felt really good. I thought I really needed some mindfulness listening today. It was fantastic."

✳ A young boy had just arrived in our classroom and had his first mindfulness practice. He shared: "I feel more relaxed and good after doing the puppy mindfulness. I felt like I had more energy to play and have fun with my friends. At the start it was a bit harder but I just relaxed. I could feel Teddy's little paws and his heart. I felt like he wanted to scavenge for crumbs but I remembered to bring him back and as soon as I came back he would too and smile up at me. I sent love to my Grandpa, Granny, and great-grandparents and my aunts and uncles and everyone in my family. I felt really good after it. Thank you for doing this with me, Ms. L."

✳ "I was relaxed. It was like sparkle powder."

✳ "When I started to relax, I felt really calm. When Teddy came to me he didn't seem to want to ever go away and he was so calm. He snuggled me so much that afterward I felt like he was still there. I felt like sparkles were hanging over me."

I am absolutely blown away by the power of these simple, yet deeply meaningful practices.

## Resources

### ADULT BOOKS

Tara Brach. *Mindfulness Meditation: Nine Guided Practices to Awaken Presence and Open Your Heart (Audio CD)*. (Louisville, CO: Sounds True, 2012).

Joseph Goldstein. *Mindfulness: A Practical Guide to Awakening*. Louisville, CO: Sounds True, 2013.

Susan Kaiser Greenland. *The Mindful Child: How to Help Your Kid Manage Stress and Become Happier, Kinder, and More Compassionate*. New York: Atria Books, 2010.

Thich Nhat Hanh. *Peace Is Every Step: The Path of Mindfulness in Everyday Life*. New York: Bantam, 1992.

Rick Hanson. *Hardwiring Happiness: The New Brain Science of Contentment, Calm, and Confidence*. New York: Harmony, 2013.

### CHILDREN'S BOOKS

Barbara Helen Berger. *Grandfather Twilight*. London: Puffin Books, 1996.

JoAnn Deak, Ph.D. *Your Fantastic Elastic Brain*. Illustrated by Sarah Ackerley. San Francisco: Little Pickle Press, 2010.

Rana DiOrio. *What Does It Mean To Be Present?* Illustrated by Eliza Wheeler. San Francisco: Little Pickle Press, 2010.

Lemniscates. *Silence*. Washington, DC: Magination Press, 2012.

Kerry Lee MacLean. *Moody Cow Meditates*. Somerville, MA: Wisdom Publications, 2009.

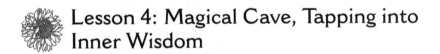 # Lesson 4: Magical Cave, Tapping into Inner Wisdom

## Cave Meditation

Brain research confirms the power of mindfulness to affect and change our level of well-being. It triggers brain wave patterns associated with relaxed alertness, activates positive emotions, increases empathy and offers many other benefits. Most importantly, it leads to greater happiness.

## Building Strengths of:

- Mindful concentration
- Social and emotional well-being
- Relaxation
- Loving-kindness
- Listening
- Self-regulation

## Materials

- An open mind
- Time

## Ages

- Preschool to adult

## School Curriculum Connections

- Oral language
- Written language
- Listening skills
- Science
- Fine arts
- Social and emotional learning

## Home and School Practice

Over the years I have been teaching mindfulness in schools, the most requested mindfulness exercise is the mind journey. If I am substituting in a class for an hour or for a day and I ask my students what they would like to do, they always say, "Please take us on a mind journey." Many times people walk past my darkened classroom and assume we have left the building, only to find the children sprawled out breathing deeply on a journey within. My own children would request a mind journey almost every night as a way to relax the body before falling asleep. You can use this mind journey to a magical cave as a read-aloud until you are comfortable creating your own adventures. Have fun!

The Magical Cave is by far the most popular mind journey I use with students. It takes the children from a safe place, with an animal guide to a magical cave. I am absolutely astounded at what the children see in the cave. I do not guide this part, but time and time again, year after year, my students meet with pets and grandparents who have died. It is such a sweet, rich moment when they reflect on these inner passages. Here is one I did recently where a magical unicorn takes them up the hill.

## Here You Go—Get Settled

I allow the children to find a spot to lie down and put their coats under their heads and get very comfortable. We are lucky to have yoga mats in the school, so they're warm and supported. If you are at home, tuck your child into bed or snuggle in a chair and begin this mindful journey.

### Say These Words Slowly While the Vision Forms

"Close your eyes and imagine you are in a beautiful meadow. It is a lovely summer day. All around you are wild flowers. You feel incredibly safe and happy lying there. A beautiful butterfly comes into your vision; its wings are shimmering in the sunlight. It is like no other butterfly you have ever seen before. There are rich golden iridescent colors catching the light. The butterfly beckons you to follow it. You get up and begin to walk down the hill and at the bottom is a lake. Close to the shore, you see a little blue rowboat. It has your name on it and you know it is okay to use it. Inside are beautiful pillows, all puffy and soft. You snuggle in and let go of the rope that is tied to the shore. The boat begins to gently move across the lake. The butterfly moves on slightly ahead of you, guiding the passage of the boat to the other side of the lake. As you get to the shore, you feel the boat bump up against the sand. You peek over the edge and the shore is covered with semi-precious jewels, all polished and shiny. You tie up the boat and see a pathway heading up a hill. The butterfly flies on ahead and you follow it up the pathway. Part way up the hill you come to a gate. It has a lock on it. Somehow you know how to open the gate. Open the gate now and go through. As you keep going upwards you hear a little noise in the bushes beside you. You know it is safe, as the butterfly is not afraid. In the bush a beautiful unicorn begins to show itself. It has the most incredible eyes. It looks at you with such love. The unicorn lowers itself down on its knees and you get on its back. It begins to gallop up the hill and the butterfly hangs onto your shoulder. You snuggle into the unicorn's mane. At the top of the hill is the opening of a cave. It has huge stalactites and stalagmites. Crystals are all over the walls. The unicorn stops at the cave entrance and you see a light toward the back of the cave. As you look closely, you see it is a fire. You, the unicorn, and the butterfly enter and sit by the fire. You snuggle deeply into the unicorn and relax. You can hear the unicorn's heartbeat. In this cave you can ask a question. Maybe you are worried about something or need to know something. You ask the question. You may not get the answer today, but it will come. You can let go of your worry now. Feel your body relax. As you look around the cave you may see someone or something. It may be a pet or just swirling colors. All is okay. It is there to give you a message. See if you can hear it.

It is time to go now. Thank the cave and all you have learned there. You can come back any time. Get on the unicorn's back and travel back down the hill to the gate where the unicorn returns to the bush. Look deeply into the unicorn's eyes and know all is well. You go further down and snuggle back into the boat. Before you push off to the other shore, see if you can remember the message you received in the cave. The butterfly guides you back to shore and you return to the meadow. Snuggle in....

Now come back to here and now. Hug yourself and know you will be with this one always.... Honor this one that you are hugging."

*At this point we sit in a quiet circle and I either have the students draw, write, or orally express what they saw, or I have them share the messages they received. If you are at home, your child can simply fall asleep.

## Resources

### ADULT BOOKS

Tara Brach. *Mindfulness Meditation: Nine Guided Practices to Awaken Presence and Open Your Heart (Audio CD)*. Louisville, CO: Sounds True, 2012.

Thich Nhat Hanh. *The Blooming of a Lotus: Revised Edition of the Classic Guided Meditation for Achieving the Miracle of Mindfulness*. Boston, MA: Beacon Press, 2009.

Jon Kabat-Zinn. *Guided Mindfulness Meditation: A Complete Guided Mindfulness Meditation Program from Jon Kabat-Zinn (CD—Audiobook)*. Louisville, CO: Sounds True, 2012.

Jack Kornfield. *Guided Meditation: Six Essential Practices to Cultivate Love, Awareness, and Wisdom (CD—Audiobook)*. Louisville, CO: Sounds True, 2007.

### CHILDREN'S BOOKS

Lauren Alderfer and Kerry Lee MacLean. *Mindful Monkey, Happy Panda*. Somerville, MA: Wisdom Publications, 2011.

Thich Nhat Hanh. *A Handful of Quiet: Happiness in Four Pebbles*. Illustrated by Wietske Vriezen. Berkeley, CA: Plum Blossom Books, 2012.

Thich Nhat Hanh *Planting Seeds: Practicing Mindfulness with Children*. Illustrated by Wietske Vriezen. Berkeley, CA: Parallax Press, 2011.

Kerry Lee Maclean. *Peaceful Piggy Meditation*. Park Ridge, IL: Albert Whitman Prairie Books, 2004.

 # Lesson 5: Weaving in the Good

When we are mindful, we're not looking for our experience of things to be different. Mindful presence helps us slow down enough to activate the natural curiosity with which we all come into this world—the sense of wonder and awe that delights a child. There's magic all around us if we take the time to see it.

## Building Strengths of:
- Mindful concentration
- Social and emotional well-being
- Loving-kindness
- Self regulation
- Self compassion
- Caring for the planet

## Materials—Plate Weaving

- Paper plate
- Tape
- Scissors
- A ball or two of old yarn
- Up-cycling used materials

## Ages

- Five to adult (little ones will need help stringing their plate)

## School Curriculum Connections

- Oral language
- Listening skills
- Social studies
- Physical education
- Fine arts
- Social and emotional learning

### *Home and School*

Do you remember someone in your life weaving or knitting? The repetitive movement of their hands as they created a scarf or sweater? I would often hear my mum's knitting needles clicking from the other room as she sat for hours happily creating a sweater for one of us kids. These days fewer people know how to knit, weave, or crochet but all is not lost to past generations. We can bring back this beautiful art in small and big ways and at the same time bring health and well-being into our minds and bodies! You don't even need to knit.

Repetitive movements are common sense: we rock babies in cradles and sit in rocking chairs because rocking has a powerful calming effect. Dr. Herbert Benson, founder of the Benson-Henry Institute for Mind-Body Medicine at Harvard, recommends the repetition of a word, sound, phrase, and muscular activity to elicit your body's relaxation response, which allows a lower heart rate, blood pressure, and muscle tension.

Repeating happy phrases while weaving is gold for *Awakening Joy*.

### Arts and Crafts Activity: Rag Rug, Wool Bowls

Start by collecting old wool, t-shirts, and fabric; then you can get started on "Weaving in the Good." This art activity combines mindfulness, neuroscience, and art. It is easily adaptable to the home or classroom. In the classroom, students enjoyed weaving for months after I introduced this idea. I have to admit that for some students who had difficulties with fine motor skills, this exercise could have become a tangle of frustration, but with the help of their peers, all the kids had a mini rug by the end of the week.

You can just do the mini project as outlined below or take on a much larger project and reap the benefits of an actual usable rug, woven together with good intentions and happy memories.

The process can take an afternoon or a week, depending on what you want to create and how much regulation you want to build. You can keep these treasures for years to come as they are infused with the energy of "Weaving in the Good."

James has shared over and over in *Awakening Joy* that if we can give whole-hearted presence to what we are doing, life becomes more fulfilling. So with a whole heart, gather your supplies and have a wonderful creative time with your child.

## Mini Plate Project

Oh, so easy! The directions may seem complicated, but once you get started it is really easy!

Step 1: Cut an odd number of small slits around the outside of a paper plate. Make sure that there is an odd number, or else it will not work out right.

Step 2: Take a piece of yarn and wrap it around the paper plate so that it crosses in the front and the yarn is parallel in the back. Tie the piece of yarn in the front.

Step 3: Tie a piece of the same color yarn to one of the ties on the front of the plate. This way you have an odd number or weft or spokes.

 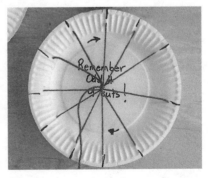

Step 4: Start from where the yarn is tied and then weave over one piece of the yarn over, and then under. Over and then under. After you have woven several over and unders at the top, then pull the string tight. Repeat the weave.

## How Neuroscience Weaves into the Project

As your child is weaving, they are building mindful concentration. Be gentle; this is about learning two new skills at once, the skill of weaving and the skill of mindful awareness. While they are weaving, ask your child to think of wonderful experiences. "Feel the experience in your body, remember how it felt on your skin and in your mind." Notice your breathing and stay as present as possible while moving the wool in and out. Chant phrases while weaving. Instead of saying "over and under," while they weave the wool, you can make up phrases like: "breathing in, breathing out"; or "loving you, loving me"; "I let go, I let in."

Meena Srinivasan, a children's mindfulness teacher, has a chant based on a practice from Thich Nhat Hanh that the children can sing while they weave:

---

Breathing in, I see myself
as a flower, human flower.

Breathing out, I am
beautiful just as I am and
I feel very fresh.

Breathing in, I see myself
as a mountain.

Breathing out, I feel solid;
nothing can move or
distract me.

Breathing in: Mountain

Breathing out: Solid

---

## Bigger Project: A T-Shirt Rug

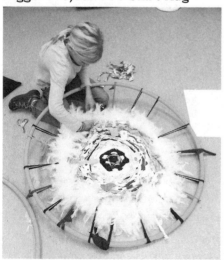

This project was one of the biggest, messiest, and most communal activities of the year. People from all over the school would stop in to see how the hoop rug was coming along. T-shirts were donated from little hands walking past the room at all hours of the day. Children would come back later to try to spot their shirts that had been woven into the rug. Children shared their experiences of joy and learning.

❋ "It was really fun cutting up the shirts. I mean we just got to cut up our clothes and make something new!"

❋ "It took a long time and sometimes it was hard because we would get mixed up with the pattern. In the end it turned out really cool."

❋ "It was super relaxing and a big project. I like working big!"

❋ "Awesome! After it was made, we kept the rug in the classroom and got to sit on it. I could see my shirt in the pattern. Did you know that in the olden days, this is how rugs were made?"

## Before Even Beginning: Awaken Joy

Choose and bring in an old t-shirt full of happy memories. Each shirt will be woven into our communal rug.

Help your child make pleasurable experiences become as full-bodied and intense as possible. Do visualization with your child or children and feel the experience of happy memories for at least fifteen seconds. Dr. Rick Hanson shares: "As the intensity of an experience increases, so do levels of the neurotransmitter norepinephrine, which promotes formation of new synapses; the more that an experience fosters new synapses, the more that it gets woven into your brain. And as an experience becomes more pleasurable—particularly if it was more rewarding than your brain initially expected because you

deliberately intensified it and opened to it through taking in the good—dopamine levels rise as well, which also promotes new synapses."

Before each shirt is cut up, have the child speak aloud of how the shirt is special to them. This can help with the step above and enable children to truly soak in the happy memory.

One little boy, Raven, got so excited that he asked to take home a hula-hoop and he wove all weekend to make his cat a sweet spot. His father sent me the picture on page 67.

## Happy Rugs

We created rugs on hula-hoop looms as happy rugs. If someone wanted to sit on one, they were infused with good thoughts and memories. The children told me that just sitting on one would make a person feel better. Everyone was given a chance to sit on the rug. It is now in a special spot and whenever anyone wants to feel good, they go and sit on the rug.

## How to Make a Hula-Hoop Rug

### Materials
- Hula hoop
- Scissors
- Old t-shirts (about eight to ten for a small rug)
- Laughter, patience, memories, and a dash of mindfulness

### Ages
- Eight to adult, but younger ones can do it with help

### Directions:

Cut t-shirts across into one-inch wide strips that form loops. You will get eight to sixteen strips per shirt depending on the size of the shirt. Use four adult-size t-shirt strips and wrap the hoop as shown. You will then have eight spokes. Use one more half strip to tie in the middle so you have nine spokes. Whatever size you make you *must* have an odd number of spokes.

Make a pile of one-inch wide t-shirt strips. Connect them together to create one long piece of t-shirt.

Daisy-chain the loops together, just like you would join two rubber bands. You could also sew or knot them. Other more advanced ways to join the pieces can be found on the Internet.

Start by tying the first circular weaving thread into the middle. Then you can go round and round clockwise, weaving up-down, up-down. When the

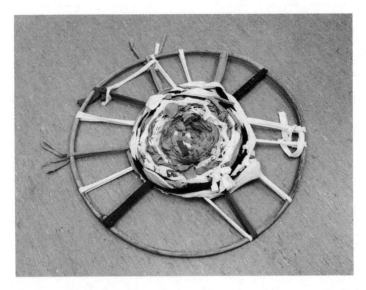

rug gets to be about eight inches across, separate the spokes so you have double the number of wefts. You will now have eighteen.

Keep weaving outward.

When you are about four inches from edge, cut and tie the weft spokes.

Remove the rug from the frame and you have a usable "Happy Memories" mindfulness rug.

To bring social studies into this practice, talk to the children about the origins of weaving, looms, and cultures that weave as an art form. You can also discuss sustainability, up-cycling, and how to protect our planet's resources.

## Resources

### ADULT BOOKS

Rick Hanson. *Hardwiring Happiness: The New Brain Science of Contentment, Calm, and Confidence*. New York: Harmony, 2013.

Sarah Holmes. *Crochet Toothbrush Rag Rug Pattern Collection*, by. (Charleston, SC: CreateSpace Independent Publishing Platform, 2000).

Sarah Swett. *Kids Weaving: Projects for Kids of All Ages*. Illustrated by Lena Corwin, photography by Chris Hartlove. New York: Steward, Tabori and Chang, 2005.

### Children's Books

Charles L. Blood, Martin Link. *The Goat in the Rug*. Illustrated by Nancy Winslow Parker. New York: Aladdin, 1990.

Omar S. Castaneda. *Abuela's Weave*. Illustrated by Enrique O. Sanchez. New York: Lee & Low Books, 1995.

Ginger Churchill. *Wild Rose's Weaving*. Illustrated by Nicole Wong. Terre Haute, IN: Tanglewood Press, 2011.

Kathleen Monaghan and Hermon Joyner. *You Can Weave! Projects for Young Weavers*. Worchester, MA: Davis, 2001.

# Gratitude Grows

3

## James: Practices for Grown-Ups

GRATITUDE IS A particularly potent ally in awakening joy, as it helps expand the mind as well as the heart. With a grateful heart we have a container and the space to hold the difficulties we meet. Gratitude is a way of saying "Yes" to life, seeing what's good as well as dealing with the things that need our attention.

You don't have to wait for moments of gratitude to descend on you. You can consciously cultivate them through practice. For some people, gratitude is the most powerful turning point in awakening joy. One of the main effects of practicing gratitude is that our "appreciation radar" is out much more consistently and we start seeing what is good in our lives.

While writing *Awakening Joy*, I, James, visited my then eighty-nine-year-old mom in Los Angeles. I happened to be writing the chapter on gratitude. I brought with me lots of research on the benefits of this wonderful quality of heart and shared it with her. I must confess that I had a slightly hidden motive, as my mom, by her own admission, was someone who tended to complain about things.

After I read her some of the studies, I asked her what she thought. When she said she was impressed, I wondered out loud how it would be to take on a gratitude practice. She raised her eyebrows and replied, "James, dear, I know I'm very blessed, but I've been looking at the glass as half empty all my life and I don't think I'm about to change now."

I continued, "Mom, if you could change, would you?"

She responded, "I suppose if I could, I would, but don't hold your breath. I don't think it will happen." I then suggested that we play a game to see if it's possible to change to a good habit just for the fun of it. I said that since she knew her life was blessed, how about if every time she complained I followed it with the reminder word "And ..." to which she would respond, "And my life is very blessed." Fortunately, she had the kind of spirit that was up for playing games and she agreed.

What an eye-opener it was for her. As the complaints rolled off her tongue, I caught each one with a playful "And ..." to which she gave her agreed-upon reply. We shared an amazing week as we laughed together at her incessant mind habit of focusing on the negative! What's more, as she said out loud how her life was blessed, she started to actually feel the truth of it. I kept up the game with her through many phone calls in the weeks after I left, along with a friend of hers in Los Angeles who was in on the game. The most remarkable thing of all was that she started to truly change. She's now a YouTube star, sharing her experience in a very funny video that went viral called "Confessions of a Jewish Mother: How My Son Ruined My Life."[2]

Of course, she still had her share of complaints. But remembering how blessed she was became her mantra for the final five years of her life. Every conversation was peppered with that recollection. She truly experienced a shift that had an astounding effect on her and others around her. I shared in *Awakening Joy* a poem that she wrote to me for my birthday seven months after that game began. Even though she was losing her eyesight, it didn't deter her from a having a miraculous change of perspective.

> Ninety is just fine with me, I no longer rant and rave
> About where the world is heading and my exclusive job to save.
> I wallow in contentment and know that I am blessed
> Awakening to the joy of living at its best.
> I'm happier than I've ever been and truly mean each word.
> The thoughts that caused the worries now all seem so absurd.
> Though my eyesight has been dimmed I see clearer than before,
> The glass is not half empty; it's overflowing to be sure.

If my mom could change, anyone can change! Even during the last days of her life when she lost a battle with cancer (fortunately with very little pain), gratitude held her in her process. I walked into her room one morning a few weeks before the end and saw a most serene look on her face. I asked her what she was thinking and she replied, "Actually my mind was completely devoid of all thoughts except 'Thank you, God. Thank you, God.'" I asked her if I could quote her on that, to which she replied with her usual wit, "Will I get a commission?"

When I later asked if she wanted me to read any words from her at her memorial service, she said, "Yes." She told me that life didn't owe her any-

2. You can watch the video at https://www.youtube.com/watch?v=FRbL46mWx9w

thing. She had had an amazing life with no regrets and was ready to go. She didn't know what she did to have been so blessed. And then she said, "Blessed. It's such a small word and it means everything."

### Switching the Channel

When you find yourself stuck in a negative rut or just bored, look around yourself for something in this moment to appreciate. Become aware of a sense door that wasn't switched on. See what is here right now to appreciate that you hadn't noticed. By shifting your focus, you can wake up from the funk your mind is creating. When we pause to notice what we usually take for granted, a new world of possibilities opens up. It's as if we've changed the station instead of being stuck on our own little "drama channel." Or you can, like my mom, from time to time, reflect on all the good things in your life.

One of my favorite insights about gratitude is from M. J. Ryan, author of *Attitudes of Gratitude*: "Gratitude is like a flashlight. It lights up what is already there. You don't necessarily have anything more or different, but suddenly you can actually see what is. And because you can see, you no longer take it for granted."

## Try This

### Basic Mindful Gratitude Practice to Awaken Joy

One of the main ways to deepen gratitude's impact is to let your awareness fully experience it when it's here, taking time to feel it in your body and your mind. How do you know you're feeling gratitude? What does it actually feel like? You don't have to take a very long time. Just a few seconds to let it register clearly in your body is enough. Once you become familiar with the landscape in your body, you will feel it easily and naturally this way. Here is a simple gratitude practice:

1. Sit quietly in a relaxed posture. Focus on the heart center. As you inhale, visualize breathing in kindness. With each exhale allow any negativity to be released.

*(continues on next page)*

2. Reflect on some blessing in your life: a person or thing you're grateful for.

3. Invite an image of that person or situation. Take a moment to silently send a thought of appreciation to that person or to life for that situation with a simple, sincere "Thank you."

4. Let your awareness fully experience your gratitude, taking time to feel in your body the energy of that blessing in your life.

### Other Gratitude Practices

1. Daily gratitude email practice with a friend. Every day send each other a brief email about what you're grateful for that day. Doing it with a partner is a very effective way to keep the practice going.

2. Write a gratitude letter. Martin Seligman, the father of Positive Psychology, has found that of all the exercises for developing happiness, this is one of the most effective of all. Pick someone whom you feel great gratitude for—a relative, a friend, a mentor—and write a letter appreciating all the ways they've enriched your life. Then, either send it to them, or even better, read it to the person face-to-face or by phone or Skype. Michele has included the positive impact of a gratitude letter written to her grade six teacher in the lesson "Snail Mail" in this chapter.

3. Write a gratitude list. For five minutes, write down everything you can think of that you are grateful for, or people you are grateful to. Notice how it feels in your body and mind just making the list. Share your gratitude list with your buddy.

4. Gratitude Journal: An alternative to sharing a regular email with a friend is to keep a gratitude journal. Write down regularly what you were grateful for that day.

5. Expressing your gratitude directly in the moment: When we share our appreciation of others directly with them, it becomes even stronger. This is because transferring a thought into words or actions deepens its impact. The other person gets the benefit of your communication and you deepen your practice of appreciation and gratitude. During these next two weeks, when you find

something you appreciate in someone else, practice expressing it directly.

Be sure to include yourself in your gratitude practice. Send yourself appreciation for practicing gratitude and holding your intention to awaken joy.

## Michele: Infusing Children with Gratitude

When I met with James in Berkeley last year, I had never traveled before on BART, the local transit system. I arrived at Richmond station and walked up the platform very proud of myself for figuring out the bus system that dropped me at the BART and the BART map itself. Basking in my relief, it was then that I realized I was on the opposite side of the terminal to the one I needed. I had no idea how to get to my platform, and the train was due in three minutes. There was only one man on my side. He was over six foot four, wore headphones, had tattoos up and down his arms, and a hat on backwards with jewelry dripping off of him. He was looking straight ahead. Of course he was the perfect person to ask. I explained my problem and asked him how to get to the other side. He stood up and said, "I will help you." He grabbed my suitcase and began running. I followed at breakneck speed. We ran all the way to the other side and he told me this is where I could get on the train. I turned to him and thanked him and told him I was currently meeting a man and writing a book about *Awakening Joy*. I shared that he had shown me such kindness that I would write about him in the book. A huge smile broke over his face. "Thanks, you do that," he said. Needless to say, I

was incredibly grateful. I made the train, I had my suitcase and a brilliant smile and wave from the tough-looking guy on the other side of the platform. I knew after waving goodbye, my meeting with James would be fruitful. Gratitude is a verb. A moment-by-moment practice.

## Circle Around

Wiping tears, a parent stood in her first gratitude circle. Children had gathered and were passing a special stone, sharing what they were grateful for in their lives. They shared things from "having my Mom make my lunch," "snuggling my cat," and "having the best class ever," to "living on planet Earth!" After twenty-five sweaty palms touched the rock and shared, this mom said she had never witnessed such a profound sharing of honesty and truth. She had no idea this could be done in schools. She whispered if this had been part of her life as a child, she would not have felt so alone.

## Why Gratitude?

* ✳ Strengthens the immune system
* ✳ Lowers blood pressure
* ✳ Helps people sleep better
* ✳ Brings higher levels of positive emotions
* ✳ Makes us feel more joyful and optimistic
* ✳ We feel less alone
* ✳ We are more generous and kind

## Does It Work?

Eli was in my grade six class when I was a young teacher. She is now a mom with a child in our school. I am embarrassed to admit this, not because of Eli—she is an amazing person—but because I don't know where the time goes. How could I possibly have a student coming back through the doors who is now a mother herself? Her statement that follows not only shows the importance of a gratitude practice, but also clearly demonstrates how prac-

tices can stick with children years and years later. We plant the seeds, let go, and they grow.

> *I was a student of Michele over twenty years ago. I am now a parent of two children myself and still use strategies and deep practices of mindfulness I learned from her so many years ago. My husband and I have been to her parenting classes and highly recommend any lessons she writes. I will need them! We now have a gratitude circle at our dining room table every night and I so remember how she had us look in each other's eyes whenever we said hello or goodbye. —Eli*

## Snail Mail and the Sewing Machine

The lessons offered in this chapter incorporate crafts as well as the art of letter writing. The gratitude crafts are fun to do at home and require few supplies and little preparation. You can use a simple needle and thread or drag out the old, dusty sewing machine. It might even be worth a visit to the grandparents to borrow a sewing machine and to work the beautiful muscle of gratitude. You can make the crafts into bigger, more complex projects if you wish.

As the crafts help children develop small motor skills and work with number patterns, the letter-writing practices build on these and extend into literacy. On the morning of the Snail Mail lesson, I was feeling down about a world tragedy. I went into school that Monday and thought about the things we don't say to those who have touched our lives in some special way.

Well, I am happy to say that as a class we wrote letters of gratitude to our loved ones.

On a personal level, the letter-writing lesson in this chapter is my absolute favorite. Did you ever get a letter written with a scented pen on scented paper? This lesson incorporates so many beautiful lost skills: the sharing of a heart on paper, the act of crafting words, the addressing and licking of an envelope, and walking to the mailbox, all the while thinking of the recipient. Grandparents, aunties, uncles, and other adults far from the children will so appreciate receiving a physical letter in the mail. It is a gift of time. It connects us heart to heart.

# Lesson 1: Planting the Seeds of Gratitude in Quick, Easy Ways

## Creating a Gratitude Practice

Gratitude creates a positive feedback loop. When you open your own heart and express your appreciation to others, they feel your friendliness. It makes them relax and feel more comfortable around you.

**Builds strengths of:**
- Gratitude
- Caring
- Sharing
- Family vision and appreciation

**Materials**
- Journal
- Craft supplies
- Seeds
- Simple gardening supplies

**Ages**
- Preschool to adult

**School Curriculum Connections**
- Oral language
- Written language
- Listening skills
- Reading
- Science
- Fine arts
- Social and emotional learning

### Model it
Express your gratitude to others and to your own children for the things that they do. Take the time to truly share by either writing a little note or looking into your loved ones' eyes and speaking to them. Tell them what they did, how it made you feel, and the effect it had on your life. For example: "Thank

you for taking your shoes off before coming into the house. I feel so happy you remembered how important cleanliness is to me and now I have time to do a puzzle with you instead of sweeping the floor." These little actions your children take, when acknowledged, go a long way to having a more peaceful home.

### Say it

Start your morning by sharing your gratitude for simple things. "I love seeing the sunshine." "I am immensely grateful for where we live." "Wow! Annie said 'Hello' this morning and it brightened my day. I am so happy to see her." (This practice gives children the vocabulary and a model for articulating gratitude.)

### Write it

Have a gratitude journal in the house that everyone can write in. If your children are not old enough to write, have someone scribe for them. Each day, or whenever you think of it, write down something you are grateful for and watch the journal grow into a family treasure to be looked back on and cherished throughout the years. You can also have photos, magazines, and a variety of craft materials on hand so children can collage in the journal.

### Feel it

Hold hands at the dinner table and have each person say a gratitude aloud for something in their day. Children need to see their parents practicing and sharing too. This has been the strongest and deepest practice my own family has maintained for over twenty years. Every night, no matter who is at the table, people are invited to share something they are grateful for. I have had countless people tell me that this practice not only touched their lives deeply and now they have included doing it in their own homes.

### Plant it

These practices not only plant seeds of gratitude in our children, but also in ourselves. They slow us down and allow us to see the small things, the non-material things. When I look back on my own gratitude journals over the years, I see a pattern of being thankful for the beauty of nature and the love of friends and family. This has created an acute awareness of what is vitally important to my daily well-being. Try keeping a gratitude journal yourself and see what patterns emerge. Gratitude reminds us of our interconnectedness with all living things on the planet.

### Resources

#### ADULT BOOKS

Thich Nhat Hanh. *The Art of Communicating*. New York: HarperOne, 2014.

Nikolaj Flor Rotne and Didde Flor Rotne. *Everybody Present: Mindfulness in Education*. Berkeley, CA: Parallax Press, 2013.

#### CHILDREN'S BOOKS

Thich Nhat Hanh. *Mindful Movements: Ten Exercises for Well-Being*. Berkeley, CA: Parallax Press, 2008.

Gail Silver. *Steps and Stones*. Illustrated by Christiane Krömer. Berkeley, CA: Plum Blossom Books, 2011.

 # Lesson 2: On the Mat / Love Arrows

## Extending Our Care and Gratitude to Others in a Fun, Physical Way

Isn't it interesting that although we know gratitude is a direct source of joy, we often don't express it? The gratitude habit takes practice.

### Builds:

- Physical well-being
- Social and emotional learning
- Reflection-mindfulness
- Family connections
- Compassion and gratitude

**Materials**
- Yoga mat or towel

**Ages**
- Three to adult

**School Curriculum Connections**
- Oral language
- Listening skills
- Physical education
- Social and emotional learning

## *Home and School Practice*

Yoga is something all the children beg to do. "Please, please, please can we do yoga today?" My own boys joined me from the time they were little whenever I had my mat out. As children are so physically oriented, I created a lesson to pair yoga and gratitude in an easy way. If you are already a yoga practitioner, this will be a breeze to incorporate into your and your children's day. If you have never done yoga before, no problem. Think of a love warrior holding a bow and arrow. You've got it! There are also yoga books listed in the resources that follow to help you hone your practice. This pose is called The Warrior.

At school this year we have a spare classroom and a yoga mat for every child. They leave their little shoes lined up outside the room. There is something about seeing all those small boots and mismatched socks and shoes that is so colorful and sweet. On the mat, we breathe, slow down, and "get into our bodies." One of the children's favorite poses is the warrior. I have them pull back their arms and place a love arrow in their "bow" and imagine someone or a pet who needs some love today. They send their imaginary love arrows flying to their target, entering their body with sparkling light and giving them a flush of goodness. They absolutely love this. At the end, in relaxation, they all lie down on their mats and I have them think of someone or something they are

grateful for. I ask them to let the feeling sink into their bodies. As Dr. Rick Hanson says, "Why waste the good stuff? Let the brain capture the good and get the neurons firing. Neurons that fire together wire together."

We then sit in a circle and share what we are grateful for. We might also share who we know who might need a little extra love today. It is amazing to me how children spontaneously share worries that are deep inside. Many of these worries have never been articulated before. One day a boy shared that his mother had been in a car accident the week before and her brain wasn't working right. He was so worried. No one knew about this accident, as he was living with his father that week and it had not been communicated to the school. The children were able to empathize with the boy and share their good wishes for his mother. It was so remarkable. We all shared the gratitude we had for our bodies and the incredible ways the body heals. This opportunity to share, grieve, and give gratitude gave the boy an incredible sense of comfort.

## Do You Know What a Joy Buddy Is?

Gratitude expert Robert Emmons shares how important a gratitude practice is in elevating well-being. "We discovered scientific proof that when people regularly engage in systematic cultivation of gratitude, they experience a variety of measurable benefits: psychological, physical, and interpersonal. The evidence on gratitude contradicts the widely held view that all people have a 'set-point' of happiness that cannot be reset by any known means: in some cases, people have reported that gratitude led to transformative life changes" (Robert Emmons. *Thanks: How the New Science of Gratitude Can Make You Happier*. New York: Houghton Mifflin, 2007, p. 3).

James has certainly found in his course that this is true when he introduced the role of a joy buddy. The idea is, each day or week you relate how your life is joyous to a buddy through personal contact, phone calls, or writing. This continual practice builds a strong muscle of gratitude, and having a witness hear or read your joy enhances the feeling beyond measure. The amazing thing is, you don't even have to know the joy buddy intimately. You will find over time this intimacy will grow with each vulnerable sharing.

I had one joy buddy for more than two years whom I had only met for fifteen minutes at a weekend retreat. After two years I felt I knew her joy and pain better than the feelings of people I see at my workplace everyday. I now buddy with another friend who lives in a different country. I get a text at some point throughout the day sharing a moment of her joy, and I send her back the same. Just hearing her share brings happiness to me, so I get double the pleasure every day.

All you have to do is find someone willing to share the practice. What a great way for you as adults to share your vulnerable heart in the ongoing journey of parenting.

## Resources

### ADULT BOOKS

Mary Kaye Chryssicas. *Breathe: Yoga for Teens*. New York: DK Children, 2007.

B.K.S. Iyengar. *B.K.S. Iyengar Yoga: The Path to Holistic Health*. New York: DK, 2013.

### CHILDREN'S BOOKS

Tara Guber and Leah Kalish. *Yoga Pretzels (Yoga Cards)*. Illustrated by Sophie Fatus. Cambridge, MA: Barefoot Books, 2005.

Teresa Power. *ABCs of Yoga for Kids*. Pacific Palisades, CA: Stafford House, 200.

 # Lesson 3: Gratitude Flags

## Building the Gratitude Muscle One Stitch at a Time

The secret to deepening your happiness groove is to pause and consciously notice what's going on inside you whenever you feel that delightful experience of genuine gratitude. All you need is a few seconds to let your awareness really take in the sensations in your body or how it feels in your mind. The more you become familiar with the landscape of gratitude, the more it will naturally be available to you.

### Builds strengths of:
- Gratitude
- Caring
- Sharing
- Family vision and appreciation

### Materials
- Fabric scraps or pieces of drop cloth (I like to use a drop cloth from the hardware store, as it is cheap and can be used for many other projects)
- Scissors ("materials" *continues on next page*)

- Permanent pens or acrylic paints
- Needles and thread or sewing machine
- Ribbon
- Embellishments such as sparkles, sequins, buttons, beads, and tassels

## Ages
- Preschool to adult

## School Curriculum Connections
- Oral language
- Written language
- Listening skills
- Reading
- Fine arts
- Social and emotional learning

Many parents wish their children were less self-entitled and more grateful for what they have in their lives. They want to give their children a wonderful life and they also want their children to appreciate not only what they have, but also the simple beauty right before them. Here is an activity that can take place over days or weeks and leave a lasting imprint of gratitude. This gratitude flag project is not only for your child, but also for all those who have a chance to view this work of art—it will enhance a feeling of appreciation. The flags can help remind us of the things we love and often take for granted. The project can be as simple or elaborate as you wish.

## Home Practice
Our family gratitude flags have been blowing on our property for many years. Every morning I see them as I walk outside. I feel such a sense of love and

warm heartedness just reading them. I have heard that as Tibetan prayer flags disintegrate and the tiny threads breakdown, those threads are sent out into the world as prayers of love and kindness. So as your flags break down in the snow, rain, sun, and hail, imagine all those grateful blessings going out into the world.

## How to Begin

Begin with a little piece of cloth and cut it into either a rectangle or pendant shape; you can make it any size you like. I usually cut 8" × 10" pieces. These will become your prayer flags. Ask your children to use a permanent marker to draw something they are grateful for. I ask them to think about the natural

world and people in their lives rather than video games or television. You decide what you would like to focus on. If they are of age to print, they can write a sentence or word to describe their picture. Next, if you have a sewing machine, create a simple fold on one side of the flag to thread a ribbon through. If you don't have a machine, do a little running stitch by hand to create the fold. Thread the flag onto a long piece of ribbon maybe six feet long and continue adding one a day or one from every member of the family until the string is full. Hang out in the elements to blow your wishes across the world.

## *School Practice*

When I teach this practice in the classroom, each child makes one flag and we string them on a line that is over twenty feet long. We then stand in a huge circle and read out what we are each grateful for. Carrying the line, we string it up in a chosen place in the schoolyard to blow in the breeze. Parents love seeing the gratitude flags waving at them every morning and the little ones love to share which part of the flag-chain they created. By seeing this flag daily, the act of gratitude is wired into the brain and nurtured in the heart.

Extension: James suggests that we write down our gratitudes in a journal in order to deepen our happiness groove. By taking the time to think of three or four things we are grateful for each day, we start to see what really matters in our lives. Every child in my classroom has a gratitude journal. At some point in the day we take fifteen minutes to freely write what we are grateful for in the moment. When it is difficult to think of anything, I ask them to remember that they have the luxury of a bed, breakfast, and a school to attend. I don't say this in a dismissive way but as a way of recognizing that small things are meaningful. We can be deeply grateful and appreciate each one of them. To take this one step further, have the children share one or more gratitudes in the group or with a friend. Articulating their gratitude also increases happiness and awakens joy.

## *Resources*

### Adult Books

Sarah Ban Breathnach. *Simple Abundance: A Daybook of Comfort and Joy*. New York: Grand Central Publishing, 2009.

Meena Srinivasan. *Teach, Breathe, Learn: Mindfulness in and out of the Classroom*. Berkeley, CA: Parallax Press, 2014.

### Children's Books

Eve Bunting. *The Memory String*. Illustrated by Ted Rand. Boston , MA: Houghton Mifflin Harcourt Books for Young Readers, 2015.

Eve Bunting. *Fly Away Home Paperback*. Illustrated by Ronald Himler. Boston, MA: Houghton Mifflin Harcourt Books for Young Readers, 1993.

Phoebe Gilman. *Something From Nothing*. New York: Scholastic Press, 1993.

Tony Johnston. *The Quilt Story*. London: Puffin Books, 1996.

Patricia Polacco. *The Keeping Quilt Paperback*. Riverside, NJ: Simon & Schuster, 2001.

# Lesson 4: Thirty-Eight Years Later— Snail Mail

When we slow down enough to relax our mind we let ourselves be touched by the simplest things—a child's laughter or the beauty of a flower. That is one of the benefits of stepping off the treadmill of our minds and really being present. When we're grateful for what is here right now, we can let ourselves be surprised by life.

## Building Strengths of:
- Care
- Well-being
- Kindness
- Connection

## Materials
- Pen
- Paper
- Envelope
- Stamps
- Time

## Ages
- Five to adult

## School Curriculum Connections
- Oral language
- Written language
- Listening skills
- Reading
- Fine arts
- Social and emotional learning

## *Home and School Practice*

### When Mail Went by Ship
When I was a little girl, my mother had us write to our grandparents, who lived in both Australia and England. I would hear my mum plunking away on the typewriter tidbits of news every week. Writing created a thread of living energy between the two countries.

As a child I would enclose a little letter every month or so. The letters were a way of connecting with the loved ones we rarely, if ever, saw. I still remember the excitement of getting my own letter. When my grandmother died, I found out she had kept every single letter written from us in Canada, over a thirty-year span. Within those letters was the history of a young woman, my mum, who immigrated to Canada in the fifties, married an Englishman there, and had a family. I can imagine my grandmother's gratitude, as she and my grandfather knew through the post that their daughter was flourishing in a new country.

## Modern Day

With email, Facebook, texting, and calling, we rarely take the opportunity to slow down and write. This lost art of the pen combined with gratitude is our lesson of the day.

### *Pen, Paper, and an Open Heart*

I often hear adults talking about a teacher or person who changed their lives. I ask them if they ever told that person. Almost always the answer is "No." As a teacher, I wondered if my own students had people who had made a great impact on their lives. Armed with this thought, I went into a class of twenty-eight eleven-year-old children.

For the sake of simplicity in this classroom exercise, I narrowed the category from "anyone" who had changed their lives to a teacher who had touched their lives.

The children brainstormed a list of every single teacher who had been important in their lives. Students were excited to share why that particular person was special to them. It took far longer than I ever imagined just to create the list. The board was absolutely full of names and appreciations.

Two little boys had tears in their eyes when they shared. The teacher they had loved the most had died of cancer. They wanted to know how they could appreciate her. Another child sitting close by suggested they write to the teacher's husband who was still alive. They eagerly took on the task. After we wrote all the names on the board, we did a mindfulness practice. We brought the life-changing person into our awareness and acknowledged the impact they had on our lives. I put on quiet music and had them write their thoughts down for about a half hour. I had an outline of how to write a letter on the board so they had a framework to work from.

I shared with the students that my favorite teacher was Miss Mallow. In grade six she let a friend and me do school work outside on the grass and gave us each our own drawing journal. This sense of freedom she conveyed and her honoring of individual choice are such key parts of the way I teach now. I wondered as I put pen to paper if I would ever find her again.

## The Beauty of Technology

When they felt complete, the students brought their letters to me and we Googled addresses. There was no one we could not find. We then learned how to address an envelope and where to put the stamps and return addresses. These were mailed out during the final weeks of school. Many students came to me and asked to write several letters, because they couldn't choose only one person.

## By the Way

I did find Miss Mallow and she expressed how deeply touched she was to get a letter from me after so many years. She was actually living within hours of my home. My partner and I took a trip this summer to see her and her husband. Last week she wrote and told me that after receiving my letter, she contacted a teacher of her own and expressed her gratitude.

Several teachers who received letters contacted me and said it had made their day and made teaching seem so much more worthwhile. They were deeply touched to get an actual letter in the mail and have placed their letters in a very visible spot to remind themselves of the positive impact they have on young lives.

## Extensions

After writing a letter, you could also have your child or students read the letter aloud to the person they chose to honor.

You could put a special thank you in the local newspaper.

You can share the power of gratitude with those you come in daily contact with by simply acknowledging aloud your appreciation.

### *Resources*

#### ADULT BOOKS

Margaret Shepherd and Sharon Hogan. *The Art of the Personal Letter: A Guide to Connecting Through the Written Word.* New York: Broadway Books, 2008.

Carol Sperandeo and Bill Zimmerman. *Lunch Box Letters: Writing Notes of Love and Encouragement to Your Children.* Richmond Hill, ON: Firefly Books, 2007.

#### CHILDREN'S BOOKS

Allan Ahlberg. *The Jolly Postman.* Illustrated by Janet Ahlberg. New York: LB Kids, 2001.

Paul Amelchenko. *Children's Letters to Dog.* Minocqua, WI: Willow Creek Press, 2009.

Nancy Loewen. *Sincerely Yours: Writing Your Own Letter (Writer's Toolbox).* Illustrated by Christopher Lyles. Mankato, MN: Picture Window Books, 2009.

Patricia Polacco. *My Rotten Redheaded Older Brother.* New York: Simon & Schuster, 1998.

# Joy in Difficult Times

4

## James: Practices for Grown-Ups

WHEN MY WIFE, Jane, began teaching English as a Second Language to adult immigrants and refugees in Berkeley, she decided to take a language immersion course in Costa Rica to learn a new method of teaching. She was excited to think of spending three weeks brushing up her Spanish in a rainforest paradise of a safe, friendly country. The program included spending many hours a day in a language school and living with a family far from town who spoke no English. Excited about the adventure, she had no idea of the challenges she would face.

Planned months in advance, the trip turned out to be a few weeks after the September 11th terrorist attacks. Cautious but determined, she decided to fly anyway. The tension was high at the semi-deserted airport and the plane was eerily empty save for a handful of passengers and TSA agents. This added to her anxious mood, setting the tone for the weeks to come.

She soon realized her Spanish was more than rusty. She could speak in only the simplest of sentences with her host family, unable to share her complex feelings in a foreign language. As she read about the continued threats to the Bay Area, including a plot to blow up the Golden Gate Bridge, and contemplated her son's recent difficulties as a high-school freshman, she felt worried, sad, and lonely. She missed her friends and family. Her classmates were mostly in their twenties and Jane soon realized her brain had thirty extra years of mileage and was no longer in tip-top academic shape.

One memorable incident occurred while trying to withdraw money from an ATM machine on a very muggy day. After waiting in a long line, when her turn finally came, she couldn't figure out the instructions. As she struggled in her attempts, she became anxious about the locals standing in the rain behind her, waiting for this fumbling *gringa*. She became so flustered that after a while she simply went to the back of the line again, hoping the next time she would be calm enough to have more success.

Her Costa Rican adventure became a very miserable three weeks. Feeling overwhelmed and out of her league, she was truly humbled. At the time, she had no idea that this experience would turn out to be a very important gift that deeply informed her career teaching immigrants and refugees from all over the world.

She understood, as never before, the culture shock and loneliness of her students in Berkeley who had been completely uprooted from their homes. They included professionals willing to start at the bottom in order to give their children better opportunities, traumatized political refugees, and recent arrivals who needed to support their families and send money home. All were trying to navigate a fast-paced high-tech culture with minimal tools for the most basic tasks. She enjoyed offering them a community where they felt safe, respected, and capable of learning. In response, her students would shower her with gratitude, often reluctant to leave her class even when they were ready to advance to the next level.

Jane looks back on that difficult trip as a transformative experience that revealed to her an inner strength she hadn't known she possessed. More importantly, she realized that patience, compassion, support, and community were as essential as the many language lessons she enthusiastically shared.

## The Transforming Power of Suffering

The practice of opening to suffering is a vital part of awakening joy. The more we understand suffering and are willing to come to terms with it, the greater the possibility of developing a mind that is not afraid of the hard stuff when it comes.

By learning to open our hearts to everything, including difficulties, we discover that beneath the pain lies wisdom, compassion, and love. And we find a courage we didn't know we had. Look back on your own encounters with suffering. Is this true for you? Have your hard lessons stretched you and helped you access strength and wisdom you didn't realize you had? Have they helped deepen your compassion?

Awakening joy does not mean living in denial. Even though I wrote a book called *Awakening Joy*, I sometimes find myself feeling a real sadness at the state of the world. Besides the natural disasters like tsunamis, tornadoes, and earthquakes, to witness the level of human suffering driven by greed, hatred, or fear is very painful. If we deny these sorrows, we're living in a dream world. But to feel hopeless and wallow in despair is not the answer either. Our happiness or suffering is not about what is happening to us as much as our relationship to what is happening.

You needn't pretend that things are going swimmingly when they're not. Start by allowing yourself to be right where you are. When things are hard, we can't just slap on a happy face and think we should get over it. We can, however, compassionately hold our sorrows in a way that doesn't increase our pain. In dealing with a major loss, for example, we need time to go through the grieving process. It's healthy and important to grieve the loss of a loved one or a major change in circumstances.

Your willingness to use difficult situations to practice greater awareness will help deepen your understanding of the human experience and life. What you learn becomes not only valuable for yourself but also allows you to be there for others who are going through similar situations.

In working with a painful situation, the first step is to acknowledge and honor your feelings. Mindful attention can help you directly open up to your experience. By being honestly present with your sorrow in manageable doses, you can learn to authentically feel it without being overwhelmed. This can allow it to move through you naturally in its own time without your trying to hurry it along (which only locks it in more).

When going through difficulties, it's important to remember that your pain and sorrow are not permanent. You will probably laugh again and feel moments of happiness again. Staying in the present and taking things one moment at a time makes the situation much more workable. Everything changes. Remembering this gives us courage to be with life when it's hard. Impermanence also reveals that suffering is not as solid as it appears. There are moments of well-being interspersed between the challenging moments. The more you can notice these, the less solid your suffering will seem. And the less you will suffer.

As you explore this theme yourself or with your children, keep in mind that you're not trying to look for difficulties in your life. Continue to work with intention, mindfulness, and gratitude as practices to awaken states of well-being and notice them when they're here. The idea is to simply allow all experience in, and, when life is hard, practice being with it in a wise, non-resisting way, a little at a time. I hope the lessons Michele offers in this book will help your children to learn that even though life can be hard sometimes, we can grow through the difficulties and strengthen our capacity to be with even the most challenging situations.

## Three Methods for Working with Suffering

In *Awakening Joy*, we present three different strategies that can help you with suffering when it arises. See if one or more of them works for you.

# *Try This*

### *Learning from the Past*

For many, like Jane, going through difficult times can lead us to true happiness. Our challenges shake us out of our complacency and encourage us to find deeper meaning in life. It connects us with the human experience of loss, pain, and sorrow, and draws out our compassion for others. Has your own suffering led you to search for meaningful answers?

1. Think of a challenging situation or difficult period that you've been through.

2. What lessons did you learn by going through the experience? How did it help you grow in some way?

### *Working with the Present Challenges*

1. Bring to mind a difficult situation you are dealing with in your life right now.

2. What are the emotions that you're feeling? Have you allowed yourself to feel all the feelings?

3. What are the lessons you're learning from this situation? How can you find meaning as you go through this difficulty?

## Method One: RAIN

The first method is bringing mindfulness to directly experience your actual feelings just as they are. The key is to not get lost in the story of the situation. Whatever it is—sadness, anger, wanting, or fear—go directly into feeling the bodily experience or energy of the emotion. The acronym RAIN can help you remember the process of directly opening to and working skillfully with difficult emotions:

1. **R**ecognize what you're feeling. (What am I actually feeling right now? Sadness? Anger? Fear?)

2. **Allow it to be here.** Let go of any agenda for it to change and, for a few moments, give it permission to be just as it is.

3. **Investigate** how it feels in your body on an energetic level without getting into the story or trying to get rid of it. (Bring a curiosity or interest that is simply exploring the landscape of the emotion without figuring anything out.)

4. **Non-identification** (a fancy way of saying not taking it personally)—don't take ownership of the experience as being who you are. ("I'm such an angry person.") It is not unique to you. It is simply an energy that has come to visit you. It does not have to define who you are. Your experience of anger or sadness isn't so different from my anger or sadness. You are opening to the human condition.

Explore a little bit at a time. If it's too hard to mindfully stay with it for more than a few moments, turn your attention to the breath or the body or, perhaps, do some gratitude or loving-kindness practice by thinking of someone you care about and mentally wishing him or her well. Then go back to explore the suffering when you've regained a bit more balance.

## Method Two: Holding Our Suffering with Kindness and Compassion

Sometimes it's too frightening to stay mindful and balanced with a difficult experience. We get scared when we feel we don't have the resources to face the challenge all by ourselves. In going through difficult times, perhaps the most important thing you can do is be compassionate and kind with yourself. Mindful Self-Compassion, an approach developed by Dr. Kristin Neff and Dr. Christopher Germer, offers some very effective tools. Here is their "Mindful Self-Compassion Break." You might try this, or your own variation, whenever you're going through a hard time.

1. Place your hand on your heart. (This is a physiologically soothing action that releases oxytocin, a powerful comforting hormone.)

2. Say to yourself: "This is a moment of suffering" (or some variation that resonates with you, such as: "This is really hard.").

3. Then say: "Suffering is a part of life." (You might find it helpful to reflect on all the people in the world who are going through what you are right now.)

4. Then say: "May I hold my suffering with kindness and compassion." Feel the vulnerability of your heart through your hand as you hold yourself. You might connect with both the tender self who is receiving the care and also the wise loving one who is extending it right through

your hand. Both are part of who you are. Doing this brings you into wholeness.

## Method Three: Surrounding Yourself with a Field of Benevolent Energy

Sometimes it's too frightening to stay mindful and balanced with a difficult experience. We get scared when we feel we don't have the resources to face the challenge all by ourselves. One technique to find the support and loving-kindness you need is to call on a benevolent force to help you, whether you think of it as God or a higher power or the Dharma or the Universal Life Force or spirit guides. This counteracts the feeling that you're all alone.

1. Call on the benevolence of life—however you conceive of it—to support you. Invite a field of benevolent energy to surround you. If it had a color, what color would it be?
2. Let yourself be held in this field of benevolence as a protection and connection to something larger than yourself. Relax your body. Trust in it. Feel its support, as you let yourself be held in it.
3. Know that it is always here for you if you call on it.

### Switching Your Focus

Don't think that once you see your suffering clearly, everything will automatically be fine. Even when the mind understands a wiser perspective, the body may still reverberate from the energy that's stirred up. Part of wisely opening to difficult feelings includes knowing when you're reaching the point when you're no longer feeling balanced. Trust your intuition regarding when you can open to your pain in an equanimous way.

If you're struggling or feeling overwhelmed, you need to back off. Otherwise, the mind and heart get contracted and lost.

When you find yourself overwhelmed or lost in a story that's not serving you, try looking around you for something in this moment to appreciate. Become aware of a sense door that wasn't switched on. See what is here right now to appreciate what you hadn't noticed. By shifting your focus, you can wake up from the bad dream your mind is creating. In taking a break, you can get a fresh perspective, which will give you more clarity to address what needs to be attended to when you're ready.

One way to switch the focus is to do something to discharge the negative energy. Exercise, do yoga, walk in nature, speak to a friend, or just give yourself the option to let it move through you in its own time. Someone I know uses the following strategy when she's gotten stuck and feels helpless: She has a cup of tea, goes out on her porch and lets herself consciously be "Pissed Buddha" for a while. After twenty or thirty minutes or so, the energy seems to shift by just allowing that space.

## Michele: Helping Children Navigate through Difficult Times

*If you treat them like hothouse flowers they won't survive the inevitable bumps in the road. They can only flourish in the hothouse. If you take them into anything other than a controlled environment, they will die.*

A dear friend and mother of three gave this piece of hothouse wisdom to me when I had my first child. As a new mother, I read every New Age book about parenting and attended to every demand and moan my wee one uttered. I wanted to be there for my son's needs before he knew he had them. I really worked hard. Smart, right? Loving, right?

Not really. I was creating a hothouse flower. I was exhausted and soon realized I could not and should not protect Kieran, my son, from the ups and downs in life. How was he to learn resiliency? How could he pick himself up from a fall and know he could manage on his own? I had already been a teacher for ten years when I had Kieran and had seen the effects of over-parenting, and yet I was doing what I knew wasn't helpful. I was helicopter parenting before he was out of diapers.

As a teacher I see more and more "helicopter parents." These parents flutter around trying to make sure their children never have a difficult conversation, never struggle for even a moment. They often end up speaking for their child as their wide-eyed bundle huddles silent. These parents take responsibilities for their child's success and failures.

Does this serve the child? Not in my experience or that of the many teachers I have spoken to. These over-protected children are often more anxious than their peers and feel they must connect with their parents before making any decisions. They lack self-confidence and inner knowing. They look to their parents or others before answering a question and have underdeveloped coping skills.

When children are not given tasks that are challenging, they fail to master tasks that are more difficult. If they cannot tie their own shoes or pick out their clothes, how can they be expected to make important decisions?

## How to Build Resiliency

If we can do our practices when times are fun and easy, it helps us be able to really put in a concentrated effort with them when things are difficult. I view charging a battery as a metaphor for daily practice. If we can do the practices day after day and slowly charge our batteries, then when we need to use our reserve in times of struggle, we will have a deep charge to draw from. We will have solid roots and a deep foundation.

This doesn't mean we deny our sadness, anger, fear, or pain, but that we let it in and allow it to flow through us rather than run away from it. We also teach children to express their emotions in healthy ways rather than stuffing them down and exploding. We teach children to shine the light on the positive, resting the mind on good moments. We teach children to empathize with others. When we do this we feel less alone and less entrenched in pain. As a result of these practices, we can bounce back from adversity more quickly.

I love this description of resilience by Paulo Coelho from *The Alchemist*: "The secret of life, though, is to fall seven times and to get up eight times." It gives me courage to allow my children to fall, learn, build resiliency, and get up stronger.

This chapter offers ways to help your child regulate their emotional state, remember good times, and spotlight the positive. Because of built-in survival mechanisms, our brains are naturally wired to pay more attention to negative events than positive ones. One key to changing how we see the world is to pay attention to the positive events. Teach your children to notice the joyful moments. Teach them how to fall, brush themselves off, and try again. Show them through your own actions how to take a baby step toward what they fear rather than run away from what scares them. Teach them that life is a bumpy road and that they have the resiliency to thrive and survive.

# Lesson 1: Building the Muscles of Self-Regulation and Discipline

The more you are motivated by kindness and the desire to act from the goodness of your heart, the greater the possibility of awakening joy. If we build the muscles of discipline daily, they will be there for us in both easy and difficult times, all of which are part of the human experience.

## Builds strengths of:
- Resiliency
- Perseverance
- Love of self
- Self-regulation
- Emotional intelligence
- Well-being

## Materials
- None

## Ages
- Two to adult

## School Curriculum Connections
- Oral language
- Listening skills
- Reading
- Physical education
- Social and emotional learning

## *Home and School Practice*

### Discipline Is Not a Bad Word

As teachers and parents, we know it takes repeated practice for children to begin to pick up new habits. Sometimes it feels as if we will go crazy repeating instructions. As a primary teacher, I lay out directions visually and orally and often show children kinesthetically. Still, they need repeated practice. Just when I think I will lose my mind trying to teach my students to be organized, winter break comes and my students are magically lining up, putting things in their cubbies, and have their day planners on their desks. I must admit this doesn't last if we don't keep reminding them, but it is much easier to reestablish the habit once it is engrained. Some people shut down at the word "discipline," but in this sense it is not used punitively, but is rather a way to strengthen the self by creating positive habits.

Christine Carter, in *Raising Happiness*, says, "Self-regulation, as the psychologists call it, is like a muscle. The more you use it the stronger it gets. One of the best things you can do to create a new habit is to exercise willpower or self-control in some area of your life, even though that area may have not relation to the new habit."

Who knew that practicing self-discipline, like brushing your teeth or making your bed, was transferable into other areas of your life?

What a great way to help our children and ourselves build muscles. As the children get older they may find a daily mindfulness practice will be much easier to come back to than people who have never had any form of daily practice before. What a gift.

## How Do We Build These Habits?

So what are a few ways we can build these habits of self-discipline? While I am said to be one of the most "flowing" teachers in the school, I try to balance flow with structure. I want children to have freedom as well as a framework of self-discipline they can use to grow from. The following practices can be used at home or at school. After a while, I find, children ask for structure. "Ms. L., you forgot to do journal writing today! The day planners are not out on desks yet so we can't start!"

## Try These Habits

Simply gifting your child with the responsibility to make their bed, brush their teeth, and get their backpacks ready every day for school can go a long way to exercising the muscle of self-discipline. In my experience, children at school who have everything done for them have a great deal of difficulty organizing their desks, assignments, and personal items. They have never had to do it so they honestly don't know how. I still have parents, of sixth grade students, coming into the classroom desperately organizing their child's desk in hopes of finding a "missing" assignment.

Give your child a little checklist that you make up together with a small list of daily practices. This will create the habits of discipline. The kids love to check off the tasks and feel a great sense of accomplishment at the end of the day. The list might include: brush hair, brush teeth, practice an instrument, and clear the table after dinner.

Following directions is vital. Children come to class unable to follow three small directions in a row. I find having the children repeat the directions back and picture themselves completing the task creates a level of mindfulness that goes a long way in anchoring the job in their minds. A few great ideas to build the muscles of following directions are:

✳ Hand slapping games
✳ Doing simple puzzles together

* ✳ Following patterns of color or shape when threading beads onto a string
* ✳ Building Legos or models that require step-by-step directions
* ✳ Sewing a simple pattern
* ✳ Creating step-by-step drawings
* ✳ Cooking using a recipe
* ✳ Building with wood
* ✳ Painting by number
* ✳ Repeating back what is said

Playing simple direction-following games like "Simon Says" and "Follow the Leader" makes children more mindful of listening to the oral word.

## Make Them Wait and Build Persistence, Resilience, and a Sense of Accomplishment

"Cameron's parents just gave him a car, Mum. They even put on insurance and pay for the gas! All the kids have a new iPhone. Their parents just gave it to them. I really want that new toy Mum. Pleeeease can I just get it now and pay you back in a month or two?" I have heard all these lines and more from my own boys.

Children have become accustomed to getting what they want when they want it. Parents are having a more and more difficult time instilling will power, self-control, and delayed gratification. Allow your child to wait for gratification.

I must say making my own children wait has been a tough one for me. Many times it would have been

easier to just give my boys something they truly wanted. When I was tempted, I tried to remember the principle that children grow in positive ways through waiting and taking steps to achieve a goal. These practices of self-discipline allow children to learn to think before they act and to become problem solvers. It also strengthens self-esteem. So with my own boys, I encouraged them to save, plan, and wait until whatever "thing" they wanted was available to them.

Kelly McGonigal states in her book, *The Willpower Instinct*, "Like a muscle, our willpower follows the rule of 'Use it or lose it.' If we try to save our energy by becoming willpower couch potatoes, we will lose the strength we have. But if we run a willpower marathon every day, we set ourselves up for total collapse. Our challenge is to train like an intelligent athlete, pushing our limit but also pacing ourselves." In other words, little steps of willpower each day will build persistence and discipline.

## Resources

### ADULT BOOKS

Kelly McGonigal. *The Willpower Instinct: How Self-Control Works, Why It Matters, and What You Can Do to Get More of It*. New Hyde Park, NY: Avery, 2013.

Shauna Shapiro and Chris White. *Mindful Discipline: A Loving Approach to Setting Limits and Raising an Emotionally Intelligent Child*. Oakland, CA: New Harbinger Publications, 2014.

Daniel J. Siegel and Tina Payne Bryson. *No-Drama Discipline: The Whole-Brain Way to Calm the Chaos and Nurture Your Child's Developing Mind*. New York: Bantam, 2014.

### CHILDREN'S BOOKS

Stan Berenstain and Jan Berenstain. *The Berenstain Bears Get the Gimmies*. New York: Random House Books for Young Readers, 1988.

Kevin Henkes. *Waiting*. New York: Greenwillow Books, 2015.

Lisa Regan. *Wait Your Turn, Tilly*. London: Wayland (Publishers) Ltd., 2013.

David Ezra Stein. *Interrupting Chicken*. Somerville, MA: Candlewick, 2010.

Mo Willems. *Waiting Is Not Easy! (An Elephant and Piggie Book)*. New York: Disney-Hyperion, 2014.

# Lesson 2: Spotlight on the Positive

If you happen to be in a phase of your life that is easy and relatively unchallenged, you can just continue to incline your mind toward well-being and remain present for uplifting states as they come.

**Builds strengths of:**
- Resiliency
- Well-being
- Self esteem
- Neuroplasticity

**Materials**
- Flash light
- Paper and pens

**Ages**
- Five to adult

**School Curriculum Connections**
- Oral language
- Written language
- Listening skills
- Reading
- Science
- Social and emotional learning

### Home and School Practice

Children, like adults, often arrive with a headful of negative thoughts. I remember being told, "Don't be too big for your britches," meaning, in my family, not to think too positively about myself. Now brain science shows that "Neurons that fire together wire together." This means that our thoughts create pathways in the brain. I want those positive connections wiring up for my students!

### Wire Them Up

At a weekend lecture by Dr. Rick Hanson, I learned that our brains are wired to look for the negative. I shared this with my students. Looking for the negative was an evolutionary way to stay alive. Look for danger or be eaten by the beast looking for food. Now that we are no longer part of the food chain, it is up to us to move our thoughts from the negative to the positive. Simply noticing our own negative thoughts is a huge step toward rewiring our brains.

## Weed Thoughts

It's important to tend to our garden of thoughts. To demonstrate the concept of negativity bias, I write on the blackboard the many negative, dark, or "weed" thoughts that I have had that morning. I am as truthful as possible and the children sit riveted, hearing that their teacher has negative self-talk too.

I list things like: My dress doesn't fit like it used to. When will I ever get up early enough to have a calm exit in the morning? I can't seem to remember anything these days. What is wrong with me?

I also tell them how when I was their age, my mum would stand at the top of the stairs if I were past curfew and say, "I thought you were dead!" and she would go on to tell me all the things she had been imagining. I have to admit my mum was a nurse so she saw her share of accidents and tragedies. These images combined with her anxiety led to many sleepless nights for my dad. I share with the students that her worry built in a wiring of acute anxiety for me. I ask how many of them have parents who worry. We all laugh at this question and many children share.

Finally, they begin to open up and their anxiety thoughts roll out.

Here is a sample of a few thoughts in a sixth grade class:

"I will never be good at math." "I am so weird." "My family fights all the time and I don't know what to do." "I am stupid." "My hair is gross today."

## Changing Negative to Positive

I give the children a sheet of paper that has been divided into two. On one side they write down one or more of their own negative thoughts, the type that tends to run around in their heads. Then we take that thought and shine a spotlight on it changing it into a positive thought. This is where I bring out my magic thought changer, a flashlight, and shine it on their paper. We talk about bringing something dark, scary, or unsupportive out into the light. The children love taking a turn to shine the light onto their own "weed" or negative thoughts.

We then bring our attention to the other side of the paper. We write down opposites or antidotes to the negative thought. For example, "I am a failure at school" changed when put into the spotlight to "Each day I do my best and while it might be challenging, things are beginning to come more easily to me." "I will never be good at math" might become "I find math challenging and little by little I take on the challenge. It is okay that I don't get every question right because I am learning." "My family fights all the time and I don't know what to do" becomes "Even though we have rough times, I create a safe place for myself and ask for help at school when my family fights." "I am stupid," might become, "Although spelling is challenging, I am musically smart. I give myself room for a spelling challenge and even if I don't pass, I tried my best."

I ask them to notice throughout the next day or week when the antidotes run into their minds. I also put many pictures of spotlight thoughts up on the overhead so that they can draw from the examples.

The students love this exercise and many ask if they can write "super private" on the top of their papers. They often believe no one else has negative thoughts or worries. I honor their process. I will come back to the spotlight many times throughout the following days, weeks, and months, until the spotlighting of changing negative thoughts to positive hopefully becomes a natural default. The kids love talking about brain science, and I love knowing we are nurturing courage and resilience. James reminds us, "When we are going through hardships, we are developing courage and strength. By opening to our pain, rather than simply enduring it, we deepen our understanding and access those qualities in us that are most noble."

## Resources

### ADULT BOOKS

Thich Nhat Hanh. *Happiness: Essential Mindfulness Practices*. Berkeley, CA: Parallax Press, 2009.

Jack Kornfield. *A Lamp in the Darkness: Illuminating the Path Through Difficult Times*. Louisville, CO: Sounds True, 2014.

Gretchen Rubin. *The Happiness Project*. New York: HarperCollins Publishers, 2012.

Lawrence Shapiro and Robin Sprague. *The Relaxation and Stress Reduction Workbook for Kids: Help for Children to Cope with Stress, Anxiety, and Transitions*. Oakland, CA: New Harbinger, 2009.

### CHILDREN'S BOOKS

Shawn Achor and Amy Blankson. *Ripple's Effect*. San Francisco: Little Pickle Press, 2012.

Thich Nhat Hanh. *A Handful of Quiet: Happiness in Four Pebbles*. Illustrated by Wietske Vriezen. Berkeley, CA: Plum Blossom Books, 2012.

Carol McCloud. *Have You Filled a Bucket Today? A Guide to Daily Happiness for Kids*, Illustrated by David Messing. Northville, MI: Nelson Publishing & Marketing, 2006.

Carol McCloud. *Growing Up with a Bucket Full of Happiness: Three Rules for a Happier Life*. Northville, MI: Ferne Press, 2010.

Cheri J. Meiners M.Ed. *Be Positive!* Illustrated by Elizabeth Allen. Golden Valley, MN: Free Spirit Publishing, 2013.

Watty Pipe. *The Little Engine That Could*. New York: Grosset & Dunlap, 2001.

#  Lesson 3: Fostering Compassionate Communication

"The very act of opening to suffering is a vital part of our awakening joy practice. We often find a courage and inner strength we didn't know we had. And in learning to face our own pain we deepen our compassion and can be there for others." —*James*

## Builds strengths of:
- Self-awareness
- Resilience
- Self compassion
- Well-being
- Self resourcing

## Materials
- None

## Ages
- Preschool to adult

## School Curriculum Connections
- Oral language
- Written language
- Listening skills
- Reading
- Social and emotional learning

## *School Practice*
On the first day back at school one September, I had my students from the year before sitting with me in a circle. In my school, we have our old class come back to their previous year's homeroom for the first week until the current year's classroom configurations are complete. By coming back and meeting in a familiar place with last year's classmates, they feel safe and can touch base before moving on into their new homerooms.

## Sharing Our Own Vulnerability
I felt a little nervous about my students leaving to go to new classes and I told them I would like to sit together and talk. We checked into what we were

excited about and what we were feeling anxious about. Having shared openly on many occasions, they willingly expressed themselves in a vulnerable way. We decided we wanted to use the "popcorn" approach to speaking. The popcorn method is to put a talking stick in the center and speak spontaneously when we reach for the stick. All people have a chance to speak and everyone agrees to listen with the utmost care to the person with the stick. As we went around the circle I told the students about my summer and the moment when I almost lost my dog, Teddy Bear, to a poisonous berry. I told them where in my body I felt that pain and what it felt like even now as I recalled it. I had a few tears in my eyes and I knew they were deeply affected, as Teddy Bear had been an active member of the class for the whole year.

## Listening to the Heart

A little boy to my right then blurted, "Ms. L., I am glad my mom didn't die last week." I asked him what he meant and only then did he say his mother had been in a terrible accident. He described to the class all the cuts and broken bones she had and how she was airlifted to a hospital in the city. I was amazed at what he was shouldering. After he spoke, at least ten other children shared how someone or something had been in an accident or had died over the summer. Grandparents, cats, fathers, mothers, brothers, sisters, and birds were mentioned in the circle. One little boy shared how his mom took him to a house that they might have to buy. She told him a car had run through it and it was a mess, and they could not even afford to buy it anyway. He was worried at the state of a place they might have to live in. He was in tears.... When I looked at the clock, a whole hour had passed and no one had interrupted or indicated they were bored or left the circle in any way. These children were only seven and eight years old!

## Taking Action

I sat for a moment and asked if anyone would like to help the first little one make a card for his mom. He smiled and called in four classmates, who spent their whole recess creating get-well cards. He tucked the cards into his backpack to take home. I asked the other little one if he could imagine any kind of house in the whole wide world, what might it have? He started to describe his dream house and all the kids piped in with ideas of slides, candy machines, and a pond. His shoulders lightened, and I asked how he felt just imagining something else. He said he wanted to draw it, so I got my best watercolor paper and two other volunteers stayed with him while they chatted and drew the best house ever. He took the drawing home to hang in his bedroom. He had a fun and comforting vision. He said that even if he didn't live in the house the children had created, it had been so much fun to work together, and he felt more hopeful.

The curriculum was incredibly rich that morning, enjoying my last moments with these kids before they moved on. I was in awe of what children carry and their vulnerability as they shared.

## *Home Practice*

### One Activity You Can Do to Build This Strength Today

Have your child think of one animal or person who might be having a hard time. It can even be someone they barely know, like someone who fell down at school and hurt herself.

When your child thinks of someone, start an action. James talks about taking baby steps and to keep in mind that everything is impermanent. So in taking baby steps, it may be that you write a letter to Grandma or Grandpa sharing your heartfelt desire for them to be well and happy. The kids could call the friend who fell on the way home and check in to see how they are feeling. It may be that they hug their puppy because he has been home all day alone while you are out at work and school. Whatever the doable task, notice it and do just one thing to honor and bring joy to this difficult time.

If it is hard to think of anyone who needs help, go outside and ask your child, "What is one thing the earth might need right now?" They may have a simple response like, "The vegetable garden needs water." Try to keep the chosen idea doable. If your child says the earth needs everyone to drive electric cars, guide them toward one doable step, they might take.

When children begin to notice that we all have hard times and that they are part of life, they are not as fearful when the difficult times come. They notice these moments pass and with strength, resilience, love, and companionship we can get through them. They have the courage to meet and greet uncomfortable feelings. I often read this poem by Rumi and discuss how by inviting in all parts of ourselves, we can relax and trust in the whole human experience. This poem also brings forward exceptional artwork in children. I have had the students paint or draw their own Guest House and see who shows up! What roars of laughter we have when we acknowledge all the characters in our heads.

## The Guest House

This being human is a guest house.
Every morning a new arrival.
A joy, a depression, a meanness,
some momentary awareness comes
as an unexpected visitor.
Welcome and entertain them all!
Even if they are a crowd of sorrows,
who violently sweep your house
empty of its furniture,
still, treat each guest honorably.
He may be clearing you out
for some new delight.
The dark thought, the shame, the malice.
meet them at the door laughing and invite them in.
Be grateful for whatever comes.
because each has been sent
as a guide from beyond.

"The Guest House" by Jalal ad-Din Muhammad Rumi, from The Essential Rumi, translated by Coleman Barks with John Moyne. © HarperCollins Publishers, 1995.

## Resources

### ADULT BOOKS

Marshall B. Rosenberg. *Nonviolent Communication: A Language of Life*. Encinitas, CA: Puddledancer Press, 2003.

————. *Raising Children Compassionately: Parenting the Nonviolent Communication Way (Nonviolent Communication Guides)*. Encinitas, CA: Puddledancer Press, 2004.

Daniel J. Siegel MD and Mary Hartzell. *Parenting from the Inside Out 10th Anniversary edition: How a Deeper Self-Understanding Can Help You Raise Children Who Thrive*. New York: TarcherPerigee, 2013.

### CHILDREN'S BOOKS

Julia Cook. *A Bad Case of Tattle Tongue*. Illustrated by Anita DuFalla. Chattanooga, TN: National Center for Youth Issues, 2008.

————. *My Mouth Is a Volcano!* Illustrated by Carrie Hartman. Chattanooga, TN: National Center for Youth Issues, 2008.

Julia Cook and Anita Du Falla. *Decibella and Her 6-Inch Voice*. Boys Town, NE: Boys Town Press, 2014.

Maria Dismondy. *Spaghetti in A Hot Dog Bun: Having the Courage to Be Who You Are*. Illustrated by Kimberly Shaw. Chicago: Cardinal Rule Press, 2008.

Beth Ferry. *Stick and Stone*. Illustrated by Tom Lichtenheld. Boston, MA: Houghton Mifflin Harcourt Books for Young Readers, 2015.

Trudy Ludwig. *The Invisible Boy*. Illustrated by Patrice Barton. New York: Knopf Books for Young Readers, 2013.

 # Lesson 4: Using Art to Remember the Good Times

### Builds strengths of:

- Gratitude
- Caring
- Sharing
- Family vision and appreciation
- Happy memories

### Materials

- Phone, camera, or some kind of recording device
- Paper, collage materials to build memory book
- Your dancing shoes!
- Happy music

## Ages

- Preschool to adult

## School Curriculum
## Connections

- Oral language
- Written language
- Listening skills
- Reading
- Physical education
- Fine arts
- Social and emotional learning

Did you know that remembering happy times can actually elevate your mood? Studies show that just recalling a happy time and savoring the memory creates neural activity in the brain that makes you happier! Wow! What a great idea to harness with activities. In the classroom, I have shared many guided meditations on recalling happy times. Hands down, after this practice, smiles are everywhere and the children say they feel great. So on a dreary day, when you and your child cannot get your engines going, try the following activity.

### *Home and School Practice*

### A Memory Book or Happiness Video

This is a lesson to anchor in the memories and create neural pathways.
Go through photos on your computer and put ones that evoke happiness into

a file. So often, we don't bother to print pictures and rarely look back at the hundreds, if not thousands that we have.

When you have the file you can print some of them to begin your memory book.

With each picture take the time to feel the sense of joy you had and now have in your body. Don't waste this experience. Remember, neurons that fire together wire together. You want to take ten to twenty seconds and really dwell in the experience. This creates more neural firing, which, according to Dr. Rick Hanson, takes that passing mental state into a lasting positive neural trait.

With your child, create a little photo album. My sons loved keeping their albums by their beds and would bring them out at night to talk about the family. We would add in pictures of the immediate and extended family as well as photos of their friends. We would also use this time to "wish them all well" as the boys went off to sleep.

If you are technically savvy, you can make an iMovie or some other form of video with pictures or movies taken throughout the year.

Older children may want to take their phones or cameras and create movies with their friends that make them laugh, smile, and feel good. They can put it to music and flush their bodies with happiness every time they watch them.

## Music

There is nothing like music to stir the memories.

A song comes on the radio or we hear it played in a shop and instantly we are transported back to what we were doing, who we were with, and how we were feeling when we heard the song being played before. Why not use this amazing part of the brain that lights up when music is played and create more happiness?

### *Home or School Activity*

Kids absolutely adore this activity. At school I have the children create a CD or playlist of songs that make them feel happy. They already listen to music all the time, so this is an assignment that energizes them. They can do it in partners or on their own. Those students who try to stick their headphones on all through the day are practically running out the door to begin this musical job. I ask that all songs presented can be played in front of a kindergartener, their grandmother, and of course me! For some, their grandmothers are much more liberal with colorful language than I am, so setting these parameters allows all children and teachers to participate in a safe, respectful environment.

## The Big Day

When the big day comes to share the music, we randomly pick a CD and put it on. The students talk about their taste in music and what feelings the songs evoke inside of them. Some children say music just gets under your skin and makes you want to dance and sing. Others say it reminds them of a great time and they feel better. Whatever is shared, we experience it as a whole group. This activity opens my eyes to the variety of music that children love. Most of the tunes, I must admit, I have never heard before.

Finally, we have a dance party. Disco balls are cheap and portable now! If they choose, they get up and move. The whole classroom is rocking out in happiness by recess.

## *Resources*

### ADULT BOOKS

Chronicle Books. *My Quotable Kid: A Parents' Journal of Unforgettable Quotes.* San Francisco: Chronicle Books, 2009.

Gloria Gaither and Shirley Dobson. *Creating Family Traditions: Making Memories in Festive Seasons.* Illustrated by Carrie Hartman. Colorado Springs, CO: Multnomah Books, 2004.

Rick Hanson. *Hardwiring Happiness: The New Brain Science of Contentment, Calm, and Confidence*. New York: Harmony, 2013.

## CHILDREN'S BOOKS

Tomie dePaola. *Nana Upstairs and Nana Downstairs*. New York: Putnam Juvenile, 2000.

Candace Fleming and Stacey Dressen-McQueen. *Boxes for Katje*. New York: Farrar, Straus and Giroux (BYR), 2003.

Roni Schotter. *Mama, I'll Give You the World*. Illustrated by S. Saelig Gallagher. New York: Dragonfly Books, 2013.

Norma Spaulding. *Molly's Memory Jar*. Frenchs Forest, AU: New Frontier Publishing, 2010.

# Integrity

5

### 🪷 James: Practices for Grown-Ups

LOOKING BACK on my younger days I can't believe some of my unaware, selfish behavior. My whole body can cringe with disbelief when I recall some really awful things that I've done. Memories from my past have come back to haunt me when I recall saying something cruel out of my own pain and insecurity or hurting someone because of my own lack of awareness. "What was I thinking? How could I have been so confused?"

Integrity, acting in alignment with our values, is one of the most effective ways to create the conditions for joy to arise. We human beings are programmed in quite an extraordinary way. We have an inner moral compass that can either lead us toward guilt and shame or inner peace. It's called conscience. Whether adult or child, as Jiminy Cricket said to Pinocchio, "Always let your conscience be your guide." If we want to bring more happiness and inner peace into our lives, all we have to do is learn to listen to that inner compass wisely.

Acting in an honorable, ethical way—walking our talk—is probably the most important modeling we can, as adults, gift to our children. As we embody integrity our children know we are trustworthy and can feel safe around us. But don't put pressure on yourself to become a saint! Just by being real and having the humility to admit when you've made a mistake, you show it's okay to be human. When my son, Adam, was young, one of my favorite Sesame Street songs was "Everyone Makes Mistakes Oh Yes They Do." We had many occasions to sing that one to each other as I showed my humanness or forgave him for his. I still lovingly sing it to myself when I blow it!

## The Power of Delayed Gratification

As most of us know, listening to our inner wisdom is easier said than done. How many times do we need to see that the momentary pleasure we get when we act impulsively is often followed by many moments of regret? It's quite amazing how short-term gratification often wins out over longer-term remorse. We can click the send button on an angry email sure that we're justified, without realizing all the mess and unhappiness we will go experience.

So a key to genuine well-being with regards to this theme of integrity is learning the power of delayed gratification: seeing the bigger picture and choosing to go for the greater happiness. Postponing our impulsive action and living in alignment with our highest values, we cannot only avoid unnecessary suffering but actually produce many moments of inner peace and joy. When I face a moment of choice between taking the easy, less conscious way or the high road, I often ask myself how this will feel a week or a month or six months from now. Each time I do, it's clear that delaying my gratification is not really depriving myself—it's actually choosing a more sustainable source of true well-being.

Here are some words of wisdom that a teenager wrote at the end of his first mindfulness meditation retreat:

> *As I write I am channeling a revelation about the secret to long-term happiness. Here it is. The real secret to long-term happiness stems from knowing that one's actions are in impeccable alignment with the truth. When there is an ingrained knowing that you are doing your absolute best to be generous and compassionate and trying your hardest not to cause harm to any other being—That Is It! There is nothing that you can possibly blame yourself for, and there is nothing that anyone else can blame you for. Suddenly an inconceivable weight is lifted from your shoulders. In essence, you are frictionless with the cycle of suffering.*

## Forgiveness and Healing from the Past

There is a price to pay for becoming more aware: We can't fool ourselves anymore. We may cringe as we look back on our poor choices. But as painful as it is, cringing isn't such a bad thing. If we're cringing it means we're no longer the same person who could do those things now. We've changed and grown.

The good news is that it's never too late to change. The key ingredient is deciding to go for real happiness and bringing more awareness to our unskillful behavior patterns. We may even see ourselves in the middle of doing something we'll later regret and still go ahead and do it. But as strange as it may seem, though it can be humbling to watch yourself like this, from the standpoint of increasing well-being, it is actually better than acting with no awareness. If you were completely unaware, you would likely repeat the same behavior in the future, have no idea how you got there again, and suffer more guilt and shame. But if you can feel the pain accompanying the action, you'll more likely be motivated to change. That is, if you don't keep beating yourself up with guilt.

Being a person who is somewhat of an authority on guilt, I can tell you it has zero value. It is self-perpetuating. You feel lousy and punish yourself by dwelling on what's been done with self-flagellation or go ahead and act unskillfully again, just confirming what a rotten person you really are. The only way out of that cycle is self-forgiveness and the commitment to learn from your mistakes.

How can we forgive ourselves when we realize we've acted unskillfully? What do we do with the guilty feelings? Rather than getting lost in guilt, we can practice what is known as "wise remorse." When you realize you've done something you regret, rather than drowning in guilt, ask yourself, "What can I learn from the experience that will help me remember to act more skillfully if a similar situation arises again?" In this way you can use the painful event as a springboard for more skillful actions in the future. And if there is an appropriate opportunity to make amends for unskillful past actions, doing so can bring about a real healing. This is an on-going process of learning that takes patience.

### Five Habits for Happiness

In Eastern philosophy there are traditionally five guidelines for acting with integrity. The basic underlying principle is to refrain from causing suffering to others or ourselves. These are not commandments but, rather, principles to help us become more conscious and make wiser choices. If we keep them in mind, they are like brakes to minimize causing harm to ourselves or others. When we live by them, they not only minimize our suffering, but also positively promote a feeling of wholeness.

1. Honor all life. The first guideline, refraining from killing, is really developing a respect and reverence for life. When we are consciously not causing intentional harm to other living beings we experience the happiness that comes from offering the gift of harmlessness.

2. Share your time and resources. The second guideline to refrain from stealing can be a practice in sufficiency and abundance. We not only avoid suffering by not taking from others, but we can also experience joy by expressing our generosity.

3. Take care with sexual energy, respecting boundaries and offering safety. Sexual energy can be a source of great joy or great pain. Rather than having the attitude of "How can I maximize my own pleasure?" we can turn it around to: "How can I give some pleasure to an inti-

mate partner or offer others safety?" When people feel respected and know we have healthy boundaries, they can feel relaxed and at ease. They can sense that we don't want anything from them other than their genuine happiness. And we feel good inside as well.

4. Speak kindly. Usually translated as not causing suffering through speech, the basic guideline is saying what is truthful and useful in a kind way. This is not only a more effective way to communicate, but it gives us a greater likelihood of being heard. It also brings us happiness as we are connected to an attitude of kindness inside us. It's important to include speaking kindly to ourselves in this guideline. Why not treat yourself as you would treat anyone else?

5. Develop a clear mind and healthy body. By not abusing substances, such as alcohol or drugs, we are more likely not to wobble in our actions regarding the other guidelines thereby avoiding harm through our unclarity. Even more, as we value a clear mind and healthy body, we give ourselves the gift of feeling mentally alert and physically more alive, which are the most supportive things we can do to awaken joy.

May your own integrity be a source of joy for you and an inspiring model for your children.

## Michele: Practicing Integrity with Children

When I was seven I snuck into my mum's wallet and took change to buy candy. At twelve I took makeup from a store. I was thirteen when I told my mum I was at a friend's and was later brought home by the police for loitering with a group of boys at the park. The list goes on. In each of those moments I felt sick with anxiety about what I was doing, but I chose the excitement of the perceived reward over the feeling of doing the right thing. These events took place decades ago and for many people they may seem like minor incidents. For me though, they stuck in my body as clear reminders that I had crossed an uncomfortable line with myself. To this day I don't remember them as an idea or visual memory but as a whole body feeling. My moral compass was out of whack.

In my early twenties, I traveled to Asia for many months and began to take karma seriously. I made a vow to try my best to follow my gut and do the right thing. At first I chose the right thing out of fear of "bad karma." Then I chose it because doing things that matched my integrity felt good.

# Try This

## Integrity Practice A: Choosing Habits to Awaken Joy

1. For one week, choose one of the Five Habits mentioned previously that you would like to cultivate as a way to bring more
   happiness and well-being into your life. You may want to choose
   one that is a particular challenge. For example, if you tend to
   speak sharply to your child, you might decide to work with
   "Speak Kindly." If it feels beneficial, continue it for another week
   until it becomes a strong habit of happiness. Or you may choose
   another habit and develop that one.

2. Think of ways in which you might act in alignment with this new
   habit. Write them down, place the paper in a prominent location
   where you can readily see it every day, and make a commitment
   to add these choices to your life. Your old habits may rebel
   and struggle for dominance. Each time you are faced with the
   moment of choice, take a breath, remember your commitment,
   and choose integrity.

3. When we act skillfully, we are planting seeds of happiness within
   ourselves as well as in the response from others. We also feel
   good when we recall what we've done. Every time you remember
   to make one of these choices (e.g., speaking kindly to your child
   even when you feel impatient), notice if you feel happier: a) in
   the moment you act skillfully b) with the response you receive
   from the other person and c) later, when you recall your action.

4. Take this one day at a time. Notice if it becomes easier to make
   your positive choices. At the end of the week, notice if your level
   of well-being and happiness has increased.

## Integrity Practice B: Healing the Past

1. Think of an incident you still regret or feel guilty about. As you
   recall the situation, notice if fear or confusion motivated your
   words or actions. *(continues on next page)*

2. Imagine that another person had harmed you in the same way and expressed regret and asked forgiveness. Could you forgive this person?

3. Now imagine yourself as a wise and kind being who understands how confusion and fear led to your actions, and forgive yourself.

4. If it is possible for you to sincerely apologize and directly ask forgiveness from someone you may have hurt, do so, without expecting any particular response.

5. Reflect on what you have learned from this situation. How might you act differently in similar situations in the future? Make a deliberate commitment to act in that way.

## Our Kids Are Watching

Our own children watch everything we do. They pick up on even the subtlest things. The example below from a teacher isn't so subtle.

*One day, I had just got back from an all-day field trip to the city with my students. Parents were picking up their tired children from the ferry. My attention was caught by a group of students huddled over by the vending machine. One child came running over to tell me that it was broken and candy was coming out.*

*What should we do? Well fifteen children and a candy machine can challenge any level of integrity to the max. We decided to tell the authorities at the head office. What stunned me was when one boy hopped in his car with his dad and left the lot. He must have told his father about the machine. The car circled the parking lot and they both got out to fill their hands with candy.—Teacher, Grade Seven*

To allow children room to find their own sense of integrity, I tell them stories of when I have not been in integrity with myself throughout my life. (No, that wasn't me at the vending machine!) They are often shocked and relieved that their parent or teacher might not have "done the right thing." This allows them to stretch into self-compassion and let go of self-criticism, while they navigate what is true to their own heart.

Your child might ask, "What does it look like to have integrity?"

It means doing the right thing even if no one is watching. Integrity means to do the right thing not for attention, applause, or rewards—but simply because it is the right thing to do.

At the beginning of every school year this quality of integrity is put to the test. The teacher leaves the room. Children peek out the door of the classroom, look down the hall, and yell, "She's coming. She's coming." Chaos breaks out and students who want to do the right thing are in tears. Over the following weeks and months we practice digging deep into integrity: modeling it, role-playing, and talking about how it feels to have this quality. We set up little scenarios that have often happened in the class and have students act them out, making good choices. These role-plays might include taking someone's school supplies without asking or moving a chair to someone else's desk at the end of the day so they have to put it away. The kids come up with huge lists of what feels "wrong." The best part of these conversations is that it all brings us to a collective agreement of what we would like basic goodness to look like in our class. We are once again building a wholesome container. Often kids don't realize how the things they do—and don't do—affect other people. Using empathy as a guidepost to navigate these difficult dilemmas makes all the difference.

To reinforce integrity, I sit with many students and point to their heart and ask:

---

✳ What would your heart say to do?

✳ Can you be true to your word?

✳ If you say you are going to do something, will you do it?

✳ Can you respect the person in front of us by speaking in a kind tone?

✳ Can you take responsibility for your actions?

✳ Can you be compassionate to yourself when you forget or act in a way you regret?

✳ Can you tell me what you would do next time?

As a parent or teacher, ask yourself:

> ✳ Are you true to your word?
>
> ✳ If you say you will take your child out to the park, do you do it?
>
> ✳ Can you talk about times when you have acted in ways you regret?
>
> ✳ Can you discuss what led you to those moments?
>
> ✳ Can you discuss how you try to meet challenges of integrity in your life today?

When I have acted in ways I regret, it has often been because I was time- or energy-crunched. I have also let go of my integrity when I am angry or surprised by someone—a thoughtless reaction.

I begin the following lesson with a story about the power of unconditional love—a story that changed the lives of those who were present to witness the event. This chapter offers your child strategies to let go of perceived wrong doings and begin afresh. The practices aid a child in developing their own moral compass. This compass is not a list of rules and regulations based on religion, morality, or rules others have created. It is something to be talked about, experienced, and developed over time. I have also included a family breathing practice as a way to strengthen family bonds. In deepening these bonds we may more easily stay in integrity with loved ones. Remember it is never too late to let go of wrong doings and fly free.

 # Lesson 1: Between the Veils: A Gift

## Feeling Deeply into the Experience of Love and Belonging

Think of a time you reached out and were kind to someone. Let yourself recall the pleasure you felt in your mind and body as you saw how happy this person was. Take these positive feelings in and let them motivate you to continue to choose skillful actions.

**Builds strengths of:**

- Connection
- Caring
- Perspective taking
- Presence

**Materials**

- Open heart, vulnerability

**Ages**

- Newborn to adult

**School Curriculum Connections**

- Oral language
- Listening skills
- Social and emotional learning

## *Home and School Practice*

We invite you to read this story and share love within the classroom or your home. One year, on the day before Christmas break, one of my students had his last day in our class. He had moved many times in the past few years and was once again being uprooted to a new town. "Tom" was a quiet boy who kept mostly to himself in the few months he was in our classroom. He would light up and come out of his shell on the days that I would bring my puppy into the classroom for a visit. He was usually very early because his mom worked and would have to drop him off long before the others arrived.

On this last morning of the year with the children so excited for Christmas, we sat in a circle and began mindful breathing. Getting the children to settle when it is not only the last day of school, but pajamas and party day, was like trying to put a cork back in a bottle of open champagne. But as the children had done mindfulness sessions almost every day, they gathered on the carpet to begin. With the lights off on that December morning, we took a collective breath and began. We often end the mindfulness time by sending love out to someone who we care for and then we complete by wrapping our own being in love.

## The Power of Recollection

I asked the students if they were willing to quietly look at "Tom" and think about a special moment they had had with him. I asked him if he was okay to receive the caring of the students in the classroom, silently. He nodded yes shyly. I recalled something Jack Kornfield had said when I was lucky enough to participate in one of his classes. "Look upon this person as if it might be the last time you will see them. Wish them well."

Now this class of twenty-two eight-year-olds had been particularly challenging. The group dynamics had created havoc in the school on many occasions. They had huge social-emotional and academic needs through the years they had been in school. I had been intentionally sharing with them each day lessons on honoring all life, being kind, and taking action from a deep sense of integrity. On many days, particularly Fridays, when the children were tired and ready for the weekend, they seemed to throw these habits of happiness to the wind and it was challenging to get them to even attend, never mind be kind or check in with their inner knowing! But on this final day of school, grace infused the space and something beautiful happened. It was as if time stopped and electricity filled the air.

## Vulnerability, Safety, and Love

Each child in turn looked at Tom and sent love right to him. I asked him if he was willing to open his heart and look into each child's eyes and he nodded yes. I asked him to allow the feeling to permeate his whole being, breathe it in, and feel it in every cell and to KNOW without a doubt, he had community and love. I told him he could take this moment with him always and draw on it in happy and tough times.

The first child in the class to give his gift was on the autism spectrum. He turned to Tom and wrapped his arms around him with a big hug. It was so beautiful. NO one said a word—a very rare moment for us—as twenty-two children in turn sent Tom love. You could see the dust particles in the sunbeams falling across our room. It was so quiet and electric. Total presence. This mindfulness session lasted almost twenty minutes. It was amazing.

There were two other support staff in the room that day and later they told me they witnessed something sacred. They were in tears.

When we finished, I asked Tom how it felt. In his quiet way, his whole face lit up. He smiled ear to ear and said "Oh so good."

I will never forget this moment. It was so unexpected as it has been such a hard go with this wild group. It gave me hope—hope that what we do each day in mindfulness practice makes a difference. Drop by drop. That it is never too late to give or receive a gift, even when times have been challenging and we want to give up. It gave me hope that we can access our true nature just by taking a breath and really tuning in.

## As Adults We Can Be Vulnerable Too

One of the most powerful moments in my life was something similar to this, when I sat and received from the heart, silently, unshielded, the total love of a group of people. We were to walk down a line of retreat participants taking the time to gaze into one another's eyes and then move to the next and the next and the next, filling with love. As I watched each participant, I saw his or her child self arise. Fifty-year-old men looked out at the world with the eyes of a toddler. As tiny children we are so proud, vulnerable, and open, and the world gazes on us with total love. With our eyes wide open we receive and smile back. I am guessing this is similar to the experience Tom had that December morning.

It can be a very scary experience to be truly open in vulnerability to love. This day with my class, though, I felt the reward of deeply felt happiness and love left in the room. There was no pushing and shoving that morning, no name calling; all that was dropped, shed, and what remained was love.

I wonder what my life would have been like if I had had this experience in grade three. The times I have yearned to be seen and loved. What effect will these twenty minutes leave on this child and all the children who were part of this moment?

This was the most deeply moving experience of the school year for me. Something arose deep inside and gave me hope and faith that love always rises, and my job was to help provide sacred space for the children, cultivate habits of happiness, continue to be present, and to love.

## Resources

### ADULT BOOKS

Jon Kabat-Zinn and Myla Kabat-Zinn. *Everyday Blessings: The Inner Work of Mindful Parenting*. New York: Hachette Books, 1998.

Alfie Kohn. *Unconditional Parenting: Moving from Rewards and Punishments to Love and Reason*. New York: Atria Books, 2006.

Marshall B. Rosenberg. *Life-Enriching Education*. Encinitas, CA: Puddledancer Press, 2003.

### Children's Books

Barbara M. Joosse. *Papa Do You Love Me?* Illustrated by Barbara Laallee. San Francisco: Chronicle Books, 2005.

Cheryl Kilodavis. *My Princess Boy*. Illustrated by Suzanne DeSimone. New York: Aladdin, 2010.

Robert Munsch. *Love You Forever*. Illustrated by Sheila McGraw. Richmond Hill, ON: Firefly Books, 1995.

Marta M. Schmidt-Mendez. *The Dog with the Crooked Tail: A Story About Diversity and Unconditional Love*. Charleston, SC: CreateSpace Independent Publishing Platform, 2014.

Nancy Tillman. *Wherever You Are: My Love Will Find You*. New York: Feiwel & Friends, 2010.

 # Lesson 2: The Ties That Bind Us

## Integrity with the Self

When we do things we know are off, it feels uncomfortable inside. This is what we call conscience. If we pay close attention, and get to know these feelings well, we give ourselves the choice to create more peace and ease in our hearts.

### Building Strengths of:
- Resiliency
- Self care
- Integrity
- Bravery
- Care of others
- Reaching out to others

### Materials
- Paper
- Pencil
- Scissors
- String or wool (six inches long)
- Garbage can or recycling container
- Willingness

## Ages
- Ten to adult

## School Curriculum
## Connections
- Oral language
- Written language
- Listening skills
- Social and emotional learning

### *Home Practice*

### The Weariness of a Child

Have you ever walked into your class and the students look weary? Does the energy ever feel heavy and unsettled? Teachers know it is impossible to teach the academic lessons when emotions are running high. I wanted to create a ceremony that was meaningful and I hoped it would allow the children to shed some of the burdens that they carry from home to school.

Over the years I see, time and time again, particularly after a family holiday for some children, the heaviness of emotion that rests on the child's shoulders and reflects in their faces. When asked, they might say there was something that they did that they now regret or that there was unrest in their household over the break. For other children the unrest may stem from a conflict at school or on the playground.

## How to Serve the Children

### Part One of the Lesson

One day I asked the children to deeply relax while we did a ten-minute guided mindfulness session. I then asked them to think of one thing that was bothering them, a regret or time they felt out of integrity with themselves. We discussed what integrity meant and wrote examples on the board. I suggested they choose a memory of something they did long ago or an event that happened today. It might be something that carried some sense of guilt, shame, or wrongdoing.

### Let Them Know You Are Human

I then gave an example from my own life and this created a sense of vulnerability and willingness to share. I shared that I had taken money from my mother's purse without asking, and even though it was a small amount, I still felt out of integrity with myself.

### Part Two—Lights Low and Have Your Supplies Ready

I had the lights turned down very low so the children could only see their own paper in front of them.

They wrote about a regret or time they felt out of integrity on the paper. They then rolled it into a tube and tied it with a six-inch cord that I had previously cut for them.

One child asked if she could write about something someone had done to her that she needed to let go of. I said of course, that whatever was sticking or arising was the perfect thing to focus on.

I reminded the children that the wrongdoing did not have to be a big thing. This was a short session and they could just start small. If something huge was arising, it might be better to do that at another time. I did this because I wanted them to feel safe and successful without tapping into something we could not manage when I had twenty-eight students and limited time.

Note: We have a counseling box where students can leave a request to speak to a counselor. I suggested that might be a good idea if they needed to look at something more deeply.

## Cutting the Cords That Bind You

With our little paper rolled up and tied up with string, one person and their neighbor stood up in the middle of the circle next to a garbage/recycling can I had placed there. They walked to the can and said, "I cut the cord of the things that bind you. May you be well!" Then the person with the paper cut it up and sprinkled it into the can.

The most amazing part of the whole exercise was that just before they cut the cord, I asked them to place one end of the string onto the part of the body where the problem was stuck or held in. Without missing a beat every child except one was able to identify the place.

Guess where most strings were stuck? The solar plexus wins the top spot.

When the whole class was finished cutting the ties, I exclaimed that the garbage can was so incredibly heavy that I bet no one could lift it. They all put up their hands to try to lift the grief! We then brainstormed ways of supporting ourselves in letting go of worries.

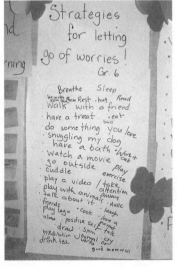

### Follow Up

At the end of the day, I asked children what their favorite part of the day was. We had had an action-packed day so I was curious if anyone would remember the ceremony. Over fifty percent said it was the most meaningful part of the day.

When you try this lesson, ask the children, perhaps a week later, if their burden has been lifted. Remind them that releasing burdens may take many, many times before they are free.

### *Home Practice*

What cords would you cut?

Take your time. You don't need to know what your child wrote. Having a sense of privacy is very important in this exercise. You can invite your child to discuss any part of the ceremony and give them ideas for support if they need it. The whole family can release burdens and fly a little lighter. Daniel Rechtschaffen reflects in *The Way of Mindful Education*, "Trying to get rid of thoughts is like trying to block the ocean waves; they just keep coming. When we go to the source of emotions we can feel them in our bodies and work with them constructively." So be gentle and compassionate while you cut the cords that bind you.

## Resources

### Adult Books

Gina Biegal. *The Stress Reduction Workbook for Teens: Mindfulness Skills to Help us Deal with Stress*. Oakland, CA: New Harbinger, 2009.

Jon Kabat-Zinn. *Full Catastrophe Living*. New York: Bantam, 2013.

Daniel Rechtschaffen. *The Way of Mindful Education: Cultivating Well-being in Teachers and Students*. New York: WW Norton, 2014.

Shauna Shapiro and Chris White. *Mindful Discipline: A Loving Approach to Setting Limits and Raising an Emotionally Intelligent Child*. Oakland, CA: New Harbinger Publications, 2014.

### Children's Books

Aliki. *Feelings*. New York: Greenwillow, 1986.

Janan Cain. *The Way I Feel*. Seattle, WA, Parenting Press, 2000.

Lezlie Evans. *Sometimes I Feel Like a Storm Cloud*. Illustrated by Marsha Gray Carrington. New York: Mondo Publishing, 1999.

Anne Miranda. *Glad Monster, Sad Monster*. Illustrated by Ed Emberly. New York: LB Kids, 1997.

Cornelia Maude Spelman and Nancy Cote. *When I Feel Angry*. Park Ridge, IL: Albert Whitman & Company, 2000.

# Lesson 3: Family Breathing Techniques to Calm the Brain and Body

## Building Strengths of:

- Self care
- Mindfulness
- Well-being
- Resiliency
- Family ties

## Materials

- Cushions
- Warm blankets

## Ages

- Preschool to adult

## School Curriculum Connections

- Oral language
- Listening skills
- Science
- Physical education
- Social and emotional learning

### *Home and School Practice*

Often we tell people to take a deep breath when they are stressed. They gulp for one or two breaths and hope for change. Relaxing is not a two-breath fix. (Although even two mindful breaths can help!) This is an endless practice, one that we need to polish daily. When your child needs to calm down, or you both do, you might try a few of the breathing techniques below. Not only are they fun and connecting but they also have the added benefit of physical touch. Touch releases oxytocin, the bonding hormone. For all the great health

benefits of this breath work, scan to the end of this section; for now, snuggle up and get breathing! The beauty of these practices is they can be done in the privacy of your own home, or modified to use in public places such as on a bus, while lying in the park looking up at trees, or while waiting at the doctor's office. They are magnificent ways to calm and distress both parents and children.

Try these practices and see for yourself.

## Mama and Papa and Baby Bear Breathing

Invite your child to lie down next to you with their back to your tummy. You can show them pictures of animals cuddled up with their little one tucked in safely. Begin by syncing your breathing to their breathing. Feel each other's tummies going up and down. Feel the gentle breath going in and out. Bring your attention to the sensations of your breath in your belly. Notice how your belly rises with each inhalation and falls with each exhalation. Ask your child to begin to feel your breathing pattern as they settle up against you. Deliberately slow down. Sigh. Do this for five full minutes and you both will be calmer. Whenever you as a parent find your attention wandering, gently return it to the sensations of the breath, returning your attention to the breath. Most parents and children fall asleep in each other's arms.

## Breathe into My Hands

It can be so healing to have another human breathe in unison with you.

Standing up at a bus stop, lying down in bed (or anywhere really), this is one of my favorite ways to calm the body. Having a partner brings attention to the body and helps anchor the mind.

How?

One person is the anchor and the other the breather. The anchor begins by rubbing their own hands together, warming them up and setting an intention to connect to the breather.

The anchor then places their hands gently on the back of the breather's head. They stay there warm and connected until the breather has taken three breaths.

Next they place their hands on the shoulders for three breaths, then the mid back and finally the low back. If you are in a place where you can touch the other's feet you can continue to there. In each place, the anchor gently holds their hands for three breaths.

When you are complete, the anchor gently sweeps the breather's body with a long light stroke, down the back, from head to feet.

Allow the breather to very gently get up while the anchor shakes off or washes their hands. Then you can switch.

Tip: If the anchor can sync their own breathing with that of the breather, they can calm their own nervous system and relax at the same time.

Kids reflect on this breathing practice:

At first it felt weird touching someone but after a while when I looked around and everyone was doing it I felt okay. When it was my turn to lie down I felt really relaxed."

"I love doing this. It feels like all the bad stuff is swept away."

"I like this but I felt embarrassed because I think my feet stank. Next time I am wearing my other socks."

"I taught this to my mom. She gets stressed a lot. It seems to help her."

## Back to Back

Sit back to back with a partner and get comfortable. Try to find a sense of balance between the two people practicing. You don't want one person overpowering or pushing the other over. Gently begin breathing into your back. You can exaggerate the breath a little until your partner feels it. See if you can feel your partner breathing into your back. No strain, just awareness. Set a little timer and try this for two to three minutes.

## Match My Breath

Did you know that extending the exhalation is a key to relaxation?

Dr. Rick Hanson explains: "Exhale slowly, twice as long as the inhalation; this helps light up the parasympathetic nervous system. Think of something, anything, that makes you feel safer, more fed and fulfilled, or more appreciated and cared about: focus on these good feelings, stay with them, sense them sinking in."

So sitting across from your partner or youngster look at each other's tummies and tune in. Try to make your breathing match. Let the little one be in charge and ask them to intentionally slow the exhalation down and you will follow. Allow for giggles and showing each other your belly buttons if you choose. Laughter also relaxes the body!

Once you are tuned in, keep your mind on the other's belly and relax. Try this for five minutes. Not only will you be calmer, but I am guessing you will also feel a deeper sense of connection to your partner.

Did you know these are just some of the benefits of mindful breathing practices?

> ...strengthens the immune system, improves digestion and builds up neurotransmitters that are involved in the moment-to-moment experience of living, our psychology. Also, when we do these practices our hormonal system benefits, both in terms of stress hormones and reproductive. It's hard to feel really in the mood if your body is redlining on stress. I reflect sometimes that if Merck or other large pharmaceutical companies could patent meditation, mindfulness or gratitude practices such as taking in the good, the practice that I particularly talk and write about, we would be seeing ads on prime-time television many times in the evening for any one of these things because the impact of these practices for physical health, particularly long-term physical health, are so extraordinary.
> —Rick Hanson, PhD, Interview with themindfulword.org, 2012

With all these incredible benefits of simply snuggling up and breathing, why not grab a warm blanket and invite your child to cuddle up? It is one of the best things you can do for your health today.

### Resources

ADULT BOOKS

Jennifer Cohen Harper and Daniel J. Siegel. *Little Flower Yoga for Kids: A Yoga and Mindfulness Program to Help Your Child Improve Attention and Emotional Balance.* Oakland, CA: New Harbinger Publications, 2013.

B. K. S. Iyengar. *Light on Pranayama: The Yogic Art of Breathing.* New York: Cross-road Publishing Company, 1985.

Andrew Weil and Jon Kabat-Zinn. *Meditation for Optimum Health: How to Use Mindfulness and Breathing to Heal.* Louisville, CO: Sounds True, 2001.

## CHILDREN'S BOOKS

Michael Chissick. *Frog's Breathtaking Speech: How children (and frogs) can use yoga breathing to deal with anxiety, anger and tension.* Illustrated by Sarah Peacock. London: Singing Dragon, 2012.

Lisa Flynn. *Yoga for Children: 200+ Yoga Poses, Breathing Exercises, and Meditations for Healthier, Happier, More Resilient Children.* Avon, MA: Adams Media, 2013.

Lori Lite and Kimberly Fox. *The Goodnight Caterpillar: A Relaxation Story for Kids Introducing Passive Progressive Muscle Relaxation and Breathing.* Marietta, GA: Stress Free Kids, 2011.

Lori Lite and Max Stasuyk. *Sea Otter Cove: A Stress Management Story for Children Introducing Diaphragmatic Breathing to Reduce Anxiety.* Marietta, GA: Stress Free Kids, 2012.

 # Lesson 4: Compassionate Listening

Relationships can bring us so much joy, yet can so easily occasion anger, disappointment, sorrow, and unhappiness. What is happening inside us is far more important than what is happening "out there." We can't control circumstances or other people, but we can train our minds to see clearly and our hearts to remain open, even in the face of pain.

## Builds strengths of:
- Gratitude
- Caring
- Connection
- Interconnectedness
- Listening skills

## Materials
- Your ears and your presence

## Ages
- Kindergarten to adult

## School Curriculum Connections
- Oral language
- Listening skills
- Reading
- Social and emotional learning

## Listen, Listen, Listen

*Too often we underestimate the power of a touch, a smile, a kind word, a listening ear, an honest compliment, or the smallest act of caring, all of which have the potential to turn a life around.*—Leo Buscaglia

How would your world have been if you had been taught the simple, yet oh-so-complex skill of compassionate listening or active listening? Imagine being heard without judgment or having someone try to fix you or get one up on you! Imagine giving the gift of truly listening to another without having to "make it all better." My many years of immersion in the skills of Nonviolent Communication and more so in the work I have done with Dr. Robert Gonzales—Compassionate Communication—have played a huge role in how I now interact in all my relationships. This is a very simple version of compassionate listening, but it works.

These are grade three students! Just imagine what continual practice will do!

---

In the short period of fifteen minutes, students reported the following;

* I felt like a huge weight left my chest
* I felt heard for the first time ever
* It was hard to be such a good listener because I had to really pay attentionto what they were saying and not zone out
* It felt so good
* I felt like I shared a problem and now I was better friends
* I felt like I had a group helping me
* My heart feels good

---

## Home and School Practice

\* Below I'll explain the practice for the classroom and how to do it at home with two or more people.

## Role-play

One of the first things I teach my students every year is compassionate listening. After any disagreement or tussle, this is the first practice I employ. The children must learn how to listen and reflect to even begin to problem solve. They must be able to hear and be present without going into their own thoughts and explanations. Mark Nepo reflects so beautifully the power of sharing by writing, "When we don't give voice to what moves through us, we become entangled with life, but not connected to life. When silent without love and pain, we can't distribute what we feel and so our heartaches and pains are intensified as they bounce around within us."

## How To

Before beginning, students simply sit, bodies facing each other at a comfortable distance. This can be in chairs or on the floor. I then ask them to look at a spot on the other's body. It may be the neck or top of the other's sweater. (This avoids chest staring in the older grades!) I request that they be respectful. Then I read the following very slowly and ask that they say nothing. I ask that they listen with their bodies.

"Just like me, this person has had hard times. They have experienced loss, loneliness, and sadness. Just like me, this person has been hurt by others. They have been sick or in pain. They have had happiness and surprises. They have been loved and cared for."

We then share aloud what it is like to know that everyone experiences these human emotions. This sharing builds a sense of compassion and empathy for the partner before beginning a role-play. It allows the children to slow down and settle. It also gets them used to being present to another without having to actually talk or do anything.

This is an example of what you might try:

> Have one student share a difficulty and have the listener not try to
> fix, give advice, talk about themselves or share anything other than
> their own open heart. At the end of the sharing I ask the listener
> to reflect back to the speaker just what they have heard—nothing
> more. Then I ask the speaker to reflect if there was anything else
> that they wanted to share. If not let the listener know, they felt fully
> heard.
>
>   Person A: Tell me something that is difficult for you in a friendship.
>   Person B: Shares until complete. (Usually a few sentences to start
> as they are short and to the point. Later they can extend into two- to
> three-minute practices.)
>   Person A: Thank you—this is what I heard. (Here they can para-
> phrase or express the main idea of what they heard without adding
> their own thoughts. We practice it and I play one of the participants
> until the kids get the hang of it.)
>   Person B: Yes, that is it; or, no there is more.
>   Person A: Did I get it all?
>
> *The truth is that empathy is compassionate energy. You don't really
> need to say anything. Words can help clarify and form a more cohe-
> sive feeling for the speaker.

*Switch*

They can go back and forth a few times and then switch partners when you
ring a bell. I ring the bell after two or three minutes. I always have a seat in
front of me if someone wants to share. This allows the children to feel safe
and held if something is really on their mind. Sitting with their teacher also
builds precious connection, for they find you are vulnerable and human too!

## The Gift

True listening is the opposite of what is modeled on TV, in movies, or even
in politics. Where can children learn this skill if we do not model and teach
them the art of presence? When children practice this again and again and
they come to a teacher or even interact between themselves, they can truly

hear each other. They can also hear deep inside themselves. It may not be easy, but it brings two people into the same space with a shift, a slowing down, and a sense of caring. It provides a reflective pause and a chance for all viewpoints to be held and valued. The loudest or angriest person does not "win." Preconceived ideas are let go and listening below anger, hurt, and pain, the longings of the heart are heard and acknowledged.

## Adults Cry

When I have done this form of active listening with adults in workshops, many have tears in their eyes and say they have *never* been listened to in such a way in their whole lives. One week, two parents happened to come in during the lesson. The children explained what compassionate listening was and the parents sat down in little chairs with a child who chose to sit in front of them. The adults said it was an amazing experience. All of the parents ended up staying for more than half an hour and shared how they were going to take this back to their own homes in hopes of creating better communication. While you open your hearts and minds to the idea of presence and compassionate listening, I invite you to rest in Tara Brach's words of wisdom: "Presence is not some exotic state that we need to search for or manufacture. In the simplest terms, *it is the felt sense of wakefulness, openness, and tenderness that arises when we are fully here and now with our experience.*"

Let's give our children this gift of presence so they can in turn be fully present to themselves and others.

## Resources

### ADULT BOOKS

Tara Brach. *True Refuge: Finding Peace and Freedom in Your Own Awakened Heart.* New York: Bantam, 2013.

Robert Gonzales. *Reflections On Living Compassion.* Portland, OR: The Center for Living Compassion, 2015.

Thich Nhat Hanh. *No Mud, No Lotus: The Art of Transforming Suffering.* Berkeley, CA: Parallax Press, 2014.

Mark Nepo. *The Endless Practice, Becoming Who You Were Born to Be.* New York: Atria Books, 2014.

Marshall B. Rosenberg. *Living Nonviolent Communication: Practical Tools to Connect and Communicate Skillfully in Every Situation.* Louisville, CO: Sounds True, 2012.

Marshall B. Rosenberg. *Nonviolent Communication: A Language of Life*. Encinitas, CA: Puddledancer Press, 2003.

Marshall B. Rosenberg. *Raising Children Compassionately: Parenting the Nonviolent Communication Way*. Encinitas, CA: Puddledancer Press, 2004.

## CHILDREN'S BOOKS

Howard Binkow. *Howard B. Wigglebottom Learns to Listen*. Minneapolis, MN: Lerner Publishing Group, 2011.

Julia Cook. *The Worst Day of My Life Ever*. Boys Town, NE: Boys Town Press, 2011.

Julia Cook. *My Mouth Is a Volcano!* Illustrated by Carrie Hartman. Chattanooga, TN: National Center for Youth Issues, 2008.

Claire Llewellyn. *Why Should I Listen? (Why Should I?)*. Illustrated by Mike Gordon. Hauppauge, NY: Barron's Educational Series, 2005.

Cheri J. Meiners. *Listen and Learn*. Golden Valley. MN: Free Spirit Publishing, 2003.

# The Joy of Letting Go

6

### James: Practices for Grown-Ups

LETTING GO is a natural continuation of practicing integrity. Integrity involves a quality of restraint in which we let go of acting on impulses that might cause harm. Now we continue to develop an attitude of wise letting go by applying it to other areas of our life and noticing the feeling of well-being that accompanies it when we do.

Letting go can conjure an image of sacrifice or renunciation, which seems far removed from joy. But wise letting go leads to joy when we realize we don't have to hold on to our "extra baggage." We are putting down an unnecessary burden—the attachment that comes from grasping onto what we think will make us happy. The secret we're learning is to wisely distinguish what we want from what we truly need. We can do this when we quiet down enough to listen carefully to the different voices in the mind. Then we're able to hear whether they are coming from a place of fear and anxiety or from a deeper, wiser, compassionate connection that truly knows what's good for us.

Meditation teacher Joseph Goldstein uses an effective image to describe the suffering that comes from holding on with attachment. He says that in a world of constant change holding on tightly is like rope burn. We don't usually realize that it's the holding that's causing the suffering. When we can wisely let go, we free ourselves of the problem.

In working with this theme there are many areas one can explore: letting go of thoughts, beliefs, material objects, and experiences. But most fundamentally, what we're really letting go of is the illusion of control—which we never really had in the first place. We may think that if we try hard enough we can make things work out the way we want. But it can't be done. Things often don't work out just the way we'd hoped. And trying to maintain control just makes us more stressed. But letting go of control is not easy since that habit is so strong. The irony is that usually the more tightly we hold on to our agenda, the more resistance we encounter from others and life.

The secret of letting go is seeing, through direct experience, the pain that comes with attachment to things being a certain way. With awareness, you can see directly for yourself that attachment leads to suffering, and you become more motivated to discover for yourself the freedom that comes from letting go.

### Letting Go of Attachment to Being in Charge

Parents and teachers have many opportunities to investigate this theme. One area is the attachment to being the authority that makes all the decisions. Of course, it's important to provide structure and be a responsible authority. But there's something inspiring about empowering children whenever possible.

When I taught fifth and sixth grades in New York City, in the early years I had the idea that it was up to me to create all the activities and lessons. It was exhausting! I remember at some point making a profound shift in letting go of the way I held my role. I became more like a conductor of an orchestra. That roomful of enthusiastic minds held much more creativity than I could ever match. Why not use it?

For example, a child might come to me with an idea like, "Mr. Baraz, wouldn't it be fun to have a talent show?" I'd respond with "That's a great idea, Marina. How would you like help to organize it? What would you need? Who would you want to work with?" It was no longer up to me to do it all myself. We were all cocreating something together. It was much more inspiring for the children, less work for me, and a lot more fun for all.

Parents can sometimes micromanage their child's choices. By letting go of complete control and letting your child decide for herself about clothes or food or entertainment choices, you're showing trust and confidence in her. (Sometimes a child is given too much power and is the one who decides for the family. That's not so healthy and is not what I'm talking about!) Mike Riera, author of *Uncommon Sense for Parents with Teenagers*, suggests that when your child is old enough to make good decisions and you basically trust his judgment, you might consider letting go of your identity of being his "manager" and shift into being his "consultant." Letting go of always being in charge can be a great gift to children.

### Not Holding on to the Way It Was

Parents and educators have an on-going opportunity to practice letting go as their children keep growing out of one stage and move into the next one. I remember when my son, Adam, was young I would experience a continual readjustment: leaving the innocence of infancy for the nonstop adventure of toddlerhood. Just when I had gotten accustomed to his current phase, he would grow into a new one. Often I'd grieve the passing of the sweet innocent boy for the new model that thought he should have more power. But that's an integral part of parenting. Letting go of what was and embracing the newer version of your child. (That includes the teenage years too!)

Teachers often go through a bit of grieving each year as they say goodbye to their students. As a teacher who genuinely enjoyed being in the classroom, I would experience the bittersweet moment at the end of the school year when I knew that these children with whom I'd spent the whole year would be moving on and never again have the same connection with me. Teachers, can you let go and allow the grieving to be held with a compassionate heart?

## Letting Go of Expectations

We all know what's best for our children—at least we think we do. And so we create all kinds of ideas about how they should behave, what choices they should make, or what they should achieve. This is a sure set-up for suffering for you and for them. One of the greatest challenges for parents and teachers—for anyone actually—is letting go of our agendas for our children and supporting them in being just who they uniquely are.

When Adam was growing up, his favorite shirt that he wore all the time said "Find Your Own Way." That became his central philosophy. Other than when he needed some clear guidance and structure, Jane and I would encourage him to make his choices. And after all these years it seems like he usually does know what's best for him such as which schools would best help him develop his interests or what career would best utilize his gifts. And he is one confident young man. Can you let go of your ideas and expectations and support your children in discovering who they really are and what they have to offer this world?

## Generosity, the Full Flowering of Letting Go Practice

Generosity is the most beautiful expression of letting go. When we share things with others, whether it's our resources, our time, or our caring, we feel a greater heart connection through the very act of letting go. Think of a gift someone has given you that you like—perhaps a vase that you have in your home or a favorite sweater. Don't you think of your connection with them when you see it? I have a favorite cup in my bathroom that was part of a wedding gift set from our friends Roger and Frances thirty-three years ago. (In this world of impermanence, the other three have broken.) Every time I pick it up I think of them and wish them well. The stuff we share is the currency of our caring.

Generosity brings us joy and it is something that can be consciously practiced. How wonderful to encourage our kids to appreciate the natural joy that comes from generosity! We experience genuine delight in giving with no ulterior motive. We share because it feels good. The Dalai Lama calls this "selfish altruism," which he says is skillful. Whenever you are being generous, don't miss that good feeling. Notice how good generosity feels. That way you reinforce the wholesomeness of the act and awaken more joy.

It's important to include ourselves in our generosity practice. We're not trying to be martyrs by giving more than is appropriate. If we do, our generosity will be coming from a feeling of depletion instead of abundance. That is one reason nourishing ourselves is so important. Not only is our own well-being increased, but others also benefit from our self-care.

It's just as important to receive graciously when someone is being generous with you. Being the recipient is, for many people, more difficult than being the giver. You don't do anyone a service by turning generosity away with a response like, "Oh, you shouldn't have!" Receiving with appreciation and delight is actually an act of generosity itself. It lets the giver enjoy the good feeling of their giving heart. If you choose to work with generosity pay attention to receiving graciously, particularly if it's easier for you to give than to receive.

## Letting Go as Simplifying

The essence of letting go is bringing greater simplicity into our lives. When we simplify and get rid of clutter, we uncomplicate our minds. One aspect of simplifying can involve letting go of material things. How much do we really need? Our consumer society is constantly telling us all the things we need to make us happy, but it's just not so. We crave simplicity. The spacious feeling that comes from cleaning out our closet is actually more invigorating than acquiring more stuff.

It's useful to remember the Ven. P. A Payutto's clear articulation of "wise consumption"—how we know when "enough is enough":

> It is an awareness of that optimum point where enhancement of true well-being coincides with the experience of satisfaction. Consumption . . . balanced to an amount appropriate with well-being rather than to the satisfaction of desires. In contrast to maximum consumption leading to more satisfaction, we have moderate, or wise consumption leading to well-being.—P. A. Payutto p 187-188 as quoted in Stephanie Kaza, *Hooked!: Buddhist Writings on Greed, Desire and the Urge to Consume*, Boston, Shambhala, 2007.

This practice of finding the point of optimal well-being requires mindful attention. But it saves you from going overboard, which can turn pleasure into suffering. (Will that extra portion of dessert really bring you more happiness or more indigestion?)

## Try This

### Letting Go as Finding Balance in Your Life

An area of letting go that can lead to more happiness is bringing more balance to an overcrowded, busy life. We create suffering by taking on more than we can possibly handle. Even if the choices are pleasant ones, doing too much throws our lives out of balance. As Peace Pilgrim, a wise twentieth-century American sage, says: "If your life is in harmony with your part in the Life Pattern, and if you are obedient to the laws which govern this universe, then your life is full and good but not overcrowded. If it is overcrowded, you are doing more than is right for you to do, more than is your job to do in the total scheme of things." *Peace Pilgrim Her Life and Work in Her Own Words*, Ocean Tree Books (March 1992) p. 23.

1. What is making my life complicated or out of balance these days?

2. What would I need to simplify or let go of to bring my life more into balance?

3. Try the following experiment: Pick an area to take on as a practice of simplifying. This can be as simple as practicing not looking at email more than you need to. If you want to add something to your schedule, make sure to delete something else.

4. Every time you make a choice for simplifying by letting go of stuff that's overcrowding your life, notice how good it feels to practice a way that better serves you.

## *Letting Go of Our Stories*

One of the most profound letting go practices is to relinquish the stories and beliefs we tell ourselves about who we are and how it all is. While some of our stories are important and can inspire us in very positive, impactful ways, we often hold onto ideas that evoke feelings of smallness, fear, separation, or contraction that don't serve our well-being. These kinds of stories that obscure what's true are a major source of our suffering. They may involve beliefs about our past, our limitations, our potential, what others think of us, our expectations, or any interpretation that causes us confusion or fear. The stories often include words like *always* or *never*, as in "I can never ..." or "She always ..."

What can you do about them? The practice of letting go of a limiting story is extremely liberating and leads to great spaciousness and joy. Whenever I'm suffering or confused, one of my main personal practices is to simply ask myself, "What story am I believing right now?" The moment I ask this, I see the emptiness of the thought and let go of the story. I'm out of my prison and can see things from a clearer perspective. Thoughts are as real as we believe them to be or as empty as we see them to be. You may find, as I do, that using this reflection is an effective way to free the mind of the tyranny of negative thinking.

## Try This

Take five minutes to reflect and write your own responses to these questions. Consider sharing them with your buddy or a friend:

1. What story do you believe that keeps you from experiencing well-being and joy?

2. What would it be like if you saw it as just a story and could let it go?

3. What story could you substitute that would be more supportive of your well-being?

4. What would you need to understand or remember in order to let it go in the future?

## Michele: Practicing Letting Go with Children

"Letting Go ... I don't think I want to do this at all," was what my colleague said when I mentioned this chapter. "I want to skip that chapter, okay Michele? It sounds far too painful. I want to hang on."

Wait, please read on. Letting go is awesome.

Does letting go mean my life will be out of my control? Does it mean that I have to give up all my material wealth? I had these questions too until I understood what letting go truly meant. Now I embrace it.

I have learned that I cannot hold on to anything! Rats! I thought I could. Now I see how holding on pulls me out of the moment and creates incredible suffering.

When I was growing up, my parents thought they were creating safety by telling me how things would be for me. I only rebelled. They tried to hold onto me as a little girl but I was growing into a young woman. The tighter they held, the more I rebelled. They told me they would live long lives. Astonishingly, they died young. We, as parents, cannot make these promises or control the lives of our children or loved ones. Have you ever had success with trying to control all outcomes? Unfortunately, it doesn't work. Now when I feel caught in telling myself how I think things should be, I breathe and let go. This letting go can be incredibly difficult in bringing up children. As a mother, I try to meet each moment afresh and let go into it. As I write this, I am breathing into this one as my younger son gets his driver's license tomorrow! I know there will be a lot of moments of letting go after this.

### Parents Want to Hang On

I have had countless parents come to me as a teacher saying they want their child to be a certain way. They expect them to get straight A's because their brother did. They want them to be a star athlete because they loved sports. They want them to buck up and be more of a boy or a young lady. They want them to have different friends. They want their divorced partner to be more involved. The list goes on. Can you see that trying to change the things on the list above is like banging your head against the wall?

I ask parents if they can love their child just as he or she is. Can they let go of a perceived outcome for their child, partner, or friend? In this letting go I am not suggesting that they stop guiding their kids. The struggle comes when the parents go against what is. The lesson below is one that shows children the impermanence of life.

## Blow It Away—the Sand Mandala

*You mean they are really going to work on it for a week and then just blow it away?* My class was stunned when they heard of the ancient Tibetan Buddhist practice of creating sand mandalas. Luckily for us, there was a Tibetan mandala being created not more than a five-minute walk away. This was my lead in to the joy of letting go, the theme of this chapter. We went down and watched the monks create the mandala and went back to visit over the days it took to create. Some children participated in the final act of watching it blow into the ocean. They witnessed this act of creation and letting go. There is a lesson on making your own mandalas in this chapter.

## Children and Teens Are Clingers and Barnacles

The children will say, "It's always been like this. I should be better at math but I'm not." "We fought at lunch and I will never let it go." "I want to be rich and buy an iPhone but I can't." "Life sucks and I feel it all the time." "I have to stay popular and be part of the group, no matter what." "She has to be my friend forever." "We said we would." "I felt great at the party last night and I want that feeling always, even if I have to drink to get it." "My cat died and I will never ever be happy again."

Letting go, like all the other practices, is not something you just do once. It is a practice you do over and over and over again. This doesn't mean we can't enjoy life, but we can ask how much of our energy we want to put into pursuing it. Letting go means allowing things to be as they are. Not grasping at the good or pushing away the adverse. Just allowing all to be as it is. You are not fixed to how it should be. It is to know that change is just the way things are. It is inevitable that good things and bad things will come our way. If you are attached to security and how things should be, you are in for a rough ride.

# Lesson 1: Letting Go

When you stop holding on so tight—to ideas, beliefs, objects, or belongings you cherish, and precious concepts of who you are—you live in a way that lets you flow with life. You discover that letting go is something you do for yourself, not to yourself.

**Building Strengths of:**
- Perspective taking
- Resilience
- Perseverance
- Humility
- Letting go

**Materials**
- Paper
- Scissors
- Paper shredder (if available)
- Sand or table salt
- Colored chalk
- Grater
- Bowl
- Stick (Pencil sized)

**Ages**
- Seven to adult

**School Curriculum Connections**
- Oral language
- Written language
- Listening skills
- Social studies
- Fine arts
- Social and emotional learning

## *Home and School Practices*

### Magically

At the time I was taking the Awakening Joy course, the topic of the month was "Letting Go." It just so happened that Tibetan lama Tenzin Tsundu was creating a sand mandala steps away from our school. My class and I discussed what this particular lama had to let go of when he crossed the Himalayas in 1957 to gain refugee status in Dharamsala, India.

### Sand Mandala

We had been practicing mindfulness all year and I knew I could take this class to witness the creation of the mandala. They would respect the space and sacredness of the event.

In the morning we had our own lesson on letting go. I asked the class to brainstorm all the things we don't want to let go of in life. We started by relating to what a baby has to let go of as they grow into a toddler. The children spoke of how difficult it is to give up a blanket, soother, stuffed animal or lovey, or a mother's breast. We then talked about all the stages of life up until the end of life.

We had three visitors in our classroom that day of various ages. They spoke about letting go of children at home, our aging bodies, and career dreams.

## Write It Out

We then spoke of things we would like to let go of. The list grew fast and furiously. The list included "Feeling bad about myself," "My old doll," "Being bossy," "Fighting with my sister," and various other things.

Finally, I had each child take out their own pencil and write what they would personally like to let go of. I said they could write as much private stuff as they liked, and they might write at least one thing they could say out loud. Heads were down and pencils scratched the paper. All the adults wrote as well.

## A Magical Machine

I told the children I had a magical machine that could help with letting go. I went to the office and dragged down the portable electric shredder. (It was the same shredder we used for chapter 1, Lesson 3, "Shredder—Start with the Negative and Move to the Positive." It's an item with many powers!) If I had been at home, I would have built a roaring fire for this magical event to take place.

I declared, by sharing with the group what they would like to let go of, on some level it would be transformed. I told them it might not happen in that moment and some things were very much out of our control. What we could do is *intend* to release the hold they had on us.

## Say It, Repeat It

We sat in circle and each child walked up to the shredder and said, "I am letting go of _____." The rest of the class responded by clapping and shouting, "Let go! YES, YES, YES!" They watched their worries be eaten up and shredded. When it was all done, we opened the shredder and I asked how they were feeling.

Many spoke of feeling so light and happy.

To top off the day we were able to sit with the Tibetan lama in the afternoon and watch the mandala form. The children were deeply respectful and many said they had never been in such a sacred space before. The mandala was let go into the ocean the following Sunday and many of the students and families were in attendance at this ancient ceremony of "letting go." The children were introduced to the ceremonies and ways of another culture and it opened a door to deeper study of the Tibetan people.

## Activities:

Make your own list of things you would like to let go of. Cut them up or shred them.

Create your own sand mandala bowl using colored salt or sand. Use the mandala as a practice of letting go.

## How to Make a Sand Mandala Bowl

1. Either collect some fine sand from the beach or open a box of table salt and pour it into a bowl. You can sift it to remove the chunks. (You will need at least 2 cups of material.)
2. You can make one or many colors of sand. Take a colored stick of sidewalk chalk or chalk pastel, and using a vegetable grater, rub the stick over the grater until you have powder.
3. Mix this powder with the sand or salt until you have colored sand.
4. Take the colored sand and put it in a bowl.
5. Find a beautiful stone to place toward one edge, leaving enough room to draw patterns.
6. Using your pencil-sized stick, draw patterns in the sand.
7. Lift your rock and shake the bowl or use your hand to wipe the pattern free.

Although this doesn't take any-where near the time it takes to create a mandala, all the children will have endless fun creating patterns and "letting them go."

## Take It a Step Further

Make a variety of colored sands. With chalk, sketch a mandala on a piece of plywood. Use the colors to fill in the design. You can build a little funnel by gluing or taping two popsicle sticks together at an angle to make a little trough. Then you can run the colored sands down them to fill in the design just like the monks do when creating a sand mandala.

Paulo Coelho speaks of the action of letting go in his novel *The Alchemist*. "'Don't think about what you've left behind,' the alchemist said to the boy as they began to ride across the sands of the desert. 'If what one finds is made of pure matter, it will never spoil. And one can always come back. If what you had found was only a moment of light, like the explosion of a star, you would find nothing on your return.'"
—Paulo Coelho. *The Alchemist*. San Francisco: HarperOne, 1988 P. 127

## *Resources*

### ADULT BOOKS

Brene Brown. *The Gifts of Imperfection: Let Go of Who You Think You're Supposed to Be and Embrace Who You Are*. Minneapolis, MN: Hazelden, 2010.

Barry Bryant. *The Wheel of Time Sand Mandala: Visual Scripture Of Tibetan Buddhism* Ithaca, NY: Snow Lion, 2003.

Paulo Coelho. *The Alchemist*. San Francisco: HarperOne, 1988.

Skyhorse Publishing. *Mandalas: Coloring for Artists*. New York: Skyhorse Publishing, 2015.

### CHILDREN'S BOOKS

Gail Silver. *Anh's Anger*. Illustrated by Christiane Krömer. Berkeley, CA: Plum Blossom Books, 2009.

Tibetan Mandalas Colored Sand, by Papo. Available at:
http://www.amazon.com/Djeco-Sand-Art-Tibetan-Mandalas/dp/B000TZGA3M

# Lesson 2: Drawing from the Inside Out

## Chalk Pastel Art: Before and After Fifteen-Minute Progressive Relaxation

When you let go of thinking that things should be a certain way, you open yourself up to the fact that there are usually a number of options that you hadn't considered.

### Building Strengths of:
- Creativity
- Open-mindedness
- Love of learning
- Self-awareness
- Self expression

### Materials
- Chalk pastels
- Large paper (11 x 16 inches or larger)
- Quiet space
- Time to do a meditation (between twenty minutes and an hour)

### Ages
- Preschool to adult

### School Curriculum Connections
- Oral language
- Listening skills
- Fine arts
- Social and emotional learning

### *Home and School Practice*

### Drawing from the Inside Out

My curiosity was alive and thriving one morning as I entered the school. I wanted to see if the children could draw the effects of a mindfulness session without using oral language in any way. I didn't want to make suggestions or preprogram what the kids might draw. The only instructions in the lesson were that it might include the shape of a face. This was going to be an experiment and I wanted it to come from deep inside.

I took my grade three class to a quiet space. They had been training in mindfulness practices all year. I began by giving them each a giant (2 x 3 feet) piece of paper. We went into a wide-open room and I gave them packages of chalk pastels.

I chose chalk pastels for this exercise because they can cover a lot of space quickly and colorfully, and they add a dreamy quality to the art. I also chose pastel because we had used them before and the children knew about shaking the pastel dust into the garbage and not letting it blow across the room. In this way the school custodians were happy too!

I had the children draw a basic face and then use the pastels to show their mood. I asked them not to judge, but to just pick up color after color and see what arose.

They began to rub pastels on paper.

After about five minutes (don't go too long or they will move into their heads and start judging the art) have them put down the chalk and fold their papers over so they cannot see the drawing anymore. Only one half of the blank paper will remain.

Next, I took them on a mind journey to deeply relax the body and said, "Breathe and relax. Remember a time when you felt very safe and happy. Someone might show up in your mind or it could be an animal; just sit with it until you feel full. Then open your eyes and pick up the pastels. *Go for it.*"

Honestly, you could not hear a sound except chalk scratching across the pages.

We laid all the art pieces out down the hall and looked at them with the children and a few teachers. After the mindfulness session, we noticed the artwork had a softness and dreamy quality. Many students talked about a deep sense of peace. Many drew pets that had died. They worked all the way through recess, not wanting to stop until they were finished.

These pictures graced the hallways of the school for several weeks. Many parents spoke to me about the profound effects of listening to their children share about this progressive relaxation time. One mother came to me in tears and said that her son spoke of a grandfather he had drawn that he had never had a chance to meet. The child had said to his mother matter of factly that his grandfather was present with him when he was deeply relaxed. There is so much unknown. I am aware that introducing children to a mindfulness practice helps them deeply relax into places and spaces that they don't often get to visit; it allows for a gentleness that may relax our unseen boundaries. More and more, little by little, by offering children various doors, they will befriend and access their inner being. Many children go home and teach their families the relaxation practices of the day, allowing the waves of relaxation to ripple out into the world.

## Resources

### ADULT BOOKS

Hannah Davies and Richard Merritt. *Calming Therapy: An Anti-Stress Coloring Book.* Philadelphia, PA: Running Press, 2015.

Laura Deutsch. *Writing from the Senses: 59 Exercises to Ignite Creativity and Revitalize Your Writing.* Boulder, CO: Shambhala, 2014.

Betty Edwards. *Drawing on the Right Side of the Brain: The Definitive, 4ᵗʰ Edition.* New York: TarcherPerigee, 2012.

Dina Wakley. *Art Journal Courage: Fearless Mixed Media Techniques for Journaling Bravely.* New York: North Light Books, 2014.

### CHILDREN'S BOOKS

Drew Daywalt. *The Day the Crayons Quit.* Illustrated by Oliver Jeffers. New York: Philomel Books, 2013.

Shane Derolf. *The Crayon Box that Talked.* Illustrated by Michael Letzig. New York: Random House Books for Young Readers, 1997.

Peter H. Reynolds. *Creatrilogy Box Set (Dot, Ish, Sky Color).* Somerville, MA: Candlewick, 2012.

Fiona Watt. *The Usborne Book of Drawing, Doodling and Coloring.* Illustrated by Erica Harrison and Katie Lovell. London: Usborne Publishing Ltd, 2010.

# Lesson 3: Letting Go of Constricting Beliefs and Wiring the Brain for Success

Whenever you're suffering or confused you might ask yourself, "What story am I believing right now?" This allows you to see the thought as a mere mental fabrication and let go of the story.

**Builds strengths of:**
- Confidence
- Caring
- Sharing
- Family vision and appreciation
- Self-confidence

**Materials**
- Voice recorder

**Ages**
- Preschool to adult

**School Curriculum Connections**
- Oral language
- Written language
- Listening skills
- Reading
- Science
- Social and emotional learning

Apparently fear of public speaking, or glossophobia, is one of the most common phobias in North America. Most people cope with the fear of public speaking by avoiding it all together. Throughout their lives people may pass up job opportunities, relationships, and the joy of pure self-expression by succumbing to this fear. If we start supporting children at a young age to speak in front of peers in safe ways, rather than closing doors, it will open a myriad of possibilities. These practices of letting go of constricting beliefs are vital to our happiness.

## *I Cannot Open My Mouth*

I remember my own experience with public speaking when I was in a culinary skills class in ninth grade. We were to demonstrate a recipe to the whole class and speak the directions aloud. I was absolutely terrified. What would the kids think of me? What if I didn't look competent? I couldn't utter a word. The teacher kept saying aloud, if you don't do this, you will get a D ... you will get a D. I was confronted with fear. Freeze, fight, or flight? I froze, then flew, and never forgot. I was not given a moment of compassion by my teacher or classmates, and I certainly didn't know how to be self-compassionate.

Dr. Kristen Neff, an expert on self-compassion, writes in *Self Compassion: The Proven Power of Being Kind to Yourself*, "How do we release ourselves from this deep-rooted tendency to wallow in black goo? By giving ourselves compassion. Research shows that self-compassionate people tend to experience fewer negative emotions—such as fear, irritability, hostility, or distress—than those who lack self-compassion."

### *School Practice*

### My Own Students

I wanted my own students to have more freedom and ease in speaking, so I started introducing public speaking at an early age. I also teach them to develop a self-compassion mantra. I let the children know that I still get nervous, yet to do my job and express my passions, I must speak out. I invite them to let go of their fears and try to speak out too!

### Being Held in Compassion While Taking a Risk

One day, I asked my students to prepare a two-minute speech on what they would like to see and do if they were to visit China. Students could use cue cards and were asked to practice before coming to class the following week. We talked about body language and how to look confident even if you are not feeling it. If you can teach the children about the physiology of fear—sweating, anxiety, blood rushing to the organs, and foggy thinking—they will be able to step back and hopefully notice and label the experience as fear and begin to talk themselves through the challenging situation.

As the day came to a close, I was pulled aside by at least four students ask-

ing if they could speak just in front of me. They did not want anyone else to witness their talk. I thought it over, and as I knew this class very well, I told the whole group this:

> "If I were to let you go without speaking today, I would be doing you a huge disservice. What I know about brain science is that you will once again wire the neural pathways that confirm that you cannot speak in front of an audience. You will create a pathway so strong it will limit your greatness.
>
> "Look around at this group. There will be times when you might accept an award and be unable to speak. What if you want to be a politician in governing this country and cannot share your values? What if you become the next NHL hockey player and cannot go on camera? What if your family needs someone to speak for them at a celebration or memorial? If today I say, "No, you won't have to do this speech," you once again have confirmed that you cannot. You will remember back to this moment in sixth grade and say this is where you grew even more phobic and more constricted. You are only eleven years old. I cannot aid in this tragedy. (I tried to look very serious at this point, and actually I was.) You are in front of the most compassionate group of people I have ever met. They care that you try. They don't care if you are nervous, stumble, or whatever. They support you and they ask that you let go of the constricting belief that you cannot do this.

"So let's say this self-compassionate mantra together.

"'Even though this is hard and I may sweat, stumble, or mumble, everyone feels this way at times. It is a part of the human experience. I am worthy of a try. I have good friends here and they will support me.'"

## Creating a Safe Place to Take Risks

### Offer—Don't Push

(By this time, eyes were very wide and one of the children who had said she was scared put her hand up and said she would like to come up and try.) I asked what she needed to support herself and she said her best friend on one side and me on the other. It also happened that on that day my little dog Teddy Bear was there, and she held him tight while I held the paper on which she had written her speech. With tears in her eyes and shaky hands, she set her feet on the ground and read her speech. Yes, her face went red; yes, she stumbled; yes, she went too fast; yes, we all held a collective breath, but the roar of clapping was heard all the way down the hall when she finished. The brilliance of her smile as she skipped to her desk was pure joy. I stopped and asked her to truly look around and take in the joy of the moment. She was installing this newfound sense of courage and success. She had changed her thought patterns and let go of a limiting belief. Throughout the day she raised her thumb to me and I to her as she had overcome something so huge with such courage. In my heart I bowed to her and the human spirit.

## Home Practice

So here are some tips for you to encourage your own children to build this capacity.

* At an early age, let kids play with their voices. Let them know nothing is "right" or "good." Just let there be sound. You can capture it on camera or video and play it back. Get them used to seeing themselves perform and share in safe ways.

* Have your children put little plays on for you or an audience. They can be incredibly simple and only take a few minutes, but the joy of sharing aloud will build courage and competence. I remember putting on plays with my boys with their stuffed animals and our pet dog sitting in all the dining chairs as their supportive audience.

* Spend time listening to your kids reading books aloud or saying the alphabet letters. This can be done at a very early age so they become

accustomed to hearing their own voices. Later they can read to a sibling or grandparents and in this way widen the audience. By the time they are called on in class, it will be easy for them to speak up.

✳ Spend family time singing songs. Put on music and sing along, pull out the karaoke, or stoke the campfire and pull out the old tunes.

✳ Encourage your kids to share in class when the teacher asks for students to present things or to read aloud. Let them practice at home. In the older grades we don't often do "sharing" any more, so children miss many opportunities to speak aloud.

## School Practice

✳ As a teacher, start with small easy shares where safety is built in. Children can share in small groups or stand with a friend.

✳ Encourage older children to model this sharing in front of the younger children to inspire them.

✳ Also, allow children to take leadership roles in the classroom by taking the roll call, guiding mindfulness sessions, giving directions and leading school-wide assemblies.

✳ Students can also lead mindfulness activities.

## Vulnerability, Connection and Self-Compassion

✳ Reveal your own vulnerability by reading a speech or presentation in front of your children. I once gave an entire opening speech for a presentation to my grade three class for practice. They were so compassionate and supportive that when I actually went to do the speech, I just drew them into the room when I was presenting and I felt a great deal of comfort. I too still get nervous and scared!

✳ Share the brain science of how we wire in negative patterns and they become stronger and more fixed into our neural pathways. What we rest our attention on goes from a state to a trait. Rick Hanson's book *Hardwiring Happiness* explains this with much ease and readability.

✳ Have your child tell you all the possible times it may be helpful to give a public speech. Connect this idea to things they love to do and see how it can serve them in the future. Little steps to success go a long way.

✳ Have your child practice self-compassion self-talk before speaking in public. They might say to themselves, "Even though I am going to talk in front of the class and I will probably be scared to death, I will get through this. It is easier now that I am more prepared. Actually I have something to share and my friends will support me." (As a teacher, I do

this aloud and all the kids repeat. This allows us to air all the possible scenarios for anxiety and the children realize everyone has some level about
anxiety and they are not alone. Children also share with their classmates
ways to overcome the tension.

Tara Brach, in her book *True Refuge*, offers these comforting words and
suggests that you repeat them several times. You may also put your hand over
your heart as you say them.

---

This is the suffering of fear.
Fear is part of being alive.
Other people experience this too ... I am not alone.
May I be kind to myself ... may I give myself the compassion I need.

---

## Resources

### ADULT BOOKS

Carmine Gallo. *Talk Like TED: The 9 Public-Speaking Secrets of the World's Top
Minds*. New York: St Martin's Press, 2014.

Fred E. Miller. *No Sweat Public Speaking!: How to Develop, Practice and Deliver a
Knock Your Socks Off Presentation with No Sweat*. University City, MO: Fred Company, 2012.

### CHILDREN'S BOOKS

Keith Baker. *The Talent Show: A Mr. and Mrs. Green Adventure*. Boston, MA:
Houghton Mifflin Harcourt Books for Young Readers, 2012.

Stan Berenstain and Jan Berenstain. *The Berenstain Bears Get Stage Fright*. New York:
Random House Books for Young Readers, 2013.

Katharine Holabird and Helen Craig. *Angelina and the Tummy Butterflies (Angelina
Ballerina)*. New York: Grosset & Dunlap, 2013.

Cecilia Minden and Kate Roth. *How to Write and Give a Speech*. North Mankato,
MN: Cherry Lake Publishing, 2011.

Rob Scotton. *Splat the Cat: Splat the Cat Sings Flat*. New York: HarperCollins, 2011.

# Lesson 4: The Power of Touch

Generosity is an active form of letting go, and it is a sure avenue to happiness. You're not only giving away something; you're connecting lovingly with others through the act of sharing.

**Building strengths of:**
- Compassion
- Connection
- Contribution
- Well-being
- Love of others
- Love of self

**Materials**
- Warm hands
- Warm heart
- Time
- Massage oil or cream

**Ages**
- Birth to adult

**School Curriculum Connections**
- Oral language
- Listening skills
- Science
- Social and emotional learning

## *Home Practice*

### Birth of Touch

When my sons were born, I would massage them as often as I could with rich oils. My eldest had jaundice when he was born, so he had to lie under the sky-lights while the soft light of winter sunshine touched his body daily. I remembered seeing pictures of children in India being massaged every day. There was a memorable connection made to their mothers and fathers as parents massaged each limb of their tiny baby. I read of how infant massage enhanced the parent-baby bond, promoted a body-mind-spirit connection, and increased sense of love, acceptance, respect, and trust. Touch also enhances communication and, above all, creates a listening heart.

So through their lives I massaged my boys, a little here, a little there, often just on the face or hands to get them to fall asleep. In my experience, this created a wonderful sense of connection and unseen benefits came to pass.

## Big Ol' Teenagers

Now, so many years later, my seventeen-year-old son comes in from his job as a grocery clerk and plops down on the couch. His size-thirteen feet take up a whole cushion. He complains about how tired he is and is unable to articulate much. As I have been away for a week on a road trip, in this moment I yearn for a deep connection with him.

I ask him if he would like to lie on the carpet by the heater and get a little massage. This is something that used to help him relax when he was little and it has been months since he did this, as his life is so busy with friends, work, and school. Snuggling is definitely not what he wants to do anymore.

In this case, though, it is clear he can use a little connection. I slow way down and feel the deep breathing of this six-foot-four young man who is still my child. I bless him as he falls into a deep sleep. I can mother him for a moment and listen deep inside as I did when he was a little child. I feel my parents, long passed over, who have never seen or held him, come and stand by me and somehow have a moment with him too. The ancestors gather in. Now still sleeping wrapped in many wool blankets, he rests deeply and I feel my heart bursting with love and connection.

## How To

How does this become a practice of letting go?

## Steps

1. Find a lovely warm space and warm some massage oil in your hands.

2. Invite your child to simply breathe while you gently begin massaging the body.

3. Only touch what is comfortable for both of you. It might be the feet, hands, neck, and back, or if your child is small you may want to massage their whole body. Be respectful.

4. As your child begins to relax, ask them to focus their mind where your hands are touching their skin. Have them breathe into any tightness, fatigue, or discomfort.

5. Slowly, very slowly, sync your breathing with your child. Take your time.

6. In your mind you can ask that anything that needs to be let go is released with love and care from the body.

7. When you feel complete, gently stroke your child from head to toe three or four times.

8. Shake your hand and release any old energy back to Mother Earth.

9. Wrap your child in a blanket and allow them to deeply relax in this snuggly cocoon.

10. Ahh . . . enjoy letting go and the power of touch.

### School Practice

Children can come into the classroom starved for touch—touch that is safe, nurturing, soothing, and relaxing. When introducing this exercise, I teach them that they have body ownership: a right to control how their body is touched. If they feel uncomfortable in any way, they can sit out or snuggle with our classroom pet or a stuffed animal. Certain children may have a history of trauma; please gently allow them to just sit out and watch. They might enjoy participating by sending happy thoughts to the people practicing. Quite honestly, in all the years I have been teaching I have rarely had a child sit out.

I usually introduce this practice partway through the year as students are much more comfortable with each other and the new students have met friends they can partner with. The following breathing/touch technique is a lovely way to connect at home and have children connect with each other in the classroom. It allows children to focus their minds and breathe in different parts of their bodies.

## How to

I allow children to choose someone in the class they feel comfortable with for this exercise. If there is a student left over I ask if they would be willing to be my partner. I have never been turned down yet!

I demonstrate the full exercise with a student before starting this lesson.

Start by having Person A curl up in child's pose. The other person (Person B) stands behind them and gently puts their hands on the other's head.

(To do child's pose, sit on your heels touching your big toes together. Separate your legs. Lay your torso or tummy down between your legs resting on your thighs while leaning forward. Now place your forehead on the floor or mat and bring your arms and hands parallel to your sides. You can have your palms face up. Relax.)

Person A breathes three or four breaths into the hands of Person B. Person B can also sync their own breathing to A so they become very connected.

Person A then slowly moves hands down, having B breathe into their upper back, mid back, and feet. When they are completely finished, they slowly sweep hands from head to toes three times and let the person in child's pose just rest for a minute.

The kids love this safe touch. Once they are past giggling and have done it more than once, it becomes natural and they immediately get a partner and start.

### Resources

#### ADULT BOOKS

Nitya Lacroix, Sharon Seagar, and Francesca Rinaldi. *Whole Body Massage: The Ultimate Practical Manual of Head, Face, Body and Foot Massage Techniques*. London: Southwater, 2009.

Vimala Schneider McClure. *Infant Massage—Revised Edition: A Handbook for Loving Parents*. New York: Bantam, 2000.

#### CHILDREN'S BOOKS

These four children's books deeply touched our lives and created a sacred space to love and be loved as we fell asleep each night. I hope your families enjoy them too!

Margaret Wise Brown. *Goodnight Moon*. Illustrated by Clement Hurd. New York: HarperCollins, 2007.

Sam McBratney. *Guess How Much I Love You*. Illustrated by Anita Jeram. Somerville, MA: Candlewick, 2008.

Robert Munsch. *I'll Love You Forever*. Illustrated by Sheila McGraw. Richmond Hill, ON: Firefly Books, 1995.

Nancy Tillman. *On the Night You Were Born*. New York: Feiwel & Friends, 2010.

# Loving Ourselves

# 7

## James: Practices for Grown-Ups

WHEN I WAS growing up I did not like myself very much. Insecure and shy, I had a hard time believing that anyone would like me, other than my close friends. I often felt like a fraud and feared that I would be discovered. If someone told me that it would possible to love myself I wouldn't have believed them. I'm here to tell you it's possible. But it means looking past our own filters of self-judgment to discover the goodness that everyone who likes us sees.

We all want to be happy. Even stronger than all the doubts, judgments, and self-destructive voices, is a pure force wishing for our happiness right inside of us. It's rooting for our well-being. All our actions are motivated by the idea that they will help us feel better or feel less bad. Unfortunately, often we are confused as to what leads to true happiness. The process of learning to love ourselves means accessing and then empowering this force, so that it wisely directs our choices toward what is truly good for us.

This theme of loving ourselves follows naturally from the theme of letting go because when you let go of the limiting stories of who you think you are, you see that you're truly lovable and worthy of love. When you can love yourself or even just begin to appreciate who you are, you allow all your wonderful qualities to shine through.

Then you can tap into your true goodness, see the gifts you've been given and experience the joy of sharing them with others. If loving yourself seems like a stretch, then just being kind to yourself or wishing yourself well can begin a profound and life-changing process. Besides feeling good on the inside, this becomes a great gift to everyone you meet, especially your children. They can easily see how we treat ourselves and that becomes a significant example. So learning to genuinely like and even love ourselves is a key to their well-being.

It's amazing how rare it is to genuinely appreciate who we are. How many of us have a low self-image driven by an inner critic? These thoughts of self-judgment often come from an underlying sense of unworthiness. Seeing yourself as unworthy is missing the truth of who you are: a perfect expression of life with the same True Nature (some call it Divine Spirit or Kingdom of Heaven) as every other living being, right within you. As a teaching from *The Course in Miracles* puts it: "Believing in your littleness is arrogant, because it's preferring your own opinion to God's."

## Forgiveness: A Prerequisite for Loving Ourselves

In order to love ourselves, we need to accept ourselves just as we are with all of our imperfections. The subject of forgiveness came up with the theme of integrity in chapter 5. With this theme of self-love it is again a significant part of our practice—not only forgiving yourself regarding past actions but also for any way you see yourself as not good enough.

If we only see our faults, we just perpetuate the feeling of not being good enough. We cut ourselves off from recognizing who we really are (when we're not acting from fear or confusion). The crucial task in learning to be kind and loving toward ourselves is to remember our basic goodness, along with all our other positive qualities.

Jack Kornfield, in his book *The Art of Forgiveness, Lovingkindness, and Peace*, writes about the Babemba tribe of Zambia who offer a radically different possibility of forgiving ourselves.

> In the Babemba tribe, when a person acts irresponsibly or unjustly, he is placed in the center of the village, alone and unfettered. All work ceases, and every man, woman, and child in the village gathers in a large circle around the accused individual. Then each person in the tribe speaks to the accused, one at a time, each recalling the good things the person in the center of the circle has done in his lifetime. Every incident, every experience that can be recalled with any detail and accuracy, is recounted. All his positive attributes, good deeds, strengths, and kindnesses are recited carefully and at length. This tribal ceremony often lasts for several days. At the end, the tribal circle is broken, a joyous celebration takes place, and the person is symbolically and literally welcomed back into the tribe.[3]

Maybe you need to forgive yourself because you can't accept some part of who you are: your body or your mind or your limitations. As Robert Bly says,

---

3. Jack Kornfield, *The Art of Forgiveness, Lovingkindness, and Peace* (New York: Bantam, 2002).

"Every part of us that we do not learn to love will become hostile toward us." Forgiveness requires us to let go of any ideal standard that is impossible to measure up to, a merciless perfectionism not based on wisdom.

Learning forgiveness and compassion for ourselves takes time and patience. It doesn't happen overnight. But as with our other practices, by inclining the mind that way we are planting powerful seeds that will bear fruit. Whenever you have a moment of self-forgiveness, be present for the wholesomeness of the feeling. Let your awareness register how that moment of forgiveness feels in your body and in your mind.

### Loving-kindness for Ourselves

With sufficient self-forgiveness and compassion, we can open our hearts to truly wish ourselves well. A famous teaching says that we can search the whole world over and not find anyone more deserving of love than ourselves. But as most of us know first-hand, it's often harder to feel the same kindness toward ourselves that we would have toward someone else.

Imagine meeting someone who got your jokes, had similar tastes, and really understood your take on things. In short, someone who really got you. How would you feel about meeting them? You'd probably be ecstatic! There is only one person in this world who fully fits that description. But, unfortunately, they inhabit your skin so you don't appreciate those qualities from the inside. Michele's lesson on "Being My Own Best Friend" is a playful portal into loving yourself. Einstein has a phrase that describes this predicament: We live in an "optical delusion of consciousness." It's only from our limited vantage point that we don't see the truth of who we are. If you met yourself, you would probably be asking, "Where have you been all my life?!"

### Letting in the Love

Here's a practice that supports self-love, inspired by John Makransky's book *Awakening Through Love: Unveiling Your Deepest Goodness.* He talks about the fact that there is kindness coming toward us all the time. By being present for it, we open our hearts and feel connected to life all around us. I practice this perspective in the following way: Whenever someone smiles at me, opens a door, sends any goodwill my way, I think of it as life letting me know that I am worthy of kindness and love. The people who are sending it are agents of that loving energy from life. Don't miss it. Feel the connection to them and, even more, see that life wants to support you and send kind energy your way. This has been a very powerful practice for me. I hope you try it and see for yourself how potent it can be.

### Take Good Care of Yourself

We often hear the phrase, "Take good care of yourself." This is the essence of learning to love yourself. If you quiet down enough to listen carefully to the wisdom inside, you can know what care is appropriate at any given time. When we take good care, we stand up for ourselves, and can honestly see what's needed. One of the most important acts of self-care we can do is to speak to ourselves in a kind and caring manner.

Bringing a kind, compassionate voice to your self-talk is a crucial piece of self-love. Be aware of the tone of your thoughts to help you discern between the voice of judgment and the voice of wisdom. If you hear a harsh tone, you can be certain that is not the voice of wisdom. It will likely be telling you what is wrong or what can go wrong. This is a sure way to not experience well-being. The wiser voice will keep you focused on what will genuinely support you.

Taking care of yourself also includes making choices that support your physical well-being—what food you put into your body, exercising and stretching your body, and giving it the rest it needs. Of course, you've been hearing this kind of advice your whole life. But try connecting with the conscious motivation of being kind to your body because you appreciate it and want to treat it well. It will have a powerful impact in developing a really healthy mental attitude toward your body, which is a great way to deepen self-love.

One way to get in touch with this wisdom that wants to take good care of you is to ask directly, "What do I need right now for my well-being?" or "What do I need right now to thrive?" Listen for the honest response that comes. There is no right answer. Whatever message follows, the key is to act on it in a way that supports the intention of kindness toward yourself. Perhaps what's needed in the moment is more focus, structure, and discipline. Can you give that to yourself in a kind way? Or maybe the message that comes through is to nourish yourself more by taking a break, calling up a friend, or having some fun. Can you do that without feeling guilty? You might have a strong sense that it's time to step out of your comfort zone and try new things. Whatever you do, keep asking what you need to take good care of yourself. Listen to the wisdom coming through. Then empower it through action.

### Your Wholesome Qualities Are Yours and Not Yours

One might well wonder if getting in touch with all your wonderful qualities can become one big ego trip. We are not doing this to inflate our egos. That's a sure set-up for later ego-deflation or resentment from others. An important attitude in appreciating our strengths is not taking ownership of them. They are gifts life has given to us that we can't really take credit for (in the same way we don't have to blame ourselves for our shortcomings). We can be grateful for these qualities, appreciate them, use them wisely, and realize that their source is bigger than who we are.

### Recalling Our Goodness

Imagine if we could do some version of the Babemba tribe's practice for ourselves! Recalling one's good deeds is actually a powerful practice to counteract our tendencies toward guilt and shame. Try this:

1. Take some time to recall as many of your good deeds as you can. What made you act that skillfully? Can you see the goodness that wanted to be expressed?

2. Notice how it feels when you recall your goodness.

3. When you get self-critical, recall some of your past good deeds and see if that lessens the negative self-talk.

### A Forgiveness Practice

When we judge ourselves for our shortcomings or how we think we're not good enough in some way, we add additional pain to the situation. In some teachings this is called adding a second arrow on top of the first. Instead of self-judgment we can bring self-compassion to our judging mind. This is a huge step in practicing true kindness to ourselves.

If self-judgment is a challenge for you, try the following exercise that I shared in the live class:

1. What do I need to forgive myself for?

2. What would I need to understand in order to truly forgive myself?

3. Imagine someone else filled with self-judgment about this issue. Would you be able to forgive him or her?

4. Let the wisest and most compassionate part of you forgive that confused being who doesn't feel good enough. Let yourself feel the wholesomeness of your compassion. *(continues on next page)*

### Classic Loving-kindness Practice

One way to take good care of yourself is to practice sending thoughts of loving-kindness to yourself.

1. Take some quiet time (ten minutes) and experiment with slowly and silently repeating the loving-kindness phrases below to yourself:

   *May I be happy.*
   *May I be peaceful.*
   *May I be kind to myself.*
   *May I love and accept myself just as I am.*

2. As you say each phrase, if possible, have an image of yourself that corresponds to the phrase. See yourself in a happy moment and send thoughts of well-wishing to the image as if you're splashing a blessing over it.

3. You can also direct these phrases toward your body or some part of your body that you want to develop a healthier relationship with. Your body has been doing the best to serve you for a long time. Send it some kind and appreciative thoughts.

This practice can have real power, especially if we say the phrases slowly and connect with our intention and the meaning behind the words. Use whatever phrases you resonate with. Two of my personal favorites are: "May I be safe from inner and outer harm" and "May I be kind to myself." You might pick three or four and say them consistently so they become more accessible.

### An Exercise to Develop Loving-kindness toward Self

In traditional loving-kindness practice, we get in touch with our noble qualities before sending thoughts of well-wishing to ourselves. A variation came to me during one loving-kindness retreat and it enabled me to understand myself from a fresh perspective with profound results.

Have you ever wondered what it is about you that others appreciate? You may take for granted all sorts of qualities that touch those around you: perhaps your good-heartedness, humor, thoughtfulness, and caring, to name a few. Try following these instructions, pausing for a moment to connect with each point, to help you get in touch with your wholesome attributes.

1. Bring someone to mind who genuinely loves you. Imagine that they're here with you.

2. Feel the special energy and love that you share.

3. Imagine, for a moment, that you can inhabit their reality and look at yourself through their eyes. What qualities do they see in you that touches them? Your kindness, your sincerity, your playfulness? Notice all of them.

4. Take some time to feel all of those qualities from their perspective.

5. Now move from their vantage point back into your own self and, from the inside, feel these same qualities. Appreciate them. Delight in them.

Wish yourself well with thoughts like, "May I be happy. May I be peaceful. May I share my love well. May I see all the goodness inside."

Keep in mind the qualities that surfaced in the exercise. Feel their wholesomeness. You might write down the qualities you saw and appreciated about yourself in your journal and reflect on them regularly these next two weeks.

## Michele: Practicing Loving-kindness with Children

The other day, I spoke with Rosemary, a ninety-five-year-old friend of mine. Her age doesn't define her, but it gives you an idea of the time this amazing woman has spent on Earth. She is the most inspiring woman I know. She lives life fully with such beauty, integrity, and wisdom. Last week, I heard from her lips, for the first time, that she is now an old lady. I was shocked and asked how this change in perspective came about. She replied that it was because she now had to use a walker. Right after stating that, she said, "You know, Michele, aging really is beautiful. I wouldn't know how kind people are if I had not lived to this age. Truly, people open doors, and help me

about. I have learned about a whole new level of kindness in the world and it is sweet. My mind feels exactly the same but my body is not."

On a beautiful summer day this year, I asked her what loving herself meant. She leaned back in her chair, took a breath, and said, "In my day and age, you were taught *not* to love yourself. You were seen as selfish to even think of yourself. It was not a virtue at all. I was told by my mother, in a sorrowful way, that if no one else loved me she would—as if I were not lovable at all. I believed it." She said in her almost one hundred years of living that loving herself was the most revolutionary and radical practice she had been part of. Rosemary let her mother's ideas go. She stated that loving herself was the only way she could love and influence others.

Then she picked up this little poem by Thich Nhat Hanh on her tea table and read it to me:

> *To be beautiful means to be yourself. You don't need to be accepted by others. You need to accept yourself.* —Thich Nhat Hanh

We want to share with our children that any time we are comparing, judging, or simply being negative, we are draining ourselves of love. Often the most enlightening question I ask children when they are in the vortex of self-judgment is: If you had a best friend what would you say to them in this situation? Or if this were your little school buddy, what would you say to them?

To help our children love themselves, share that it is important to:

* Validate our feelings, "It's okay to feel uncomfortable, sad, wrong, awkward, and generally out of sorts sometimes." These feelings often point us toward what we are yearning for.

* Let go of perfectionism.

* Let go of judging ourselves when we fall down.

* Listen to our inner world, our own heart.

* Reassure ourselves that what we are experiencing will pass.

* Be grateful.

* Comfort ourselves by talking to ourselves as if we were a young child.

* Look after ourselves.

* Remind ourselves how we feel when we do something we feel good about.

* Finally, one very powerful message I share is: You are with this one until the day you die; you cannot exchange your body for another. How will you care for this one and love this one?

### Oh, Parents, You Don't Get Off the Hook

Demonstrate self-love by not putting yourself down in front of the kids. Even better, totally stop putting yourself down. If you are saying you are too fat, stupid, or whatever, your children will certainly follow. Look at the list above and love yourself too!

Rosemary's parting words to me on that summer day were:

*I used to think I would be wise when I reached a certain age. I am not. I thought I would have certainty. I do not. I don't honor having a fixed knowing about things. I am not the person that just says she knows. I will keep learning until I die. I am glad to be part of the human race—trying to be a better person.*

I take this wise wisdom and offer three practices in this chapter "Loving Ourselves" that bathe us in self-love and teach us how to be our own best friend.

Have fun.

 # Lesson 1: Cloth of Self-Compassion

A parent loves her child and wishes the best for him even when he is having a tantrum. In the same way the most powerful and healing expression of love is one that includes the whole package. When we love unconditionally, those on the receiving end know they are deserving of love not just because they are sweet and kind, but because they are worthy of it just for whom they are.

## Builds strengths of:
- Self-compassion
- Ability to acknowledge and meet difficulties
- Learning to empathize, not sympathize
- React with caring, instead of criticism and self-judgment
- Social and emotional learning

## Ages
- Preschool to adult

## School Curriculum Connections
- Oral language
- Written language
- Listening skills
- Social and emotional learning

## Materials
- Soft piece of cloth three to four inches square

## *Home and School Practice*
When they are babies, we want our children to self-soothe. We are thrilled when they find their thumb, lovey, or blanket, and go back to sleep so we don't have to be their only source of comfort. As children get older, they need ways to soothe themselves too. It can be a challenge for little ones to go to school without the familiar sounds and smells of home. Giving children a little bridge from home to school goes a long way in starting the road to self-compassion.

## A Little Comfort

My students loved this self-compassion activity and at the end of the day all twenty-five left the room with a sacred, soft cloth against their cheeks.

Try it at home and make one for everyone in the family.

For this activity, I found a length of the softest fabric I could find. I cut it up into eight-inch squares. Any size will do. You choose. If you enjoy sewing, you could run a little hem around it to bring in more of a handcrafted element.

I told the students that research shows when we put our hand over our heart or against our cheeks the body releases oxytocin and we feel good. I told them I was going to give them a special cloth that we would infuse with love.

## Funny but True

Even though I had the idea of a self-compassion cloth, the children naturally took it a step further. I had cut the cloth at lunch to prepare for my afternoon class. I then snuggled my puppy Teddy and rubbed lavender hand cream on my hands before entering the classroom. When I handed the cloth out, one little boy sniffed it deeply and said, "Wow this is a great cloth, it smells like you and Teddy Bear. I feel so happy!" His eyes shone and his smile beamed. Be careful what you rub your hands on. You want the smell to be pleasant and associated with compassionate feelings.

To infuse the cloth, you can hold it with your child and think of people, animals, or indeed anything you love. When your child says it's okay to stop, the cloth is full of love!

## If It Is Hard to Care for Yourself

Sometimes when children find it difficult to be self-compassionate, they can find the doorway to self-compassion through thinking about their care for another. Ask them to imagine how they would send love or care to a dear pet or friend. They could see the cloth of caring on this being. Then see if they can bring that same love to themselves. When your child is hurt or upset, remind him that he can soothe himself and be kind to himself.

## We Say Aloud to Ourselves

We practiced before doing a classroom public speaking activity.

*It is hard to talk in front of the class. Even though others may react or giggle I can try. I may stumble. Everyone gets scared and nervous. This is normal. I am still learning. I may not do it perfectly but I will try.*

## We Hug Ourselves and Love Ourselves Up

Every time I do a relaxation or yoga session with the kids, I end with having them give a hug to themselves. I get them to wrap their arms around their backs, telling themselves that they are their own best friend and they will be with themselves always. I ask them how they can be a little kinder to themselves today.

## *Resources*

### ADULT BOOKS

Tara Brach. *Radical Acceptance: Embracing Your Life with the Heart of a Buddha.* New York: Bantam, 2004.

Brene Brown. *The Gifts of Imperfection: Let Go of Who You Think You're Supposed to Be and Embrace Who You Are.* Minneapolis, MN: Hazelden, 2010.

Mark Nepo. *The Book of Awakening: Having the Life You Want by Being Present to the Life You Have.* Newburyport, MA: Conari Press, 2000.

### CHILDREN'S BOOKS

Patrice Karst. *The Invisible String.* Illustrated by Geoff Stevenson. Camarillo, CA: DeVorss & Company, 2000.

Kimberly Kirberger. *No Body's Perfect*. New York: Scholastic Paperbacks, 2003.

Eric Litwin. *Pete the Cat: I Love My White Shoes*. Illustrated by James Dean. (New York: HarperCollins, 2010.)

Debby Slier. *Loving Me*. Cambridge, MA: Star Bright Books, 2014.

 # Lesson 2: Family Bead Necklace

There is only one of you, and if you let yourself be the best one of yourself possible, you may also like what you see. In time you may even love yourself.

## Building Strengths of:
- Family and community ties
- Art expression
- Reflection-mindfulness awareness
- Love of others

## Materials
- Wire to string beads
- Beads
- Willingness
- Stick about two or three feet long

## Ages
- Newborn to adult

## School Curriculum Connections
- Oral language
- Written language
- Listening skills
- Fine arts
- Social and emotional learning

## Home Practice

### A Family Bead Necklace
When each of my boys was a year old, I invited friends and family to come and celebrate each son's first year on the planet by creating a Family Bead Necklace. Each participant in the ceremony was asked to think about the child and bring a bead reflecting the qualities they would like to gift the child within his lifetime. People gathered on the day in a big circle with the year-old child present.

We sat in a large circle on the floor with each person holding his or her bead. Every guest in turn looked at the celebrant and said, "I give you this bead that signifies (whatever they chose) and ask that you are gifted with this in your lifetime. I value this quality because I ..."

My boys received all kinds of beads. Some had musical notes imprinted on them, symbols of the whole world, crystals for clarity, and certain rocks for their medicinal qualities. People who had never been in sacred circles told me they felt comfortable. The ritual for some seemed more normalized as they were gifting a small child.

The symbolic beads were then strung on a wire and made into a loop to be hung in the child's room. My sons are now young adults. They both still have their necklaces and see them as special, sacred items.

### Keeping the Intention Alive

We also cut colored embroidery thread and asked all the participants to tie the thread around their wrist and leave it there for one month. Each time they glanced at the thread, they were asked to bring to mind the quality they had blessed the little one with and see the child as whole, happy, and healthy each time they looked at the thread.

The feedback I have had over the past twenty years from the people who partook in this ceremony was that it was deeply moving. Many later adopted the sacred ceremony and made necklaces for their children as well.

### School Practice

### A Classroom Talking Stick

Here is a similar ceremony you can bring into the classroom by creating a talking stick. Have the children bring in beads or shells symbolizing what qualities they would like to bring into the classroom. Sit in a circle and have the children tie their bead onto the stick with colored embroidery thread. In the past, some kids brought in little beads with stars to symbolize the ability to reach out for success. Other students brought in beads with soccer balls, as they really wanted an active year. I like to add beads that symbolize confusion, frustration, and the ability to try again when we fall down. I want the full gamut of the human condition acknowledged by the children. The students loved see-

ing their precious beads on the stick. Each time we used the stick, it became a more sacred object in our classroom. Find a place to hang it on the wall so it can be seen by all throughout the day. The stick symbolizes that all students have a voice and unique intentions for the year. We honor all beings. We all have one voice.

## Resources

### ADULT BOOKS

Evan Imber-Black and Janine Roberts. *Rituals for Our Times: Celebrating, Healing, and Changing Our Lives and Our Relationships.* New York: Jason Aronson, Inc., 1998.

Shari Maser. *Blessingways: A Guide to Mother-Centered Baby Showers—Celebrating Pregnancy, Birth, and Motherhood.* Ann Arbor, MI: Moondance Press, 2004.

### CHILDREN'S BOOKS

Geoff Blackwell, ed. *Humanity: A Celebration of Friendship, Family, Love & Laughter.* Auckland, NZ: PQ Blackwell, 2010.

Anabel Kindersley and Barnabas Kindersley. *Children Just Like Me: Celebrations!* New York: DK Children, 1997.

Patricia Polacco. *The Keeping Quilt.* New York: Simon & Schuster, 2001.

Nancy Tillman. *On the Night You Were Born.* New York: Feiwel & Friends, 2010.

# Lesson 3: Being My Own Best Friend

## Lessons in Self-love and Appreciation

**Building Strengths of:**
- Self-love
- Humor
- Appreciation

**Materials**
- Mirror

**Ages**
- Five to adult

**School Curriculum Connections**
- Oral language
- Written language
- Listening skills
- Reading
- Social and emotional learning

James inspired me to create this lesson after I read this, which he wrote in the introduction to this chapter:

> Imagine meeting someone who got your jokes, had similar tastes, and really understood your take on things. In short, someone who really got you. How would you feel about meeting them? You'd probably be ecstatic! There is only one person in this world who fully fits that description. But, unfortunately, they inhabit your skin so you don't appreciate those qualities from the inside.

### How to Introduce Your Best Friend

You have to have a bit of a poker face for this practice to introduce it well. You might want to go and check your own face in the mirror before you start!

I had a very open-hearted grade three/four class one year. I had had some of the students for two years, so we had already built a great deal of mutual trust. I like to joke and play and I love surprises, so I wanted to give this idea a try. Earlier in the day, I had the children imagine a special friend, a friend that could be their "best friend." We brainstormed together what qualities that friend might have. I said that everyone's best friend is different. I might prefer a playful, spontaneous best friend, while some people would not. The students suggested friendship qualities like *honesty*, *trustworthiness*, *humor*, etc. ... I differentiated internal from external qualities, distinguishing *money*, *good-looking*, or *tall* from internal qualities like *kind*, *compassionate*, or *generous*. This is a *key* differentiation so make sure they are honing in on internal qualities.

## The Joke

I had all the children sit with me and I told them that the principal and I had scoured far and wide and we had even gone to the city to find the perfect best friend for each one of them. The principal and I had actually both been away that week, so this worked well.

This amazing friend had agreed to meet them today. They were right in the next room! I had the principal then take each child next door, where we had put up a curtain. Behind the curtain was a mirror and when they pulled it back they were looking at themselves. This in itself is a bit risky, but I had prepped them by telling them that whomever they saw, they would be kind.

Next, each child was invited to sit and look at themselves for ten or fifteen seconds. They were to simply thank their friend. They are used to this type of acknowledgement, as we do gratitude circles several times a week and we thank friends all the time.

Then the children went to another room without returning to the classroom and wrote in their journals.

* Who can be your best friend? (I wrote, "can be," as many children—and adults—do not always like themselves.)
* Who will be with you always from morning until night?
* What qualities would you like your best friend to have?
* What qualities does your best friend have already?

Then the kids drew their friend and wrote them a little hello letter.

*Just to note, every time I do a relaxation or yoga session with the kids, I end with having them give a hug to themselves, telling themselves that they are their own best friend and will be with them always. I had done this for months, so they had heard it many times before.

The children loved this playful exercise and I am sure it hit home that we can be our own best friend.

Extensions: At home and throughout the week, invite your child to look in the mirror and tell themselves something kind. You as parents can do the same thing and then share the following questions: "How does it feel? What is hard about this? What is easy? Does it get any easier over time?"

If we start loving ourselves at a young age, maybe we can befriend ourselves much more easily as we grow older.

"Why do we have to listen to our hearts?" the boy asked. "Because, wherever your heart is, that is where you will find your treasure."
—Paulo Coelho, *The Alchemist*

## Resources

### Adult Books

Sylvia Boorstein. *Happiness Is an Inside Job: Practicing for a Joyful Life.* New York: Ballantine Books, 2008.

Julia Cameron. *The Artist's Way.* New York: TarcherPerigee, 2002.

Kristin Neff. *Self-Compassion: The Proven Power of Being Kind to Yourself.* New York: HarperCollins, 2011.

J. Thomas. *The Dalai Lama: The Best Teachings of The Dalai Lama, Journey To A Happy, Fulfilling & Meaningful Life.* Charleston, SC: CreateSpace Independent Publishing Platform, 2014.

### Children's Books

Karen Beaumont. *I Like Myself!* Illustrated by David Catrow. Boston, MA: Houghton Mifflin Harcourt Books for Young Readers, 2004.

Maribeth Boelts and Noah Z. Jones. *Those Shoes.* Somerville, MA: Candlewick, 2009.

Dharmachari Nagaraja. *The Buddha's Apprentice at Bedtime: Tales of Compassion and Kindness for You to Read with Your Child—to Delight and Inspire.* London: Watkins Publishing, 2003.

R. J. Palacio. *Auggie & Me: Three Wonder Stories.* New York: Knopf Books for Young Readers, 2015.

Natasha Anastasia Tarpley. *I Love My Hair!* Illustrated by E. B. Lewis. New York: Little, Brown Books for Young Readers, 2001.

# Lesson 4: Teaching Our Children about the Media

When you stop focusing on what you don't appreciate and start seeing yourself as a unique, mysterious, changing being, you allow your best self to shine through. And the joy of that radiates out to the world.

## Building Strengths of:
- Perspective taking
- Love of self
- Love of others
- Optimism

## Materials
- Paper
- Pens of various colors
- Magazines
- An open mind

## Ages
- Five to adult (You may be surprised how children as young as five are influenced by the media. Modify to suit your age group.)

## School Curriculum Connections
- Oral language
- Written language
- Listening skills
- Reading
- Social studies
- Fine arts
- Social and emotional learning

### Loving Ourselves

Loving ourselves is difficult with the media bombarding us with all kinds of messages, telling us we are not good enough and nowhere near up to par. Even at the young age of seven or eight, children have a clear idea of what is cool and what is not! You may not have TV but the messages are everywhere in our wider culture.

Just acknowledging the impact of these influences and creating an awareness of how the media impacts us on a daily basis goes a long way in creating a discerning mind. I found after this lesson, children came up to me all year long with examples of how the media tries to manipulate children and adults into feeling "not quite good enough."

### Home or School Practices

Gather a group of your child's friends or set this lesson up in class. You may be quite shocked at how deeply children are affected by the images of media. You may also see how you may have grown accustomed to the images flashed daily in front of your own face.

Looking at these ideas is a way of allowing children, or any of us, quite frankly, to see how the media has created an image in our minds of what is okay and what is not. This lesson is set up to show children that who or what we may seek to emulate or venerate in the media does not match our truest vision of a beautiful person. After digging into this lesson, I can guarantee that you will want to explore this topic more completely throughout the year.

### Self-Esteem Down the Tube

I first created this lesson over ten years ago when I was asked to teach a course on building self-esteem with grade seven girls. These are girls who were only twelve and thirteen years old, yet that year we had three girls in our classes diagnosed with eating disorders. We all found the exercise eye-opening. I recently retaught the lesson to my grade threes.

### Describe Her

I start by having the children imagine in their heads a typical girl in the media. This could be a girl in a movie, TV show, or in a magazine. I put a large piece of paper up on the wall and start to draw as they describe her. As I draw, I ask questions like, "What color hair does she have—is it straight or curly? What color are her eyes? What does her nose look like?" We move down her body and

they call out all the parts they want me to draw onto the girl. I draw in what most of the children agree on and move fairly quickly so they can blurt out gut responses. (If you are working with older students, you can call her Media Woman). I then ask them to describe her life right down to the kind of dog she might have. You may be astounded at the consensus! I have had children describe that she can have a mole, but only on her upper lip—and then they proceed to tell me exactly what size it can be.

After I have drawn Media Girl to their specifications, I draw Media Boy. I have included pictures below of what the children described.

If you wish, you can supply magazines and have them actually cut out pictures of the eyes, hair, clothes, etc., and create a mock-up girl and boy (or someone who is transgender).

When we have finished and taken a big breath, we continue.

## Who We Truly Admire

Take a breath yourself. All is not lost. The magic is starting to happen.

I have the children close their eyes and think of a girl they truly admire. Really see her. Then I ask them to call out her description. Invariably she has short hair, long hair, curly hair, and straight hair. She may have brown eyes, green eyes, or blue eyes. She may be a variety of shapes and sizes. It doesn't matter. The children may say they never even noticed what she wore or where she lives.

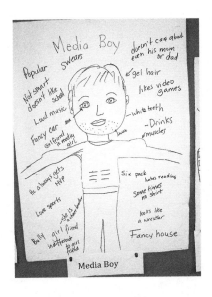

Media Boy

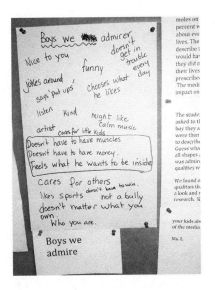

Boys we admire

## Pause at This Point and Let Them Take This In

This is a big "aha" for the children. I really push this point: the outside does not define her; the qualities of her inner being do. We list all her qualities and why we find her so admirable. We then repeat the exercise with a boy.

I put those qualities up on a poster board and reflect on how the media image is so far from what we admire and value. We talk about how we can stay true to our own selves and love ourselves, building on admirable qualities.

There are so many links and online resources you can add to this lesson. We are all affected constantly by the outer world on a very deep level. It is good to come back to self-love.

Finally, I ended with a quiet guided mindfulness session on the sweetness of loving ourselves just as we are.

### *Resources*

#### ADULT BOOKS

Tara Brach. *Radical Acceptance: Embracing Your Life With the Heart of a Buddha.* New York: Bantam, 2004.

Brene Brown. *The Gifts of Imperfection: Let Go of Who You Think You're Supposed to Be and Embrace Who You Are.* Minneapolis, MN: Hazelden, 2010.

Pema Chödrön. *When Things Fall Apart: Heart Advice for Difficult Times.* Boulder, CO: Shambhala, 2000.

#### CHILDREN'S BOOKS

Shari Graydon. *Made You Look: How Advertising Works and Why You Should Know.* Illustrated by Michelle Lamoreaux. Vancouver, BC: Annick Press, 2013.

Dev Petty. *I Don't Want to Be a Frog.* Illustrated by Mike Boldt. New York: Doubleday Books for Young Readers, 2010.

# The Joy of Loving Others

8

## James: Practices for Grown-Ups

RELATIONSHIPS ARE OFTEN the barometer of our happiness or sorrow. They are the major source of our greatest joy as well as our deepest suffering. When we share an easy flow of love, we feel connected, secure, and at home within ourselves. When we're lonely or isolated, depression and anxiety are often not far away. Having focused on a healthy connection with ourselves, we now naturally move into how we create happiness through connection with others. This includes not only people close to us, but also everyone we encounter in our lives.

### The Power of Forgiveness: The Doorway to an Open Heart

Even with those closest to us—sometimes especially with those closest to us—frustration and anger can be triggered in a moment when others disappoint us. When this happens, the doorway to greater connection is forgiveness.

It's good to realize that the person who benefits the most from your forgiveness is you. You are the one who suffers when your heart is closed in anger. Being consumed by ill will is likened to picking up a hot coal to angrily throw at someone and not realizing we're the ones getting burned. Holding onto bitterness is like drinking poison and hoping that the other person will get sick. Understanding that we're creating our own suffering can motivate us to change. If you find yourself contracted, disconnected, and suffering because you're caught up in anger, forgiveness may be your key to awaken joy.

An essential quality of forgiveness is empathic understanding. Last year I met a thirteen-year old girl from Trinidad named Lael-Anne who was wise beyond her years. Though she hadn't quite figured out the details, she told me about an invention she was working on that was guaranteed to bring peace into the world. She had my attention! She called it a "Perspective Helmet." Once you put it on, you can immediately understand the perspective of another person. I agreed that such an invention would be a major contribution toward world peace and address most other man-made problems in the world.

We are all products of our conditioning. We see the world that we're familiar with. I remember seeing a poster that showed a sad little boy. The caption said that a child raised in a home with domestic violence is seven hundred more times likely to experience domestic violence in his or her adult life. Who is to blame? It's just a perpetuation of confusion over generations.

People do hurtful things because they're lost in stress or confusion. Without condoning the action we can forgive the confusion that led to an unskillful response. This doesn't mean we don't get angry. But we might begin to replace anger with compassion.

When your heart is contracted in anger at someone's hurtful action, it might help to imagine what their mind state is. Sometimes I imagine them as a small child doing the best they can and being lost in their own habits of confusion. You might try saying something like, "I forgive your confusion," allowing your heart to soften as you let go of the hot coal. You might notice the relief that comes with just a moment of forgiveness.

Although someone's actions may seem bizarre to us, they make sense to them. The Dalai Lama suggests keeping in mind that the other person's words and actions are *not about you*, but about *their internal reality*, which has intersected with yours in a way that doesn't meet with your hopes and expectations.

If you're not yet ready to forgive someone, then forgive yourself for being just where you are, particularly if you judge yourself for feeling the way you do. We can't hurry up the process. Hurt sometimes takes a while to heal. But know that you're the one who benefits most in forgiving another. So be open to the possibility of forgiving them sometime in the future, not only for their sake, but for yours as well. As Desmond Tutu says, "Forgiveness is the highest form of self-interest. I need to forgive so that my own anger and lust for revenge doesn't corrode my own being."

## The Power of Loving-kindness

We're naturally drawn to those people around us who are kind and loving. Expressing kindness and goodwill toward others causes love to come back to us. We have a tremendous power to draw out different qualities of those around us by what we look for. A major support for loving-kindness is the ability to see the goodness in others. If you keep looking for the good, you'll have a much better chance of finding it. Not always, of course, but your odds increase tremendously. When you know someone appreciates you, you can relax around them and be yourself.

Just like us, everyone wants to be happy, safe, and loved. This is especially true of children. When I was a schoolteacher, the special challenge I gave myself at the start of each year was to find the key to every child's heart. Some kids radiated so brightly you practically had to wear shades around them. Others were shy or had learned to get attention by acting out. But I knew every one of them wanted to feel safe and accepted for who they were. Looking for their goodness gave me a much greater chance of bringing it out.

Of course, we should have reasonable expectations of respect and cooperation. But the more we have a particular idea of how they're supposed to be, the more they will disappoint us. When we genuinely appreciate others just as they are and wish them well, they relax and enjoy our company.

As part of his practice, a friend who took my *Awakening Joy* course adopted an experiment of connecting with people he passed on the street. "I decided that I would say good morning to everyone I saw on my walk around Marina Bay," he reported. "I was amazed at the smiles and reactions I got just from taking the time to acknowledge they were there." As we connect positively with others, we allow the goodness and generosity of spirit to flow through us and awakens that in others. Our hearts naturally open, we feel happy, and it comes back to us.

### Sympathetic Joy

Another way we can experience the joy of connection is tuning into the happiness of those around us. This is sometimes called Sympathetic Joy. It's very easy to experience this around children. We delight in seeing them happy. We all know this feeling when we root for someone to do well. Most movies give us chance to delight in the hero or heroine's triumph.

Delighting in a child's joy is one thing. Delighting in other adults' joy can sometimes be a different story. We may feel envy when we hear of someone else's success. But there's no quota or limited supply of happiness. Just as we're affected by someone else's anger, we can be affected by another's joy and tune into that energy. If someone else is happy, we can delight in the fact that there's a little more happiness in the world. We can let their happiness rub off on us. As the Dalai Lama says, if our happiness depends on our own well-being, it's limited. But if it can be activated by the happiness of others, we increase the possibilities by seven billion!

### Connection through Playfulness, Fun, and Laughter

One of the best ways to enjoy connection with kids is by having fun with them and letting ourselves be playful. Besides feeling close to them, it is one of the most important ways to reduce stress and get out of our heads. This is one of the best things about being around children. They know how to play! When you're with your kids, let them remind you of the kid right inside. Playfulness and humor are crucial to genuine happiness. They can all too easily get squeezed out of our "important" agenda. Keep your heart light—be playful, silly, and have fun. It will directly connect you to joy. As one friend puts it, "If you can't laugh, it's just not funny."

Our culture has become increasingly cut off from valuing play. According to one study, "Individuals who spend some time just having fun are 20 percent more likely to feel happy on a daily basis." In another study of hundreds of adults "those who enjoy silly humor are one-third more likely to feel happy."

If you find you're taking yourself way too seriously, try lightening up. Get out of your head by doing something playful or silly. It might be just the right prescription. Have as much fun and laugh as much as you can. It's not an accident that laughter makes you feel good. Research has shown laughter to release endorphins (the body's natural pain killer), reduce the stress hormone cortisol, relieve tension in the body, counteract depression and anxiety, and strengthen the immune system.

Many of us need permission to have fun and be able to laugh, so here it is. I'm not only giving you permission—take it as an assignment! Don't feel pressure to have fun. Just know that it's available, if you're open to it. Howard Thurman put it beautifully: "Do not ask yourself what the world needs. Ask yourself what makes you come alive, and then go and do that. Because what the world needs is people who have come alive." Connection with others helps us come alive.

## Try This

### Forgiveness Practices

Forgiveness works both ways. Sometimes we do something that hurt others and we regret it. Other times we're on the receiving end of others' hurtful words or actions. Until we are able to come to some resolution with such conflicts, we spend lots of energy either in guilt or anger. Forgiveness is what frees up that energy and allows our hearts to open to life and greater well-being. When we've been humbled by our own unskillful actions and need to ask for forgiveness, that can be a springboard toward forgiving others. Here are some forgiveness practices that I would encourage you to try at home:

Asking for forgiveness:

1. Bring to mind someone who you may have acted unskillfully with. Imagine him in front of you.
2. Get in touch with any remorse you have. Reflect on your state of mind and the confusion or ignorance that would cause you to harm them.
3. Apologize by saying silently, "I'm truly sorry for any harm I might have caused you. I ask for your forgiveness."
4. Imagine them hearing your sincerity, taking in your words, and forgiving you. Notice how that feels.

Extending forgiveness:

1. Bring to mind someone who has acted unskillfully toward you and caused you to suffer in some way. Imagine them in front of you.
2. Reflect on their state of mind and the confusion or ignorance that would cause them to harm you.
3. Extend forgiveness by silently saying, "For any harm you may have caused me intentionally or unintentionally, I forgive you. I forgive your confusion."
4. Imagine seeing them take in your words and feel your forgiveness. Notice how that feels.

### Loving-kindness Practices

It's easy to practice consciously directing thoughts of well-wishing and goodwill toward others. You might hold your close relationships as practice vehicles to develop an ongoing openness of heart. When you feel affection naturally flowing, bring mindful attention to that feeling and directly connect with the joy of that good feeling. If you verbally express your love, the feeling will increase still more!

Here is a basic loving-kindness practice. You can do this internally as a meditative exercise or silently, when you are with others during your daily activities.

1. Formulate an image of the person to whom you wish to send loving-kindness as you reflect on their good qualities.
2. Send them these kinds of thoughts (or others that come naturally to you): *May you be happy. May you be peaceful. May you share your love well.*
3. Pay attention to how it feels in your body or mind to wish them well.

Practice this same spirit of well-wishing with others you encounter, besides those close to you. As you're waiting in line at the grocery store, instead of seeing everyone as being in the way, an obstacle slowing you down, try practicing sending them thoughts of kindness like, "*May you be happy. May you have a good day. May you share your love well.*" It's a much more pleasant experience than feeling stuck and it transforms the situation.

The aim of loving-kindness practice is to widen our circle of connection to include all beings everywhere without distinction. One might wonder about practicing loving-kindness toward someone who causes harm to others. It helps to realize that, if someone is genuinely happy, they will not intentionally cause harm to us or anyone else.

### From Agenda to Love

The near enemy of love is attachment. It disguises itself as love but is very different. The heart that is loving is expansive without an agenda for who someone is supposed to be. You can see the difference between the two by trying this exercise:

1. Bring to mind someone you love—a friend, a child, or perhaps a pet. Focus on how much you care about his or her well-being and happiness. Notice how good it feels to simply love that being and wish them well with thoughts like, "May you be happy."
2. Now think about wanting something from him or her—attention, reassurance, affection, a certain behavior. Notice if the feelings in your body and your state of mind shift from openness to contraction, from a sense of fullness and connection to pulling back and closing down.

THE JOY OF LOVING OTHERS ✳ 195

3. Now once again let your thoughts return to the love and positive feelings you have for that individual. Notice the difference in your body and mind.

### Sympathetic Joy Practice

Experiment with this:

1. Bring to mind someone with whom you have a warm connection and who is going through a good period in his or her life. Picture them in a moment of happiness and imagine you're in their cheering section. Send them these thoughts, as if splashing them with a blessing: "May your happiness continue. May your happiness grow."

2. Do this in your mind with a number of different people.

3. Finally, imagine all the people who want you to be happy in a cheering section rooting for you as you direct these phrases toward yourself. Feel all the support from others, as you slowly let yourself take in the words.

Work with sympathetic joy by having your radar out for happiness around you. When you see someone in good spirits, say the phrases "May your happiness continue; may your happiness grow," realizing that their happiness is contributing a little more joy to the world. You can also formally include a few minutes of saying those phrases silently to yourself when you meditate.

## Michele: Practicing Loving Others with Children

Put brothers and sisters in a car for a long ride, or thirty children in a classroom setting, and the joy of loving another will instantly be put to the test. Our children have more access to privilege, opportunity, and every gadget known to humankind than any other generation. As parents and educators we deeply want our children to care about others and demonstrate love.

Loving others is actually my favorite step in awakening joy. There is something incredibly sweet when the classroom community comes together in a "love bubble." This is a transitory bubble, but when it arises it is sweet and worthy of exploration.

## I Had a New Class One Year

The children fought constantly. They were said by some parents and teachers to be "the tough class" and seemed to be deliberately "mean" to each other at every turn. I couldn't put my finger on why it was so challenging for the kids to demonstrate empathy and kindness. All I could do was stop, send myself compassion, and then slow down and do a loving practice with the kids.

Day after day my teaching partner and I set up activities to cultivate compassion. Many days I came home absolutely exasperated wondering if anything we did made a difference.

Miraculously, about three months into the year, I stopped the children and asked them if they noticed a difference in our class. They said they did. Children were "nicer, gentler, and easier to be with." They cared about each other. They were willing to partner with anyone in the group. There was a sense of calmness pervading the classroom.

Honestly, all I can suggest when times are difficult is to stay with the practices. It may take a while. When times are good, build the muscles of loving-kindness. I now trust that the practices will work even if they don't seem like they are.

## Expanding Out

It is only when we can be kind to our immediate neighbors that we can begin to share our kindness with the wider community. Classes come in fragmented, anxious, and with many cliques. How do we teach the children to love one another or at least empathetically care? This chapter contains several lessons including one on "Sparkles" that create an atmosphere of deep caring. All the lessons can be used in the home as well. I have shared a framework of several

areas to cultivate the loving of others. These are practices that help build love and compassion.

Loving others is modeled, repeated, and repeated; only then does it become part of the consciousness of the home and classroom. Below are some ideas on how to entwine loving-kindness and empathy into your everyday home and school activities. These ideas are further expanded upon in this chapter on the joy of loving others.

## Love Is a Verb

### Loving-kindness
Set up a loving-kindness practice by imagining sending love to pets, family members, friends, and those with whom we have difficulties. This will create pathways for love to flourish.

Do acts of kindness in your home, school, and community, as well as on a global level.

Read stories about acts of kindness or times we have trouble loving others, and talk about what holds us back from love and what opens our hearts to love.

Teach children what they have in common with others. I have connected my own children and students with pen pal buddies in other countries. The kids can't wait to get a letter and just chat. They feel a deep sense of caring for people in other parts of the world. They see people as equals and individuals.

### Did You Know: Loving-kindness
Barbara Frederickson and her colleagues published a study in *The Journal of Personal Social Psychology* (2008) that found practicing seven weeks of loving-kindness meditation increased love, joy, contentment, gratitude, pride, hope, interest, amusement, and awe. If there was that much change in seven weeks, imagine what we as teachers can do in ten months!

### Every Child's Love Is Unique
Remember all children are different in the ways they show their love. I have had children gaze up into my eyes and climb all over me sharing their love on a daily basis and others for whom a smile once a month was a huge act of love. I have had children appear as if they did not like me or my class, but when I ask them about it they share that they are shy and that they truly love the class. I am often gob-smacked by this admission as I pride myself in my ability to read the emotional states of my students. I must admit when a child does not

want to come to my class I have a hard time not taking it personally or trying to "fix" the situation. Connection and trust can take a long time, sometimes longer than we can imagine. I love that as a teacher I have so much to learn. So please allow the kids to choose ways of their own to express their love. Let them see and experience how you love.

## Talk and Play

### Talk about Unconditional Love

✳ Create friendship bonds by having your child do things with siblings and friends. You don't have to plan a big playdate full of activities. Just let the kids get together and find their way to connecting.

✳ Playtime also gives so many opportunities to learn to share, care, and work through problems. Try not to jump in too fast when difficulties arise. Even though as parents we *so* want to! When needed, give the children some coaching.

✳ My boys and I had a sign with our hands that showed we were feeling love for each other. We would knock our chests with two hands in the shape of a heart and send it to the other person. It is kind of corny but to this day I will make the sign and all six foot five of their body smiles. We also had a bird sound we would make when the boys were getting off the school bus and walking up the steep street we lived on. I would make that bird sound hidden in the trees, and my sons would light up cooing back to me as they ran

up to our home. It was special and it was our own. I still make it when my youngest gets off the public bus after a day at work. It kind of blends in with the other birds so he doesn't have to be embarrassed (as all teens are), but he laughs and knows I am waiting in love for him.

### Give Them Opportunities to Shine

Everyone in my class gets a job. They are all responsible to make the big picture work. We truly value their contribution. Remember the very act of doing is the reward.

### Teach Independent Thinking so Children Are Not Swayed by the Mob

Teach your child good decision-making skills. Practice checking in with your head, heart, and gut to decide what you want to do. Talk to your child about her values and how to honor those values.

Set an example of independent thinking and talk about the people in history who have rocked the world by following their hearts and passions. One of my favorite artists who exemplifies this is Frida Kahlo. My students call me a Frida Freak! I share this remarkable Mexican woman's stories of resilience and heartbreak with all my kids. A few years ago my partner and I had the opportunity to visit her home in Mexico City. I took a ton of photos and now have even more to share with the students. If you have never heard of her, please look her up and you will find a remarkable independent, passionate artist who so many students lovingly connect with.

Don't get too worked up about the small things. Keep the communication lines as open as you can. I once had a teaching mentor who was about ten years older than me. One day after hearing that my son had done something on the playground that was "inappropriate," I ran into the photocopy room and started to talk about it to her. As a mother and a teacher I was still ruminating over the incident even though it had been worked through with the people involved. My friend stopped me, looked into my eyes, and said, "Michele, this is the small stuff. It will pass. In a week or a month, you won't even remember. Let it go. There are bigger fish to fry. My kids are older. This is small stuff." I never forgot that day, partly because she was his teacher and my mentor—and partly because it proved to be true.

# Lesson 1: Sparkles

Developing a kind and loving heart may be the most important thing we do in life if we want to be happy.

**Builds strengths of:**
- Gratitude
- Compassion
- Forgiveness

**Materials**
- None

**Ages**
- Preschool to adult

**School Curriculum Connections**
- Oral language
- Listening skills
- Social and emotional learning

### *Home and School Practice*

From kindergarten to grade seven this is a favorite activity that can easily be brought into the home. Before sharing the home practice I invite you to read how it is received in the classroom.

> Twenty minutes before school is out every Friday, the children eagerly gather to do "Sparkles." I hear them telling each other, "Quick, clean up, we have to get to Sparkles."
>
> Everyone settles in with his or her backpack and belongings ready to go. The hands begin to rise. I ask them to feel into their hearts and see in what way someone has touched their lives this week. Smiles burst out as students sparkle others for "being my friend when I was on the playground," "helping me find a chair," "reading with me," "sharing a snack," "for being a good friend," "for my mom being here" and for many, the object of Sparkles is Teddy Bear, my puppy who makes guest appearances in the classroom throughout the week. He always sits on my lap for this part of the week. If I forget to get him from his little kennel, the children are quick to remind me that Teddy is part of this important moment and they want him to witness the sharing. If I notice a child does not get a sparkle, I casually ask Teddy to whisper in my ear to see if he has any sparkles and he always finds one!
>
> I ask them to notice not only how it feels to get sparkles but also to give sparkles. Where do they feel it in their bodies? I ask them to sink into the

feeling. The sender must look the receiver in the eyes and say why they sparkle them. The receiver simply says "Thank you." Many of the students ham it up and when asked where they received the sparkle—they fall to the ground with their hands over their hearts.

Slowly, more and more students take risks to share their gratitude, and friendships build. They begin to notice how to share stories of the heart. They notice that the small acts of kindness really matter.

Last week as Friday came to a close, I was feeling rather exhausted and at that moment I looked at each child and asked if they would like to know how they had touched my heart. Every child said yes! I then opened to them and found a way to acknowledge how just being who they are touches me greatly. Their softening and love was palpable and I felt renewed. Children learn to sparkle or give gratitude. We cannot assume that they know how. Many come from families where thanking each other is not part of the family vocabulary.

We were laughing in my class yesterday recalling that in September when we first started doing Sparkles, no one said anything but me! Then, over the weeks and months, as safety built and a few children took a chance and opened their hearts of gratitude, the whole place broke open. Now we have to allow at least twenty minutes for the activity as students have so much to share. I never force the issue, yet I invite and tell them that in my experience the heart grows and grows with every sparkle like in the book *The Grinch Who Stole Christmas*! Below, a little boy shares his experience of Sparkles and how he even moved it into a loving-kindness practice.

*I sparkled my friends and even my enemies. Thinking of our class pet, Teddy Bear, really slowed down my breathing and made me feel better. I sparkled my grannies and grandpas and even my great-grandparents. I sparkled everyone in my family. I really felt good after it. Thank you for doing it with me.*
—A seven-year-old boy

The smiles are huge this day and if parents come in, the tears flow. Actually parents usually arrive early so they can sneak in for Sparkles. The week is complete.

## Home Practice

Sparkles can be woven in all through the day but one of the best times is when everyone is present at the dinner table.

Let each person in the family speak if they wish and say, "I sparkle _____ for _____." The receiver of the gratitude looks into the eyes of the sender and simply says "Thank you."

Open your heart and receive the gift. If your child cannot think of gratitude, you can either gently encourage them by having them reflect on their day or ask them to share when they feel something. When they listen to you share the simplicity of gratitude, you demonstrate the smallest to largest things

that one can be grateful for. My teenage son regularly shares his gratitude for his dog, his father nearby, and his big brother who has gone off to college. It brings all we love to the table. He might not notice that his washing is done, or his breakfast is made but he has acknowledged someone important in his life in a family setting and this builds not only an open heart, but also allows me to know what brings him joy.

Many times sibling rivalry can dissolve when one child gives a sparkle to another. I noticed an example of this only yesterday when a child came to me in tears. Another student would simply not contribute in his group and was totally off-task. We talked about a few strategies he might use to be okay with what he had contributed without trying to change the other student, while sharing his frustrations and longing for cooperation and contribution with the other student. By the time Sparkles came around, I saw him take a big breath and thank the other student for coming through and being part of the group. The other boy smiled back and the wall tumbled down.

Parents demonstrating gratitude for each other and their child also sets a

tone of love in the family. Sometimes adults forget to take the time to share their vulnerability and love for each other in front of their children. These precious words are often shared behind closed doors or when the adults are alone. Children need to witness these sacred moments in order to emulate them. For example, in my family I don't recall hearing my dad or mum tell each other that they loved one another. I know part of it was the generation of holding your cards close to your chest. When my mum died unexpectedly before my dad, he cried and showed me a card that he had in his cupboard for my mum for Valentine's Day. She died before she ever got to receive it. It was her first Valentine's card in thirty years of marriage. It wasn't that my father didn't love or demonstrate love for my mother, but he didn't gift us, his children, with the skill of how to share this part of himself. I made a pact with myself that I would share this part of myself with my kids but I had to learn how. So, by saying aloud and carrying the energy of open-heartedness to your family table, you gift your children just by your very actions with more than you can imagine. You teach them simply by being. You show them how you cherish and love your partner or whomever is at the table and that you value that relationship. They see love shared and can take that gift out to others with much more ease. At first the whole process might seem awkward, but the rewards of sharing your open heart exceed the awkwardness by a million to one.

## Resources

### ADULT BOOKS

Sura Hart and Victoria Kindle Hodson. *Respectful Parents, Respectful Kids: 7 Keys to Turn Family Conflict into Cooperation*. Encinitas, CA: Puddledancer Press, 2006.

Myla Kabat-Zinn and Jon Kabat-Zinn. *Everyday Blessings: The Inner Work of Mindful Parenting Paperback*. New York: Hachette Books, 2009.

Inbal Kashtan. *Parenting from Your Heart: Sharing the Gifts of Compassion, Connection, and Choice (Nonviolent Communication Guides)*. Encinitas, CA: Puddledancer Press, 2004.

### CHILDREN'S BOOKS

Cindy Gainer and Miki Sakamoto. *I'm Like You, You're Like Me: A Book About Understanding and Appreciating Each Other*. Golden Valley, MN: Free Spirit Publishing, 2013.

Gail Silver. *Peace, Bugs, and Understanding: An Adventure in Sibling Harmony.* Illustrated by Youme Nguy. Berkeley, CA: Plum Blossom Books, 2014.

Cornelia Maude Spelman and Kathy Parkinson. *When I Care about Others.* Park Ridge, IL: Albert Whitman and Company, 2002.

 # Lesson 2: Sticky Friendships

When we love someone, we want that person to be happy. It requires a lot of surrender to trust that they will find their way there by a different route than the one we think is best.

## Builds strengths of:
- Deep Listening
- Ability to acknowledge and let go of difficulties
- Compassion
- Empathy
- Friendship
- Breaking dysfunctional family patterns
- Sharing deep emotions/building emotional vocabulary

## Materials
- Paper
- Pens
- Willingness

## Ages
- As young as four (with parental guidance) to adult

## School Curriculum Connections
- Oral language
- Written language
- Listening skills
- Social and emotional learning

### Love 'Em and Leave 'Em

So often children and adults discard a friendship after a disagreement. In many families people are cut off, ignored, or turned into an enemy image when people are unable to work out the conflict.

I find, in the classroom, a whole friendship is often thrown away when it is "not feeling good" anymore. Children will often come in off the playground and say, "You are not my friend any more because you did this or that."

Teaching children to look at the whole person and acknowledge that friend-

ships can contain ups and downs helps build lasting relationships. We must teach them strategies to get through the difficult times so the kids can refer to them when they are in the thick of disagreement.

Dr. Daniel Siegel reminds us about teaching children perspective taking during a disagreement. He says, "Reminding children that those we invest in most deeply can often be our most challenging friendships. If we can work through the challenges they can be the richest, deepest, and more transformative relationships."

## Home or School Practice

### Good Friends

Have your child write down what they love about a specific friend or various different friends. Brainstorm all the great things together on paper. Write what you, as a parent, value in friendships on the same piece of paper. Sit in that feeling of having great friends and getting along.

### Sticky Problems

Now have your child write or tell you about what they find challenging or what gets sticky in a friendship. Again put this up on paper so the children can see that inside all relationships there are challenges.

> **What broke a friendship?**
> · lied to you
> · left to a different country
> · won't share
> · left me out
> · called me names
> · was mean and I couldn't stand it anymore
> · talked behind my back
> · stole something
> · want more time than you can give
> · found a new friend and left me

Children are amazing. They can share at such a deep level. Here is an example.

## Getting through the Sticky Stuff
Ask your child to share how they have overcome a problem in a relationship, whether it was by apologizing, forgiving, letting go, or getting some help. They will have lots of other ideas to add here. Let them know how you got through a problem.

## When We Don't Get through the Sticky Stuff
Also brainstorm times you did not get over the break in a friendship. What happened? Acknowledge the challenge and pain and the sheer fact that many times friendships do fall away. Children report that when friendships broke down, they:

* never spoke again
* hung out with different people
* looked the other way
* felt bad but didn't know what to do
* never forgot
* felt relief
* felt alone
* found new people to hang out with

## Set Intention
Finally, have your child write one intention they have for a current relationship when it gets difficult or sticky. You can use sticky notes for this part and stick them in special places such as journals, deep in desks, or on the bathroom mirror. Refer to it when things are tough. Connection is one of our deepest sources of joy so we have to work at relationships. It is a living process.

> **If we got through it, How?**
>
> - phoned and asked if we could play
> - ignored problem and let it go
> - had them over and talked
> - said sorry
> - just played
> - had our teacher help
> - tried to look at it from their side

## Resources

### Adult Books

Pema Chödrön. *When Things Fall Apart: Heart Advice for Difficult Times*. Boulder, CO: Shambhala, 2000.

Michael Gurian. *The Wonder of Boys*. New York: TarcherPerigee, 2006.

Gordon Neufeld and Gabor Mate. *Hold On to Your Kids: Why Parents Need to Matter More Than Peers*. Toronto: Vintage Canada, 2013.

Rosalind Wiseman. *Queen Bees and Wannabes: Helping Your Daughter Survive Cliques, Gossip, Boyfriends, and the New Realities of Girl World*. New York: Harmony, 2009.

### Children's Books

Jan and Stan Berenstain. *The Berenstain Bears and the Trouble with Friends*. New York: Random House Books for Young Readers, 1988.

Jan and Mike Berenstain. *The Berenstain Bears: The Forgiving Tree*. New York: Random House Books for Young Readers, 1988.

Alexis O'Neill. *The Recess Queen*. New York: Scholastic Press, 2002.

Herman Parish. *Amelia Bedelia Makes a Friend*. New York: Greenwillow Books, 2011.

Bob Sornson. *The Juice Box Bully: Empowering Kids to Stand Up for Others*. Northville, MN: Ferne, 2010.

Mo Willems. *Leonardo the Terrible Monster*. New York: Disney-Hyperion, 2005.

# Lesson 3: Pen Pals

## Building Global Connection and Compassion

When you know how to listen to that voice inside, you begin to live in a way that aligns you with life. You find yourself increasingly in the right place at the right time.

### Building Strengths of:
- Compassion
- Perspective taking
- Global unity
- Reflection-mindfulness awareness

### Materials
- A pen pal
- Paper and a stamp

### Ages
- Five to adult (the little ones might need a scribe)

### School Curriculum Connections
- Oral language
- Written language
- Listening skills
- Reading
- Social studies
- Fine arts
- Social and emotional learning

### *Home and School Practice*
Do you remember the excitement of getting a letter in the mail with foreign stamps affixed to the envelope? Do you recall the thrill of hearing from someone from far away? Over the years, I have tried to build connections between my students and students in other parts of the world. We are currently writing to friends in Uganda, Mexico, and Costa Rica. I have personally met many of the organizers and deeply value these connections.

### Social and Emotional Benefits of a Pen Pal
Hearing first-hand stories from an international pen pal can encourage children to take someone else's perspective and to think outside of themselves.

Many of our pen pals live in politically unstable and economically challenged countries. Children are given an opportunity to become less egocentric when they are connected to the world at large.

Another benefit of having a pen pal is creating empathy. Being friends with a similarly aged child in another country helps kids realize that they have many things in common and enjoy playing with the same things. They read aloud the letters and share that these children have hopes and dreams, families and pets, just like they do. Their pen pal might love sports or have a sister, just like them. Even living in very different environments, there are so many things that make kids the same everywhere. The ability to see commonalities amongst the differences is a beautiful gift.

Children learn about world geography with excitement. This creates curiosity and hopefully worldview perspectives. They are always looking on Google Earth, the classroom globe, or a map to see where their new friend lives.

Some children have started collecting stamps and envelopes, tracking how their letters arrived. My grade three class once sent letters that arrived at their destination by sled dog. Boy did that ever create some rich learning.

### Patience

As the letters are sent and arrive, children savor the time it takes for paper to pass from hand to hand. There is a gift of waiting in this world of instant gratification. The children experience the gift of not knowing and wondering if the letter will be answered and being willing to take a chance on connecting.

As James states, "We can understand interconnectedness as a concept, but knowing it through experience is what helps us to live in accordance with this reality." For children this means they can actually see how their letter impacts another child and get a living response of friendliness and gratitude.

I have never seen so much excitement in the hallways as when a huge envelope of pen pal letters arrives at our school. I quietly pin them up on the wall and wait until someone bursts out. "They have arrived!" Already, we have researched the county, the people, food, customs, and the politics, so the children have some understanding of their pen pals' backgrounds. The students have written letters telling their pen pal friends about their own days.

One year we wrote to our buddy school Uganda and they told us that they needed a medical bed to help the students who arrived at school sick. My students raised money over several months and sent it along with hand-tied bracelets. The joy they received when a picture was posted of their African pen pals wearing the bracelets was unbelievable. They knew they had made a difference and they had a significant connection with a group of kids on the other side of the world. They also loved getting letters and the children in Uganda knew they had made a difference to their friends in Canada.

I have never used pen pal organizations but ask the children directly if they have connections in other countries. Many of our students are first-generation Canadians and have a rich cultural background. They often know of someone to whom we can write. Once a young girl told me she had an extra empty suitcase as she was traveling to her mom's home country at Christmas break. The class decided how to fill the case with handmade sock monkey dolls. It took us days to make the monkeys. Each doll had a name with little embellishments made by the children in our class. They even gave them a birth certificate and travel papers! The little girl brought back joyous pictures of the other children playing with the dolls. These small acts are spontaneous and out of the hearts of my students. They make an unforgettable difference.

I love to travel, and I meet many families and children when I do. I ask if they would be willing to become pen pals and I have never been turned down. Please remember it can be very expensive to people to send letters from their country of origin. We have often accessed school funds for the cost of return postage. I hope you enjoy the rich engaging experience of connection in our world. I think the most rewarding relationships are the ones we have nurtured over many years. So you might pick one or two organizations and commit to them while watching the bonds deepen and grow.

## Resources

### Adult Books

Heather Adamson. *Homes in Many Cultures (Life Around the World)*. Mankato, MN: Capstone Press, 2009.

Linda Evans and Mary Thompson. *Art Projects from Around the World: Grades 4-6: Step-by-step Directions for 20 Beautiful Art Projects*. New York: Scholastic, 2006.

Peter Menzel and Faith D'Aluisio. *Hungry Planet: What the World Eats*. Oakland, CA: Material World Publisher, 2007.

Margaret Shepherd and Sharon Hogan. *The Art of the Personal Letter: A Guide to Connecting Through the Written Word*. New York: Broadway Books, 2008.

## CHILDREN'S BOOKS

Heather Adamson. *School in Many Cultures (Life Around the World)*. Mankato, MN: Capstone Press, 2009.

Nancy Loewen and Christopher Lyles. *Sincerely Yours: Writing Your Own Letter (Writer's Toolbox)*. Mankato, MN: Picture Window Books, 2009.

Peter Menzel and Charles C. Mann. *Material World: A Global Family Portrait*. Berkeley, CA: Counterpoint Publisher, 1995.

Stuart J. Murphy. *Polly's Pen Pal*. Illustrated by Remy Simard. New York: Festival Publisher, 2005.

Gloria Rand and Ted Rand. *A Pen Pal for Max*. (New York: Henry Holt and Company, 2005.)

# Compassion

# 9

## James: Practices for Grown-Ups

WE ARE WIRED UP to care. When we see a child fall and hurt herself, something instinctive motivates us to help. There's nothing in it for us. Just a movement of the heart that causes us to respond. Isn't that wonderful? Modern neuroscience has shown that our brains have "mirror neurons" that naturally empathize with another person's experience. The same brain cells that light up when you stub your toe also light up when you see someone else stub theirs. When we see suffering in another it evokes caring in our own heart. That is why watching a movie is such a powerful experience. We are with the hero or heroine's challenges and triumphs.

The capacity to care and respond to another's suffering is more than just a nice thing to have; it is a way to access and awaken joy. Helping others and making a difference in their lives is one of the most fulfilling ways to experience true well-being. Martin Seligman, the father of Positive Psychology and author of *Authentic Happiness*, writes that the greatest source of happiness is identifying our gifts and then using them to make a contribution to others.

Aline is a young woman whose commitment to community development and environmental protection has taken her to places like Senegal, Peru, and Siberia. Through her service work she has witnessed in all these places the heartbreak of poverty and ecological destruction. And yet her work is so fulfilling. As she puts it:

> I think it's a very human thing to want to serve. It feeds something in the soul. If people look honestly, living their values counts more than money. If you're not aligned with your values, it eats at you. When you are, something in you grows and comes alive. Each one of us has our own hidden purpose inside, and needs to uncover it and give it wings. Service is one of the things that gets us in touch with that most natural and true part of ourselves.

Just like adults, although our children are naturally wired up to care, they also have strong instincts to get what they want even at the expense of others. Giving them opportunities to experience the joy that comes from expressing their caring is one of the most important things we can do. This world needs as many compassionate human beings as we can help shape.

## Compassion Is Not Rescuing

With all the suffering around us, it would be easy to get overwhelmed or simply shut down. This benefits no one. It's essential to include ourselves in our compassion practice. Otherwise we burn out. You can be compassionate with yourself by knowing your capacities and limits. By remembering to nourish ourselves, as we respond to the suffering of others, especially our children, we have more to give and it creates a more joyful experience.

Compassion doesn't mean tirelessly rescuing everyone we see from their suffering. It's not supposed to be a heavy burden. Not only can't we prevent people from suffering, we usually can't take it away from them. Of course we don't want to see our children suffer. But suffering is part of life. In fact, sometimes our attempt to rescue them can actually disempower them. In our heroic attempt to take away their suffering, we can undermine their own growing process and prevent them from exercising their own inner strength.

A key to wise compassion is balancing our caring with another great heart quality, equanimity. Equanimity is the spacious acceptance that, although we want things to be different, this is the way they are. Equanimity is simply acknowledging, "It's like this." Feeling frustrated and distressed because we're powerless to change the situation just drains our capacity to respond.

Equanimity helps us stay centered when we see others suffer. The famous Serenity Prayer sums up the need for both action and equanimity: "Grant me the serenity to accept the things I cannot change, courage to change the things I can, and wisdom to know the difference." The more we can find this balance, the richer our compassion becomes a healing environment for others.

Often compassion just means being there for another. Instead of trying to fix someone or take away his or her suffering, your caring presence is often the most comforting thing you can offer someone in pain. If you see a child going through a difficult time, before going into action mode, first take on the practice of just being with them. Listen to their experience. Imagine what it's like for them to be going through it. If you were in their situation, what kind of presence would you want from another? Find a centered, balanced place inside that is mainly witnessing them in a loving, supportive way. You might ask them questions that help them get in touch with what they're feeling. Let go of any agenda to try to fix them. Don't miss the uplifting feeling that accompanies your loving presence.

## Mentoring

One of the most joyful aspects of being an agent of compassion is empowering another through mentorship. It's a real joy to support a young person's development and help her or him blossom into their full potential. Each of us can empower others to find their destiny. Every young person who hasn't reached his or her full potential and has a good heart is a perfect candidate to invest in. Even those who, in their confusion and ignorance, cause suffering to others have great potential. I see the process of mentoring and empowering as the following:

1. See the good in that person, including their unique gifts and talents.
2. See the potential they have to help others.
3. Believe in them and let them know it.
4. Help awaken those gifts through encouraging and supporting them to develop themselves.

By mentoring and empowering that person we are helping a seed of deep compassion and wisdom grow. It's tremendously rewarding and a guaranteed way to bring some joy into your life.

## Responding to the Suffering Around Us

Relieving the suffering of others through volunteering brings a tremendous uplift of the heart. It's also one of the most effective ways to get us out of our own suffering. For some, focusing on our family or those close to us in need of support is the ideal arena to express our caring. For others, volunteering through some social service program is a source of real joy. Some quotes on service that I find particularly inspiring:

*I don't know what your destiny will be, but one thing I do know: the only ones among you who will be really happy are those who have sought and found how to serve.* —Albert Schweitzer

*How wonderful it is that nobody need wait a single moment before starting to improve the world.* —Anne Frank

One research study showed that "volunteering contributes to happiness by decreasing boredom and creating an increased sense of purpose in life.

Volunteers, on average, are twice as likely to feel happy with themselves as non-volunteers."

If you have the time, you might consider a simple, doable project that puts you into an environment of service to someone local to you. It could be spending time with someone you know who needs support or it could be volunteering in a new setting. Don't do anything that will take an unrealistic amount of time. You don't want to resent your compassion practice! Do it as an experiment in discovering how it feels to step outside your comfort zone. Be present for whatever wholesome (or other) feelings arise as you serve another.

### Extending Compassion Beyond the Local

We only need to look at a newspaper to see all kinds of suffering in the world. If you are moved by any given situation, ask yourself, "What can I do in a small way to express my caring?" If you feel outrage over how human beings can be so insensitive or cruel to one another, don't let the outrage poison you. Go underneath those feelings to the place of real caring for those who are the victims (and perhaps try to feel compassion for the ignorance of the perpetrators).

We're all familiar with terrible disasters that leave thousands homeless, like earthquakes or tsunamis, or the suffering that comes from war. You might consider responding to situations beyond your neighborhood. Or perhaps you have concern over climate change and its consequences. If you feel helpless with regard to these victims, ask yourself how you can respond wisely, rather than feeling powerless. Stay in touch with your caring heart, which might motivate you to act from that wholesome place.

As writer Andrew Harvey advises, "Follow your heartbreak." See what you're moved to do. "Action absorbs anxiety," as Angeles Arrien says. Whatever action you take in response to suffering, whether writing a letter or sending funds, do it as a conscious compassion practice. You might try saying the phrases "May you be free of suffering," or, "I care about your suffering" (including the Earth's suffering) quietly before or after you write a letter or send money.

As you express compassion, you will be modeling for your children the most inspiring way to live. Our deepest happiness does not come from what we can get from others but how we can contribute to their lives. May it be a source of real joy for you and the children you live and work with.

## Try This

### Compassion as a Formal Contemplative Practice

You can incline your mind toward greater empathy by consciously planting seeds through formal compassion meditation. Here is a classical compassion practice. I encourage you to include this in your meditation/quiet time for a few minutes each day and see what effect it has:

1. Sit quietly getting into a relaxed quiet space. You can use your breath to do this.

2. Bring to mind an image of someone you care about, who might be going through a hard time. Feel the connection and caring you share.

3. Say either of these phrases—"I really care about your suffering" or "May you hold your suffering with compassion." Get in touch with the meaning behind the words, projecting those thoughts and feelings toward the person. Imagine they feel your caring and love.

4. Repeat this slowly for one or two minutes, staying in touch with the feeling as much as possible.

5. Direct those thoughts toward yourself, then another person. Notice how it feels to send compassion to yourself or another.

### Mentoring

In the bestseller *A Long Way Gone: Memoirs of a Boy Soldier*, Ishmael Beah writes about how he transformed from a boy who committed unspeakable acts of cruelty into an inspiring presence who has shown many the possibility of profound transformation. His road back was possible through the love and mentoring of others, especially Laura Simms, a woman who saw he was capable of something else. It's never too late for someone to change and turn their confusion and cruelty into wisdom and compassion. *(continues on next page)*

To support someone's development, you might initiate mentoring them, using the steps below:

1. Think of someone in your life who respects or looks up to you; someone who hasn't fully come into their own power or realized their full potential.

2. In whatever way that feels appropriate, let them know you believe in them and that you're in their cheering section.

3. Within reasonable parameters that work for both of you, be there for them as a guide, mentor, or pillar of support.

4. Notice how this feels inside and how it affects the relationship between you.

## Michele: Practicing Compassion with Children

Most children have a natural, spontaneous way of sharing their compassionate hearts. I am left in awe at how children can so easily forgive and let go of squabbles including things that would take some adults hours of therapy to even touch upon. A conversation and guidance on owning their part in a disagreement and discussing how they might do something differently next time goes a long way in reconnecting at the heart. In a matter of minutes, the kids often hold hands or invite each other to play again. We, as adults, can receive a lot of guidance from these wise young hearts that give so freely. Once children feel secure in their environment they can expand their hearts out to others. This chapter highlights the art of service and the gift of giving.

## *Service*

*"I slept and dreamt that life was joy. I awoke and saw that life was service. I acted and behold, service was joy."* —Rabindranath Tagore

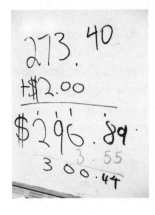

Personally, I don't use the word charity; I prefer the word service. I feel we are global citizens with responsibilities and that we are actually serving ourselves by the very act of giving. There is no ulterior motive in true giving. It is not earned and cannot be bargained for. There are no hooks or strings attached. Giving is simply an offering. This is very different than the current mentality many students have that says, "If I do that, what do I get?" It is a new paradigm that opens us to selfless contribution and it works! This is the place I want my students to be working from.

When we set up giving projects, parents shared that their children, who hated to get up in the morning, were bustling to school to get on with the work that they felt needed to be done. They felt alive.

Here are a few comments from the students:

* ✳ "I know I make a difference and I didn't know that before."
* ✳ "I can't believe that by raising money we actually bought a bed for the school in Uganda where sick children can rest. That is so cool."
* ✳ "I didn't know that real kids had problems I just saw in books."
* ✳ "Now I actually have a letter in my hand and guess what, he likes soccer too. That is so amazing."
* ✳ "I want to empty my piggy bank to help!"
* ✳ "I brought in dog food for the food bank so they can have food too."
* ✳ "I did extra chores and brought in $15 to help. It feels good that I can do something."
* ✳ "Let's do something every month to help somewhere. Can we?"

## An Opportunity to Serve—Leadership

Teachers and playground supervisors sent Jaxson, an eleven-year-old boy, to the office daily. He couldn't make it through the day without getting into a tussle, creating havoc, or getting into everyone else's business in negative ways. He was actually a natural leader but had not honed his skills to serve in positive, constructive ways.

Jaxson was in my class every Monday. He came in the first day yelling, flinging balls around, and making sure *everyone* knew he was in the class. The introverts cringed and many of the more boisterous children jumped up and started wrestling around. I thought to myself, what a year this is going to be! I could see Jaxson had a huge desire to be respected and seen and it was being fulfilled in negative ways. This yearning to be seen reminded me of myself at that age so I had a leg-hold into working with this student.

## From Me to We

This chapter includes practices of self-love and spirals out into giving to the family, community, global community, and our planet. Service can be as simple preparing a communal luncheon to larger projects like fundraising or developing a micro-financing plan. It also highlights how to hand children the reins of leadership so they can find their own ways to give back to the world and those who inhabit it. Creating opportunities to serve and make change gives kids places to shine.

I have shared some of the most beloved activities my students and my own children have done over the years to serve the planet and humankind. I can say without a word of doubt that social justice and "doing good in the world" are the most meaningful projects I ever do with my students. Children who have rarely contributed in athletic or academic ways often find a voice and a valuable place through social justice issues.

# Lesson 1: From Me to We

May your joy and happiness continue, and may good fortune follow you everywhere.

**Building Strengths of:**
- Community
- Global Peace
- Perspective
- Compassion
- Leadership
- Informed decision making
- Sustainability
- Collaboration

**Materials:**
- None

**Ages:**
- Five years to adult

**School Curriculum Connections**
- Oral language
- Written language
- Listening skills
- Reading
- Mathematics
- Social studies
- Fine arts
- Social and emotional learning

> *I would say that the thrust of my life has been initially about getting free, and then realizing that my freedom is not independent of everybody else. Then I am arriving at that circle where one works on oneself as a gift to other people so that one doesn't create more suffering. I help people as a work on myself and I work on myself to help people.*
> —Ram Dass

## Home and School Practice

### Give Them Responsibility

In September, I laid out our year's curriculum on the board, focusing on service and social justice. My intention was for my students to become even more active citizens and take on leadership roles while educating themselves on local and global social justice issues. We began reading about the challenges children around the world face, from working in sweatshops to living lives of grave poverty. We compared our own abundant lives to some of the deep struggles other people have on the planet to basically survive, never mind thrive. I explained that just by the very fact they were born in Canada, the children in our classroom had already won the lottery. They had medical care, social services, and the ability to go to school.

To create deeper global connections, I paired my students with students in Uganda, Costa Rica, and Mexico. These pen pals are people I have met through my travels and personal connections. We had been pen-palling between the schools and children for over three years at that point. My students see children in other countries as people, just like themselves, with wants, desires, celebrations, and struggles. They are not just reading about history or the lives of people in a book but holding a living document written especially to them. This living energy really opens the portal to see the disparities in our lives and the pain and challenges that others endure on a daily basis. Rather than shielding ourselves from pain in the world, we respond by doing a caring action and we open to possibility. We discussed how we could live lives of gratitude for the abundance that each day brought to us.

### The Story of Jaxson Grabbing the Reins

One September day I shared a slide show of my travels to developing countries, including Nepal and Myanmar. The unbelievable difficulties the children in those places can face each day were evident from the pictures. The challenges became instantly more real when a huge earthquake struck in Nepal that month. I had a friend, who was directly involved with victims of the earthquake, share letters from the local people. We read them aloud.

At this point my students wanted to fundraise and Jaxson, the boy I described in the introduction to this chapter, was on it. He said he had no idea how other people in the world were struggling until he took my class and he wanted to do something.

Jaxson came every recess and lunch to run raffles, game days, and even had his mom drive him to school in the evening for a fundraiser. His energy was amazing. He could go and go and pull in everyone in the school in his wake.

His mother pulled me aside one evening and said she had never seen her son so committed to anything. He told her he now knew he was on the planet to change the world for the better and he knew he could actually do it.

He took responsibility for his actions and could see clearly the impact he had on others. Students slowly began to see him as a leader and someone who "did good" in the world. It took time to change the perceptions teachers, staff, and students had of him.

At the end of the school year I asked students to write where they saw themselves in ten years and present a speech to the class. He said with absolute assurance he would be doing social justice work. He wanted to teach, create change, and travel the world doing service work. I was absolutely stunned and humbled that he received so much out of one day a week of practices. I was also inspired that he thought we had created change in the world. And we had.

## Nepal
When the Nepal earthquakes happened, I came to school in a daze. How could I help? I felt shut down and sad. I shared my sorrow with my class and showed them pictures of my travels to Nepal twenty-five years earlier. Without missing a beat, they suggested we have a Friday bake sale. Two weeks later we had prayer flags flying on the school grounds, bake sales, raffles, fun days, and school-wide education about life in Nepal. We also raised over $2000, which for a tiny school of 200 children is remarkable. The students shared that they felt empowered to make change on a personal and global level.

## How to Begin
So how do we as parents and educators even begin the process of giving? How do we make a conscious pledge to serve others? How can we look at global problems and not disengage? How do we find opportunities to help? How do we grow the deep muscle inside ourselves that knows we are global citizens? How can we create giving as a daily practice rather than something that we do on holidays or in times of dire need? How do we teach to give from compassion rather than pity? James shares this lovely quote:

*Love moves in a circle. You take it in and send it out; you send it out and it comes back to you. You are an instrument of love. The love that naturally radiates from us awakens the love in others. What really happens is that love is finding itself through us.*

## Encouraging Kids

### Service—Begin with Self-Love

Start by teaching children that the giving practice begins with nourishing our own well-being. So many people give tirelessly from a place of depletion and duty. True giving starts right at the heart with "Me"! How can we listen deep inside ourselves and hear the yearnings of our own inner being? Teach your children to listen to their bodies. Stop and ask them to focus inside to see if they need food, quiet, exercise, or company. When they feel nourished, that is the time to begin moving outwards, from me to we. We start slowly, but gradually helping out becomes a habit and a way of life. We start to look at the world with different eyes, eyes that see ways to change the world for the better.

### Service—Family and Friends

Giving is done in all sorts of ways. It might mean that your child performs an extra chore or finds a special way to give to someone in the family who needs a boost. Brothers and sisters might read to each other or walk one another to school or the park. One small thing makes a huge difference. By working side by side with others we see our choices strengthen families, friendship bonds, and communities.

Encourage your children to adopt their own causes, and then integrate those causes into your family's decision-making around giving.

One question, inspired by Marshall B. Rosenberg that I love asking my family is: "What can I do to make your life more wonderful?" When I ask this question daily and over time, I find I have come to know the simple ways in which I can give to my partner and my children that truly make a difference. It doesn't mean that I respond to every request, but I hold their wish in my heart and when I can selflessly give, I do. I also find that my family wants to give to me in this way. They truly want to make my life more wonderful. (I just have to remember this is a request, not a demand disguised as a way to get my family to do something. I have to let go of the outcome.)

## Service to My Local Community: Food Bank Filler

At school, my class would discuss at length the groups we would like to give to. There would be debate and banter. The board would be filled with causes close to the students' hearts. If someone's service group did not become a class effort, they were encouraged to work with their family or friends to fulfill their desires to support their chosen cause. Our local food bank is amazing. Students have gone on tours delivering groceries. Many people in our school population have used the food bank regularly. The kids clearly see the need in the local community for support and are able to deliver. Three or four times a year, we do a school food drive. I usually create, as a challenge, some kind of container for the students to fill. For Valentine's we made a giant heart out of cardboard and put it in the main foyer of the school. It was filled to the brim in days. Having a large visual in the school allows all children from young to senior grades a way to participate and begin to become caring, contributing citizens.

## Service to the Global Community: Wishes of Well-Being

Several years ago there was a huge earthquake in Japan. At the time I had several students who had family in Japan as well as a student whose father was an airline pilot and was actually in Japan during the earthquake. The level of anxiety for the well-being of others was palpable in our classroom. We wondered how we could possibly help. The children decided they wanted to make 1,000 paper cranes, string them together, and send them to Japan with a family that was traveling back to check on their loved ones. They also wanted to fundraise and send a sum of cash that could be used by the Red Cross.

The crane folding began in our class of twenty-eight students and quickly spread to become a school-wide project. Children opened up "crane stations" while educating other students on earthquake safety and the plight of the people in Japan. I don't know if you have ever tried to make 1,000 paper cranes, but it is a huge feat. I had no idea. It took us over two weeks as a collective— but we did it. We called in our Japanese friends who had family in the affected

cities, and ceremoniously gave them the cranes. They were so deeply touched at this outpouring of love. We formed a circle with the whole class while holding hands and saying a series of "blessings" for them to take back to Japan for us. The children told me they felt so comforted that they could do something. I love these pictures of the cranes hanging in the room. One world, one heart.

## Service to the Planet: Planting a Garden

Everyday choices impact the environment. Simply planting a seed and nurturing it brings children the awareness that life unfolds over time and must be cared for. They learn there are cycles of life. The joy of watching a child's face when little sprouts push through the earth is immeasurable. They begin to understand where their food comes from and how important it is to protect our environment.

In my classroom I have numerous plants sprouting under grow lights. The window ledge is also lined with little plants of various types. Children are invited to take snips of herbs to add to their lunches. When springtime comes,

we take our vegetable babies out to the school garden. This little plot of hammered together boards has evolved over the years but it is one of the central hubs of the playground. Children care deeply for the space and return time and time again to see the plants growing. This year two lovely cement benches were donated and everyday families are gathered by the garden watching life unfold. There is a lesson in chapter 10 called "Mindful Tea," which more fully expands on the wonders of gardening.

Here are the levels or spirals of service written out in a little list. You can photocopy and place it on your desk or have your children write it in their journal. Your children can drop the pebble of self-love into their own being and then begin to look for ways to ripple goodness out to the world. We never know which shore the goodness will wash up upon.

*I would like my life to be a statement of love and compassion—and where it isn't, that's where my work lies.* —Ram Dass

## Service Begins With Me:

*Here is just one thing to get the ripples of service flowing out from me to we*

*Service to myself:*
Do one thing you love today

*Service to my family and friends:*
Ask what can make their lives more wonderful

*Service to my local community:*
Try creating a food bank filler and take it
to your local center

*Service to the global community:*
Choose a few organizations and think of ways
to support their cause

*Service to the planet:*
Plant a seed in the garden

## *Resources*

### ADULT BOOKS

Ram Dass and Paul Gorman. *How Can I Help?* New York: Knopf, 1985.

James Doty. *Into the Magic Shop: A Neurosurgeon's Quest to Discover the Mysteries of the Brain and the Secrets of the Heart.* New Hyde Park, NY: Avery, 2016.

Craig Kielburger and Kevin Major. *Free the Children: A Young Man Fights Against Child Labor and Proves That Children Can Change the World.* Vancouver, BC: Me to We Publishing, 2009.

Nicholas D. Kristof and Sheryl WuDunn. *Half the Sky: Turning Oppression into Opportunity for Women Worldwide.* New York: Vintage, 2010.

### CHILDREN'S BOOKS

Amnesty International. *We Are All Born Free: The Universal Declaration of Human Rights in Pictures.* London: Francis Lincoln Children's Books, 2011.

Maribeth Boelts and Noah Z. Jones. *Those Shoes.* Somerville, MA: Candlewick, 2009.

Linda Sue Park. *A Long Walk to Water: Based on a True Story.* Boston, MA: Houghton Mifflin Harcourt Books for Young Readers, 2012.

Malala Yousafzai and Christina Lamb. *I Am Malala: The Girl Who Stood Up for Education and Was Shot by the Taliban.* New York: Little, Brown and Company, 2013.

# Lesson 2: Random Acts of Kindness with a Camera

Don't miss all the goodness that comes through you and touches others. It is a great source of true well-being.

## Builds strengths of:
- Self-awareness
- Mindfulness practice
- Physical well-being
- Artistic expression
- Random acts of kindness

## Materials
- Camera, something that takes photos
- Garbage bags

## Ages
- Preschool to adult

## School Curriculum Connections
- Physical education
- Fine arts
- Social and emotional learning

### Home Practice
Tonight, as I set out on my walk with my puppy and my sweetheart to the local town center, I packed my camera. I set the intention to walk looking for acts of kindness to perform. I wanted to see the world through my camera lens and change it one small act at a time. What would show up on my screen? What needed to be done?

What evolved from this exploration is a teachable lesson for my students, which can easily be translated into a family activity. If you are doing this at home, you could send the photo essay to a grandparent or friend. It would also be a great challenge to send out your photo essay to other families as a way to keep your community clean and cared for. The bottom line is you can do it just for fun. It can be as simple as a walk of caring mindfulness. Each walk can be different. See what shows up in the lens for you.

Here is my photo essay, and the simple, easy acts my partner and I did. I felt full of joy when I got home, particularly over one act, which I had walked by many times telling myself someone else would do it... They didn't and I finally did. Read on to see.

## *School Practice*

Allow students a few days to create this photo essay. Have them use their own cameras on their phones and iPads, or bring out the camera gathering dust in the cupboard at home. We are very lucky in our school to have twenty-four iPads available for students to use.

Ask the children to look through the eyes of a lens and walk for fifteen to sixty minutes looking for acts of kindness that they can perform. The acts may be simply seeing litter and picking it up. It may be that someone's jacket has been left on the playground and needs to go to the lost and found. It could be something that one hundred people walk by and the act of kindness viewer does.

Photograph the situation that needs attention and then take another photo after the act is completed. Have the kids create a photo essay using whatever form of media they prefer. Many of my students use iMovie or Keynote, as we are a Mac-friendly school. My younger students love to get an older buddy or their parents to help with this activity. We have a little computer club at school so children can get help if they need it. The students can then write, post, and show the photo essays to classmates or at an assembly in the school. It is also a wonderful way to begin a parent conference, PTA meeting, or Monday morning. It shows kindness in the world being seen and celebrated.

## Walking in Kindness and Gratitude

The first thing I saw was a plastic bag floating on an ocean wave.
I picked it up.

A plastic soft drink bottle was nestled in the bushes.
I picked it up.

I picked up doggy doo that others had left wrapped in bags
on the side of the path.
This was a hard one for me... YUCK!

I smelled this wonderful rose on the side of a path telling her how beautiful she was and how much gratitude I had for her scent.

 I carried my puppy down a steep hill to a stream to give him a drink of water even though our house was only minutes away. He so wanted to go!

I had walked past an old plastic container many times. It was a stinky float filled with goo. We picked it up out of the cold ocean, wading in fifty meters to bring it home and put it in the garbage bin. Unfortunately, it cannot be recycled as it was filled with gluey stuff.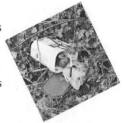

These are not huge acts, but tiny drops of "doing" in front of my camera lens and my eyes. It makes each walk more alive and celebratory. Who knows what tomorrow will bring? Maybe even today? The puppy needs to go out again!

## Resources

### ADULT BOOKS

Thich Nhat Hanh. *True Love: A Practice for Awakening the Heart*. Boulder, CO: Shambhala, 2011.

M. J. Ryan and Conari Press, eds. *Random Acts of Kindness Then and Now: The 20th Anniversary of a Simple Idea That Changes Lives*. San Francisco: Red Wheel/Weiser, 2013.

### CHILDREN'S BOOKS

Rosalynn Carter, Dawna Markova, and Conari Press, eds. *Kids' Random Acts of Kindness*. Berkeley, CA: Conari Press, 1995.

R. J. Palacio. *Wonder*. New York: Knopf, 2012.

Emily Pearson and Fumi Kosaka. *Ordinary Mary's Extraordinary Deed*. Layton, UT: Gibbs Smith, 2002.

Jerry Spinelli. *Stargirl*. New York: Laurel Leaf Publishing, 2012.

# Lesson 3: Stone Soup

## Opening Our Hearts and Homes to Friends and Families

### Based on an old folktale of generosity and sharing

As long as you stay connected to your intention to share the goodness inside of you, it will keep shining through and you will be making a significant contribution to the world.

### Builds strengths of:
- Sharing
- Perspective taking
- Connection to our Earth and food
- Creating healthy food choices
- Appreciation
- Cooperation

### Materials
- Big cooking pot
- Large spoon
- Cutting board and child-safe knives
- Smooth rock about heart size from the beach or a river
- A little love

### Ages
- Preschool to adult

### School Curriculum Connections
- Oral language
- Written language
- Listening skills
- Reading
- Social studies
- Mathematics
- Social and emotional learning

### Home and School Practice

Stone Soup is an old folktale in which hungry strangers convince the local people of a town to give them food. It is usually told as a lesson in cooperation and generosity amid scarcity. In some versions the main character convinces people that they can make soup from an old nail. But whether it's a stone or a nail, the story helps us to remember the value of co-creating and generosity.

Make Stone Soup at school and it will inspire you to make it at home. You can invite your family and friends over to make magic stone soup or share the idea with your child's classroom teacher.

## Have Vegetables Coming Out of My Ears

Each year in the fall when the harvest is over and the food in our BC gardens has begun to wither, I ask the children what it might be like to make soup with a magic stone. All we need is a spoon, a pot, water, a magical stone and a little love from their house.

Each child is asked to go home and talk with their parents about one or two things they can bring in for a collective soup. Tenderly, I see handfuls of herbs, a carrot or two, rice, beans, and bits of produce arrive. Many of our students have vegetable gardens and are very proud to bring in their harvest.

## The Whole Gang Shows Up

On this day a small group of parents, grandparents, and helpers come to help.

Each child cuts up their donation and adds it to the pot. All morning long the children stand on a little stool and smell the bubbling pot, coming back to the classroom with tales of the "best soup ever," "just getting better and better," cooking. Some of the children have never contributed to cooking a meal before. They feel so incredibly proud.

I tell them that the special ingredient is generosity and love and of course the magical stone I have brought from the beach! Several students who forget to bring anything have the opportunity of contributing by washing dishes and cutting boards. Everyone helps. Just before lunch we wipe the desks clean and bring out bowls and spoons from home. Sometimes there are still a few flowers in the garden and the tables are decorated.

## A Gratitude Circle

We form a big circle of parents, children, and anyone else in the room. A gratitude stone is passed from person to person. This can be any stone you have in the house or at school that is special to you or your child in some way.

Parents often wipe tears from their eyes on hearing the simplicity of the students' gratitude and love. "Thank you, Mummy, for coming in when you are busy, to help with this magic soup." "Thank you to Mother Earth for all this great food."

## Finally

When all the special guests are seated, we smile, breathe in, and eat. Very few students, in my experience, even vegetable haters, don't finish their bowls of soup. The special stone in the soup pot is removed and given in a raffle to a winner.

The next day we walk to our local beach and look for amazing stones to be taken home for everyone's Stone Soup.

### *Resources*

#### ADULT BOOKS

Thich Nhat Hanh. *Joyfully Together: The Art of Building a Harmonious Community*. Berkeley, CA: Parallax Press, 2009.

Jack Kornfield. *Soul Food: Stories to Nourish the Spirit and the Heart*. New York: HarperOne, 1996.

Peter Menzel and Faith D'Aluisis. *Hungry Planet: What the World Eats*. NewYork, NY: Penguin Random House , 2007.

Peter Menzel and Charles C. Mann. *Material World: A Global Family Portrait*. Berkeley, CA: Counterpoint Press, 1995.

#### CHILDREN'S BOOKS

Heather Forest. *Stone Soup*. Illustrated by Susan Gaber. Atlanta, GA: August House, 2005.

Vanessa Martir and Nancy Lublin. *Do Something!: A Handbook for Young Activists*. New York: Workman Publishing, 2010.

Jon J. Muth. *Stone Soup*. New York: Scholastic, 2003.

Tomie de Paola. *Strega Nona*. New York: Aladdin, 1979.

# Simply Being

# 10

## James: Practices for Grown-Ups

WHEN I WAS a schoolteacher in my twenties I would find a way to travel on a tight budget to Europe each summer vacation. One summer I went to Greece thinking I would just relax in paradise. It turned out that, unfortunately, I still brought my mind with me. I had scrimped and saved to be in this beautiful place yet thoughts of worry and anxiety continually swirled through my mind. At some point I saw clearly that I was pretty much missing out on enjoying my summer holiday. It was a memorable moment when I realized that I couldn't solve my all my worries right now and that life would just unfold however it would. Although it had taken me a few weeks, I finally decided to slow down and enjoy the amazing good fortune of being in one of the most beautiful, peaceful spots on Earth I could imagine. On that watershed holiday, I learned the joy of simply enjoying being where I was.

Our final practice theme, the joy of simply being, is an antidote for the intensity and frenzy of life. It is also the way to access the inner peace we're all looking for. Up until now all the other practice themes have involved some kind of *doing*—practices to cultivate specific states of well-being such as generosity, gratitude, compassion, or kindness. Now we switch from doing to simply *being*. We stop all trying and let ourselves completely rest, simply receiving the moment that's given to us right now.

William James spoke of "the ceaseless frenzy of always thinking we should be doing something else." In our manic-paced modern life, we can pride ourselves on our "busy-ness," often worn as a badge that says we're doing so many "important things." We become expert multi-taskers thinking we're getting a lot accomplished, measured by how many balls we have in the air at the same time. In actuality, it's been proven that when we're multi-tasking we cannot experience true happiness. When our brain is rapidly flitting from one task to another, it doesn't get a chance to light up the centers associated with true well-being.

Moving from *doing* to *being* doesn't mean disengaging from life. Quite the opposite. We're actually able to be present instead of toppling forward in our minds thinking about the next thing we need to do. That is how genuine connection is possible. In *The Little Prince*, the beautiful and insightful book by Antoine de Saint-Exupery, the Little Prince finds delicious pleasure in fully enjoying his flower. The wise fox tells him the great secret: "It's the time you spent on your rose that makes your rose important."

An Awakening Joy course participant found this out for himself as he shared,

> "I once considered my life to be relatively bland and uneventful. It was even hard for me to remember what had happened during the day, since it was almost by definition 'unimportant.' But I now think this is more a matter of perception than fact. Seeing the wonder in what is, rather than looking for something wonderful and disregarding the rest, has been a big discovery."

The practice of simply being is about the ease and relaxation that is available in any moment we remember to be present without thinking about the past or future or having any agenda at all. It allows our actions to come from a more centered, effective place. This state of being is not foreign to us. Neuroscience expert Rick Hanson says it's been shown through fMRI experiments: "When you are not hungry or threatened or in pain, your brain's natural state has these characteristics: It is conscious, calm, contented, caring, and creative." James Baraz, p. 275 *Awakening Joy: 10 Steps that Will Put You on the Road to Real Happiness*, Bantam, New York, 2010 (as quoted in Awakening Joy class, Berkeley CA).

## The Real Breakthrough: Loving the Absence of Stimulation

One obstacle to the peace of *being* available in each moment is our inability to enjoy the absence of stimulation. We usually think of lack of stimulation as...*boring*! We often miss the peace that's right here by relating to a moment where not much is happening as just the boring gap between entertaining stimulation. With practice, this joy of *being* can be held as a "homecoming," as the experience of coming back to your true home. As long as we're looking outside for the next experience to delight or entertain us, we miss the peace that's right under our noses.

Parents have a tendency to think they need to find some entertainment for their children to keep their minds occupied. Paradoxically, children usually need free time away from stimulation to discover their inner world of imagination. I remember when Adam was little. Those times when I stopped myself from trying to find entertainment for him and trusted he could survive were the times that his natural creativity had a chance to shine through.

In exploring this idea of enjoying simply being, notice how you deal with boredom when you feel it. See if it's possible to let yourself just relax and appreciate the feeling of not needing to do anything else than just rest where you are and enjoy being alive.

### Letting Go of "Trying" to Meditate

Sometimes even mindfulness meditation can be approached from a strong sense of *doing*, which then turns into unhealthy striving. It's true that it *does* take effort to bring your awareness into the present moment, but once you're grounded in the present, any additional effort takes you out of experiencing the ease and peace that's here right now. In order to open to that peace, you need to completely let go, *be* the space of awareness that receives experience, feeling life as it moves through you. As one great Tibetan master teaches,

> "Happiness cannot be found through great effort and willpower, but is already here, in relaxation and letting go. Wanting to grasp the ungraspable, you exhaust yourself in vain. As soon as you relax this grasping, space is here—open, inviting, and comfortable." —Gendun Rinpoche p. 11 quoted in Nyoshul Khenpo & Surya Das, *Natural Great Perfection* Ithaca: Snow Lion, 2008.

For the next week when you take time to meditate or be quiet in your own way, rather than trying to make something happen, let yourself just enjoy the peace that's here right now as you become familiar with just relaxing. Enjoy the feeling of stillness and peace.

### The Practice of Equanimity

The joy of *being* is supported by learning to develop the quality of equanimity. Equanimity is a balance of mind that allows things to be as they are. It has a quality of spaciousness, not fighting what is here. Spaciousness and balance come when we stop trying to control our world and rest in the simplicity of things as they are. We've already explored three other heart qualities—loving-kindness, sympathetic joy, and compassion—but it is equanimity that holds these other qualities in balance. Without equanimity our loving-kindness can tip over into attachment, our compassion for the suffering of others can overwhelm us, and our joy can spin us out in excessive exhilaration.

The mind filled with equanimity is relaxed, but completely engaged. There's a big difference between equanimity and apathy or indifference, epitomized in the classic teenage response, "Whatever." This apathetic attitude is really disconnected. With equanimity you connect fully with life because you're willing to be with everything as it is. You can do this when you understand that, since everything changes, whatever is happening right now, whether difficult or wonderful, will not last. That gives us the courage to be with the hard stuff and the wisdom not to hold onto the highs when they subside.

Life has ups and downs. Anything can happen at any moment. As one teaching says, "Fortunes change quicker than the swish of a horse's tail." When you understand how quickly everything can change, you see that things are really out of your control. So the peace and happiness you're looking for doesn't depend on *what is happening* to you at any given moment, but on *your relationship to what is happening.*

At times you can consciously invite the experience of *being* by inclining the mind to come into balance. One form of equanimity practice is to simply say when you are thrown, "May I come into balance of mind right now." That phrase can remind you that there's another perspective you can bring to the situation to help you relax into the present moment. Try practicing using this phrase whenever you find that you need to come back to center. The balance and spaciousness that comes with equanimity allows you to relax your grip and vigilance and receive life in an open state of being.

### Developing Equanimity

Developing equanimity involves recognizing how we can get thrown off-kilter as things change, and accessing the wisdom to bring ourselves back into balance. Take a moment to reflect on the following:

1. When do you get thrown off balance in your life?
2. In your wisest moments, how do you come back to balance? What helps you remember to keep things in a wiser perspective?

### Trust and Surrender

When we develop equanimity we loosen our attachment to things working out a certain way. This opens us to another aspect of *being*: trust and surrender. This kind of trust is not based on a belief that things will work out just the way we hope, but rather that our awareness will meet the moment when it comes. Of course, conscious planning is important, but obsessing about the future is a certain prescription for suffering. We can do our part, but we usually don't have enough information to see how things will turn out.

We easily frighten ourselves in imagining all the scary future scenarios. There's a story of a skilled artist who went to a cave one day and painted a very realistic, life-size ferocious tiger. He did such a good job that when he was finished, he threw up his palette and brush and ran away. We paint these tigers in our mind about what might happen in the future and then frighten ourselves with them. That is why coming back to the present moment is such a refuge.

By learning to trust in the unfolding and in your ability to respond to it, you keep your mind from contracting and getting in the way. Then life becomes an adventure instead of something to fear. A friend recently told me that he sees life as being like a roller-coaster ride. It's always been that. But with practice, when the big curves and drops come, he can relax into them instead of being in the grip of fearing them. And that has made all the difference in enjoying his life.

### Learning to Listen

The spaciousness produced by coming into *being* has an additional benefit: it helps us access our wisdom to respond skillfully to any situation. As the great Taoist sage, Lao Tzu wrote, "By letting it go it all gets done. The world is won by those who let it go. But when you try and try, the world is beyond the winning. To the mind that is still, the whole universe surrenders." When we become familiar with relaxing and can simply *be* we allow for a wise response to emerge from within instead of forcing things.

We move from fear to a wiser response by learning to listen to our wisdom voice, discerning it from the voice of fear. One rule that I live by is to not let fear drive my decisions. Instead I metaphorically take fear out of the driver's seat, put it in the "passenger's seat in my mind," put a seat belt around it (perhaps even a helmet) to make sure it feels as safe as possible and let the fear know I honor it and care about it. But I don't give it the keys to the car. I want the voice of inner wisdom and truth to be running things.

Think of a good decision you've made in your life. Chances are it was the voice of wisdom speaking to you—something in you felt the "rightness" of it. How does it feel in your body when you are able to hear that voice? Relaxed, open, connected, grounded? What is the tone in your mind when it speaks its truth? Probably clear, kind, and supportive. Getting to know the voice of wisdom and its ring of truth is the secret to trusting it and letting it guide you to a deeper sense of being even in challenging times. And this voice can only be heard when we stop our running around and relax into being.

### The Joy of Everyday Being

This mode of *being* is the essence of a mind at ease and is actually much more available than we realize. Most of us regularly experience moments of freedom, such as the deep feeling of connection when we let the beauty of nature touch us or the feeling of peace when we allow ourselves to enjoy a break after finishing a task. But we're usually unaware of these moments of pure being, free of worry, wanting or confusion. In missing it, we miss the deep peace that's here for us to enjoy.

When we are mentally spinning our wheels, no matter how terrific the circumstances, we still suffer. Our happiness or suffering is not so much about external conditions as it is about what's going on inside. That's why meditation practice is such a powerful tool to develop inner peace. The more we learn to be here and relax into the moment, the more that carries over to the rest of our life.

We can learn to access this place of peace even in very challenging circumstances. When we do, we can experience what my son, Adam, refers to as "abundant enoughness." We feel a sense of sufficiency, that we have everything we need—a good heart, a body that serves us, a mind that works, the seed of deep wisdom. We can feel blessed just to be alive. We can let our beingness shine and radiate out, which reminds others to do the same.

So many people fight life—"Just hang in there," they say. With that adversarial attitude, life is mostly seen as something to get *through*. With practice, we don't have to wait for luck to bring us the next good moment. This moment counts; we don't have to postpone our arrival at the here and now. The joy of simply *being* includes opening all of the goodness around us, too. For example, hearing children squealing can make us happy. In everyday being, we practice allowing our hearts to be nourished by life, to savor it, taste it, luxuriate in it.

## The Gift of Your Beingness

One of the great benefits of accessing the joy of *being* is that you not only find peace inside of you, but you also affect everything and everyone around you. By accessing that calm center, you remind others that it is there in them as well. Think of the most centered person in your life. How do feel when you're around them? Doesn't their energy affect you as well?

Think of your opening up to *being* as giving everyone around you the gift of your centeredness. Your presence will awaken balance, calm and aliveness in others as well. You don't have to go around fixing anyone. As Anne Lamott

## Try This

### Coming into Being: Pause, Relax, Open

Greg Kramer, who teaches a method of wise speech called Insight Dialogue, has a useful formula for returning to calm and inner peace even when we're caught up in a complex task like communicating. It has three parts: pause, relax, and open. Try it yourself:

1. Pause. Don't feed the internal dialogue in the mind.
2. Relax. Feel your body. Take a breath and let go.
3. Open. Receive the experience of life as it's presenting itself in this moment. Let yourself be open to the person you are with. Let go of any agenda and just let yourself be.

Whenever you're caught up and tense—or just waiting in line at the store or for your computer to boot up—try using this simple technique of "Pause, Relax, and Open." It can help open you to a bigger perspective than the drama at hand. Make it a game to "disengage your clutch."

points out, "Lighthouses don't go running all over an island looking for boats to save; they just stand there shining."

In my early years as a schoolteacher, I used to quiet the class down with a jarring desk slam to override the din in the classroom. It could work for a few moments but then the noise would soon return. In my sixth year I got interested in meditation. I decided that instead of slamming the desk to quiet everyone down, I would quiet myself down first. I closed my eyes and breathed slowly and mindfully. To my amazement, the children would look at me with curiosity and soon quiet down. It was an early confirmation of the powerful effect my own presence had on everyone around me. As you practice this attitude of beingness within yourself I hope you too see the profound effect it can have on your children.

### Fully Enjoying the Moment

You don't have to be still to open to this quality of *being*. Whenever you're fully engaged in an activity you are experiencing *beingness*. Whether gardening, dancing, having fun, or enjoying your work, you experience what is known as *flow*, a term coined by Mihaly Csikszentmihalyi. When you're in flow you become absorbed and fully engaged with the activity at hand. Thoughts about the past or future don't distract you.

Whenever you find yourself fully engaged notice how good it feels not to be concerned with the past or future. Notice and enjoy the experience of true fulfillment that doesn't need anything added or taken away. This is another experience of the joy of simply being.

## Michele: Practicing Simply Being with Children

Ever wonder how you can fit one more thing into your already packed day? Do you question if you are taking enough time to teach your children the important value of presence and slowing down? Do you want your child to listen to their inner truth and wisdom?

Life is busier than ever. Often any spaciousness we have is filled with social media, computer and screen time. We are so busy doing we forget to be.

What about reversing this busyness and learning the power of doing nothing. Just being. Allow your children to be bored without having the need to fill the space with noise or activity. It is in the bored moments that the beauty of life right before us can actually open. It is in the moments of stillness that a portal is open to our inner lives. These moments also create unique happy memories of pure presence.

Can you make doing nothing as important as doing something?

How can we teach children to appreciate the simple moments?

To get an idea, I asked children what they love doing the most with their parents when they were just relaxed and being. Here are some of kids' favorite moments and best memories of "simply being."

✳ "I like just sitting with my mom doing crafts. We don't have to talk."

✳ "When the bed is really fluffy, I love snuggling my Dad."

✳ "We watch raindrops on the window."

✳ "The house smells good when we make cookies for no reason."

✳ "If I put my head on my dad's chest, I can hear his heartbeat."

✳ "I love it when my parents play with my hair and stoke my head."

✳ "My family lays outside and listens to the crickets chirping."

✳ "When I was little we blew up an air mattress and laid under the stars. I could see so much and it was so fun. I never forgot that."

✳ "My brother and I watched a whole army of ants for hours."

✳ "Sometimes I get to go for tea just with my mom. Just the two of us."

✳ "We dance around the house and play."

✳ "We do a puzzle and just chat about nothing much."

✳ "We grab sheets and clothes pegs and build forts in our living room. We even eat dinner there."

✳ "I like to just walk with my family at the beach. We don't really have a plan we just see what is there."

✳ "Well I like a good bonfire. We tell stories and eat marshmallows and hang out."

✳ "I set up a tea party with my stuffies and my mom and dad. They come and sit and we have tea."

Think about moments from your own childhood that were times of relaxed non-doing. Moments when time stretched and the worries of the day evaporated. Use these ideas to inspire your moments of simply being.

*One day I had the children take out the class yoga mats onto the grass. We simply looked up at the clouds and watched the sky. We listened to the birds. No one spoke a sound. The children said it was the best day ever. I was worried that we might not get to math and then I just let go and relaxed. It was good for me too.* —Teacher

## What Blocks Connection

Can you guess the number one thing children say blocks their connection with others?

The cell phone!

I can be guilty of that one. When I hear a certain ring, I jump like a Pavlovian dog. The kids also said they were challenged in the following scenarios:

"When my younger brother or sister gets all the attention and they think I don't need as much."

"When my dad travels away for work and I don't see him for months, it is hard to really feel he loves me."

"When my parents fight, I don't feel connected to anyone."

"My mom acts like she is there but she is doing something when I try to be with her and I don't think she is really listening."

"I have so many activities. We go from one thing to another and we don't have time to just relax."

"My parents are just busy. We don't have time."

"The computer takes my parents away."

Remember, when reading these scenarios, to be self-compassionate. We are not present to our children all of the time. It doesn't work like that. But by making an effort to have moments that fold into more moments, we build a quality of presence and connection that enables our children to participate in life with an awakened heart.

## Teacher Pressure

I know as a teacher there are many pressures to "get through" the curriculum. I also know that some of my best teaching moments are when I allow the children to really stretch out into their creativeness, when I give the kids hours to develop ideas and access their deepest creativity. If I can slow down enough to allow the children to really see, smell, and feel their environments, they settle down and open up to learning. Try for a minute, an hour, or a day to slow down and just let go of outcomes. You will see how a lesson I shared about Fairy and Leaf people morphed into a month-long unit. It was a celebrated and rich learning time. Let the children be who they are without the pressure to finish or get anywhere. Let go of outcome and open to the unknown; simply be present to what is right before you.

I have included some of the absolute best moments that facilitated a quality of presence with my own children that we still remember twenty years later. Times when we made tea from garden plants, looked at the starry skies, and spent time in the forest. Time to simply be.

## Lesson 1: Come Play

You can discover more about a person in an hour of play than in a year of conversation.—Plato

### Builds strengths of
- Play
- Self-expression
- Friendship
- Natural endorphin release
- Connection
- Loving others
- Simply being
- Collaboration

### Materials
- Various depending on activity

### Ages
- Newborn to adult

### School Curriculum Connections
- Oral language
- Listening skills
- Reading
- Social studies
- Science
- Physical education
- Fine arts
- Social and emotional learning

*Men (and women) do not quit playing because they grow old; they grow old because they quit playing.*—Oliver Wendell Holmes, Jr.

### Home and School Practice

Many adults have come to me telling me they love the sense of playfulness I embody. I have never really been sure what that meant as I didn't know I was different from anyone else. Although I must admit I would be at "boring" meetings or gatherings wondering to myself, "When can we play?"

I once met a woman who had grown up in a very conservative house. She said she rarely played and would get into trouble if she created disorder. She was at a workshop I was part of and as she walked by I asked her if she would like one of the children's stickers I had brought to decorate my journal. I told her she could use it in her journal or wear it on her body. She was so tickled to get the sticker. She tucked it deep inside her shoe and said she would look at it every day to evoke a sense of play. She wasn't ready to wear it on the outside yet—that was far too bold. A year later she sent me a message saying she still had the sticker and she was playing a little bit more.

I spend most of my time with children and a playful puppy. Before I began teaching school, I was a lifeguard, so I have never really done a job that had any shortage of fun. I have the pleasure of teaching young children that exude play all day long. Even if I only keep up with one tenth of it, I am in joy. My students and my own sons just expect me to join in. I must admit, jumping with skipping ropes on hard pavement last week left my hip joints ready for the massage therapist, but here are some ideas to connect with your child and play again.

### Ten Ways to Play Again

#### 1. Blow

Simply blow bubbles or dandelions. (Only in wild fields; the neighbors won't appreciate this dandelion play.) Watch them float off into the sky. Get the big wands and create giant bubbles as you walk down the road and watch smiles abound.

## 2. Body Paint

Get a set of tempera paints, body paint, and stickers and create washable tattoos on your family and friends. People love painting each other, and even a simple heart drawn with care is a blessing on the face or arms. I used to set up a full-length mirror outside for my boys and give them a set of paint and brushes. They would paint their entire bodies and then run in the sprinkler. (Getting any ideas yet?)

## 3. Get On Down

Get down, if you can, and play with your pet. How could you not play with this little guy?

## 4. Feed The Unseen

Walk in nature and feed the fairies. Children love this one. I used to take my sons with little bags of nuts and raisins and they would look for tiny castles in trees that fairies lived in. They would put little gifts inside the trees and show me how to look more deeply at the beauty of nature that I was often rushing past and missing.

## 5. Get Down Further

Play Lego or create with Kiva blocks. We have had hours of fun building scenes from our minds, interacting, agreeing, disagreeing, and creating with these wonderful tools. My boys and my students would want me playing every minute, so I try to be fully present once a week to a long game.

## 6. Junk

Get a bunch of old wheels, wood, nails, and hammers and go at it. Build something just for fun. Children love this idea. This is a photo from a day that I put a huge tub of things out for our grade sixes and sevens. We had a few parents come in with saws, drills, and tools. They worked steadily for several hours and made all sorts of toys and mobile skateboards to take home.

### 7. Old Ideas Are New

Get out the old badminton, croquet, or lawn bowls. Why did we put them away? What fun!

### 8. Chalk It Up

Get some sidewalk chalk and draw. Give a piece to all your friends and children. Draw huge, draw small, write words. Ask permission and draw all over each other's drawings, adding and changing. Draw hopscotch and jump. It all washes off in the rain and you can start fresh again.

### 9. Collect Something.

Get a bag and go for a walk. I live by the beach, so we go looking for beach glass or rocks with rings on them or flowers for an edible salad. Whatever you like. It has you running, seeing, and enjoying in a different way.

### 10. Fight (with Water)

The easiest way to really play quickly is to find a group of friends or kids and set up a water fight! In playing with water you will instantly find your playful players and break the ice. I once went to the store at a retreat where we were getting very heavily into emotion and bought a set of water guns. In loving-kindness we shot at everyone, laughing until we were rolling on the grass.

**Bonus:** During play there is a huge release of endorphins, creating a feeling of connection and joy. Play can build capacities like problem-solving, persistence, and collaboration that we draw on throughout our lives.

## *Home Practice*

### Looking for the Good (for Bedtime)

James suggests a practice in *Awakening Joy* that is perfect for children. Look for the good. When you settle in at night after story time, think of different people you met throughout the day and look for the good in each one. Your child might say, "Sara Jane helped me on the playground when I fell down" or, "Peter helped me spell a word."

Notice how you feel when you do this practice. Talk about it while you play "Looking for the Good."

## Take Time to Play

Start small; even just walking outside with bare feet or singing aloud can begin to evoke a playful awareness—it is good for you and all those around you. Be gentle with yourself. This may be a new experience for you.

### *Resources*

#### ADULT BOOKS

Chris Biffle. *Whole Brain Teaching: 122 Amazing Games!: Challenging Kids, Classroom Management, Writing, Reading, Math, Common Core/State Tests.* Charleston SC: CreateSpace Independent Publishing Platform, 2015.

Stuart Brown and Christopher Vaughan. *Play: How it Shapes the Brain, Opens the Imagination, and Invigorates the Soul.* New Hyde Park, NY: Avery, 2010.

Garry L. Landreth. *Play Therapy: The Art of the Relationship.* New York: Routeldge, 2012.

#### CHILDREN'S BOOKS

Bobbi Conner. *Unplugged Play: No Batteries. No Plugs. Pure Fun.* New York: Workman Publishing, 2007.

Carmela LaVigna Coyle and Mike Gordon. *Do Princesses Scrape Their Knees?* New York: Copper Square Publishing, 2006.

Jane Drake and Ann Love *The Kids Campfire Book: Official Book of Campfire Fun.* Toronto: Kids Can Press, 1997.

Marilyn Singer and LeUyen Pham. *A Stick Is an Excellent Thing: Poems Celebrating Outdoor Play.* New York: Clarion Books, 2012.

Debra Wise. *Great Big Book of Children's Games: Over 450 Indoor & Outdoor Games for Kids, Ages 3-14.* Colombus, OH: McGraw-Hill Education, 2003.

#  Lesson 2: Fairy Garden and the Leaf People

We've all experienced those precious moments when we just relax for a minute, stop all our doing and simply allow life to move through us. That state is profound and can be consciously cultivated.

## Builds strengths of:

- Self-awareness
- Biodiversity
- Timelessness
- Awareness of the natural world
- Cooperation
- Presence in the moment

## Materials

- Natural materials such as sticks, shells, rocks, feathers, and twine
- The outdoors

## Ages

- Preschool to twelve years

## School Curriculum Connections

- Oral language
- Written language
- Listening skills
- Reading
- Science
- Physical education
- Fine arts
- Social and emotional learning

## *Home and School Practice*

This outdoor activity can easily be done at home or at school. All you need is a green space; a miniature garden or even a lone tree would work.

The smallest patch of the forest is rich with life, presence, and a deep running pulse that is often overlooked. On the school grounds we have a tiny lot of evergreen forest about sixty-five feet from the school. This green space covers a patch of land about as big as a classroom. We are also lucky enough to be steps from a huge forest and the shores of the Pacific Ocean.

In this lesson, I wanted the children to

experience a time and place engrained in my own senses growing up as a child in the Pacific Northwest. I literally spent half my childhood in the forest. The smell of earth, the cedars and hemlocks with an underskirt of salal were part of my daily landscape. It helped to ground and calm me.

## The Invitation

I invited the children to bring special items from their own yards and bedrooms that were gathered from nature. Big and little bags of sticks, shells, leather, stones, and greenery came through the door.

No plastics, glues, or man-made materials were to be a part of the project. I provided twine for binding items. Before entering the forest, I showed them many photos of tiny fairy furniture, houses, and dwellings. A group of children said they wanted to make leaf-people houses, not fairy dwellings, so of course I said yes and off they went.

In small groups I let them loose onto the forest floor. It was utterly amazing watching what evolved over a period of minutes, then hours, then days. I literally could not stop them.

The children found tiny holes, berries, feathers, flowers, twigs, and natural material and built ladders, chairs, tables, and beds with all sorts of additions to their fairy homes. Astounding, to me, was the deep reverence they had for the forest and the lands they created.

## Story Writing

Even more astounding were the stories that arose. The children were literally bursting with imagined life. I asked them if they would like to write these stories and all hands reached for the sky. Hours and days later the children said it was like no other writing assignment they had done before. I had some very reluctant writers begging to stay in at recess and lunch to write. They literally lived the experiences inside their minds. Many children invited their parents to come to the school on weekends and play in the lands of the fairies. Time slowed down, colors became brilliant, and the world became magical. We just stretched out into it letting go of all agendas.

In this fast-paced world often so removed from nature, children can reengage their senses and connect with their love of Mother Earth.

What this practice really needs is time and a sense of wonder and play. Lie with your child or children on the land and let the building of a mythical land unfold. Let there be no agenda in mind.

My group of children learned to work together, negotiate, compromise, and had a deep experience of timelessness. One of the greatest acts of service to Mother Earth is to enjoy her beauty. Children exposed to the natural world protect it and view it with a sacred heart.

## Resources

### ADULT BOOKS

Maureen Heffernan. *Fairy Houses of the Maine Coast*. Rockport, ME: Down East Books, 2010.

Richard Louv. *Last Child in the Woods: Saving Our Children from Nature-Deficit Disorder*. Chapel Hill, NC: Algonquin Books, 2008.

Richard Louv. *The Nature Principle: Reconnecting with Life in a Virtual Age*. Chapel Hill, NC: Algonquin Books, 2012.

Debbie Schramer and Mike Schramer. *Fairy House: How to Make Amazing Fairy Furniture, Miniatures, and More from Natural Material*. Sanger, CA: Familius, 2015.

Jennifer Ward and Richard Louv. *I Love Dirt!: 52 Activities to Help You and Your Kids Discover the Wonders of Nature*. Sedro Woolley, WA: Rost Books, 2008.

### CHILDREN'S BOOKS

Sarah C. Campbell and Richard P. Campbell. *Growing Patterns: Fibonacci Numbers in Nature*. Honesdale, PA: Boyds Mills Press, 2010.

Tracy Kane. *Fairy Houses (The Fairy Houses Series)*. Lee, NH: Light Beams Publishing, 2001.

Tracy Kane and Barry Kane. *Fairy Houses Everywhere! (The Fairy Houses Series)*. Lee, NH: Light Beams Publishing, 2006.

Joyce Sidman and Beth Krommes. *Swirl by Swirl: Spirals in Nature*. Boston, MA: Houghton Mifflin Harcourt Books for Young Readers, 2011.

# Lesson 3: Mindful Tea

## Creating Connection and Compassion for Mother Earth
*And you don't have to have a green thumb!*

Mindfulness is simply being aware of what is happening right now without wishing it were different; enjoying the pleasant without holding on when it changes (which it will); being with the unpleasant without fearing it will always be this way (which it won't).

### Builds strengths of:
- Sharing
- Connection to our Earth and food
- Creating healthy food choices
- Simplicity
- Celebration
- Ceremony

### Materials
- Teapot
- Teacups
- Various herbs from home or the market
- You might enjoy a plant identification book

### Ages
- Preschool to adult

### School Curriculum Connections
- Oral language
- Written language
- Listening skills
- Science
- Physical education
- Social and emotional learning

### *Home Practice*

### The Children Build
One of the most complex yet simple celebratory activities I have done at home or at school is the making of garden tea. It incorporates so many principles of mindful living, sustainability, plant cycles, and stewardship of the earth.

From the time my boys were very small, they each had their own garden. We hammered a few boards together filling the tiny plot with soil, seaweed, and compost. When we did not have space available, we would have small pots in the house ready for seeds. The boys would carefully decide what they wanted in their garden and begin planting.

## Wishing Rocks and Planting

The process of planting seeds started with tiny wishing rocks under each plant. The boys would gather special rocks from the beach and lug them up the road tucked in their little pockets or backpacks. We would look at each rock and decide where it might go in the garden. Saying a blessing as we tucked the little rock under a seed started the plant on its way. Even when they could not see any signs of life they knew the earth was holding their wishes.

## After a Few Weeks

Footsteps could be heard racing across the land. "Mum, there is a little green showing! Dad, come see!" Over time, days and weeks, the plants would grow. We would check on them from day to day. The children learned the cycles of life. They learned that life takes time to unfold. Each day as we waited for their gardens to sprout, the boys would comb the bigger garden for bits of mint, fennel, raspberry leaves, and lavender tips.

## Put the Kettle On

I taught the children which plants made tea and which ones not to use. We used their grandma's teapot. Filling the pot with boiled water, a little honey, and the herbs, I felt such a deep connection to her and her love of the garden. The lads would race to get out their special cups and the tea would brew as we chatted. To this day, earth tea is a family favorite. They don't go gathering the plants as much but if a pot is on the table, it is enjoyed.

## Simply Be

This simple, easy practice connects children to the "Joy of Simply Being." Enjoying the rays of sun, the sprinkle of rain, or watching clouds pass over the sky while awaiting the wonders of the earth. So many children only have the experience of tea from a sterile sealed bag. Why not plant a few seeds and see what joy your family can experience. Appreciate what is right in front of you and open to the incredible richness, stillness, and complexity of life in the moment. Create a life-enhancing daily ritual that is easy to do, and give it your full attention, allowing yourself to fully inhabit the moment. What do you get from this daily touchstone for your personal well-being?

## School Practice

### School Garden

The children absolutely love this practice of garden tea. I can hardly keep them out of the school plot we created. Every morning there is a story from

the garden, which has created some amazing topics for oral and written language work. I am absolutely amazed how quickly they spot a strawberry growing and even with almost 200 children, no one picks it until it is ready and the ones who plant decide how the harvest will be shared! Children who have never had their hands dirty are picking up worms, beetles, and critters and gently placing them in parts of the plot to nourish the soil. They learn that all creatures are valuable and they learn to be kind.

### Grab the Urn

On special occasions, I have a huge urn of hot water steaming in the classroom and children bring in a favorite cup. We invite anyone passing by for a taste of our tea. The children are incredibly proud of the tea and many parents come in asking how we made it. Children want to plant their own herbs. The kids learn the properties of various plants, their medicinal usage, and how to grow and cultivate seeds.

## Grow Lights in The Classroom: Woo Hoo

This year to get a jump-start, our school purchased a grow light kit for every classroom. Seedlings are started and even during the dreary rainy days in British Columbia, children see the wonders of nature sprouting forth.

Some of the books we have so enjoyed that pair so beautifully with gardening with children in this simple way are listed in the resources below.

### *Resources*

#### ADULT BOOKS

Thich Nhat Hanh. *How to Eat*. Berkeley, CA: Parallax Press, 2014.

Thich Nhat Hanh and Melvin McLeod. *Your True Home: The Everyday Wisdom of Thich Nhat Hanh: 365 days of practical, powerful teachings from the beloved Zen teacher*. Boulder, CO: Shambhala, 2011.

#### CHILDREN'S BOOKS

Eric Carle. *The Tiny Seed*. New York: Simon & Schuster, 1991.

Henry Cole. *Jack's Garden*. New York: Greenwillow, 1997.

Joanna Cole and Bruce Degen. *The Magic School Bus Plants Seeds: A Book About How Living Things Grow*. St. Louis, MO: Turtleback Books, 1995.

Lois Ehlert. *Planting a Rainbow*. New York: Houghton Mifflin Harcourt Books for Young Readers, 2001.

# Lesson 4: Full Moon Nights

Even though compassion is a response to suffering, it is not draining. Rather, it is uplifting because it activates the feeling of caring, which is a noble quality of the heart.

## Builds strengths of:
- Self-awareness
- Interconnectedness of life
- Awareness of others
- Well-being
- Develops a vocabulary of needs
- Family visioning or goal-setting

## Materials
- A place to sleep outside
- Some sort of bed to lay down on
- Hats and warm rocks if you live in a cold place
- Crystal bowl
- Giggles and willingness

## Ages
- Preschool to adult

## School Curriculum Connections
- Oral language
- Listening skills
- Reading
- Science
- Fine arts
- Social and emotional learning

## Home Practice

When my boys were very small, we put a futon bed out on the covered deck and we would lie outside and watch the stars. I set an intention with the boys to sleep out under the stars on every full moon. British Columbia, Canada, can be very cold outside at night so on winter nights we would put rocks that had been heated on the fireplace deep inside the covers to warm the bed. Then we would tuck woolen hats and blankets around us and climb into our little nest. The boys' dad preferred to stay inside so we would bid him goodnight and watch the evening fall. We placed a crystal bowl that my mum as a young immigrant had brought from Australia on the railing of the deck. We filled it with water and a few special things that we wanted the full moon to cleanse and caress. The boys would search their rooms to place a few special things in the bowl too. They would scamper outside with Lego bits, stones, and silver jewelry to add to the bowl. My parents had passed away before my boys were born so this was a way to connect with them as well as share ancestral stories

with the boys. We took the time to talk about our best, our funniest, and our most challenging moments of the day and week. We would share our hearts as tears and laughter flowed. These moments built the groundwork of a compassionate heart and a deep family connection.

As it became dusk, bats would fly and we would wait for the first stars to shine. I would have a set of binoculars by us so we could look at the night sky. The three of us snuggled up, swearing high and low we would do this forever. Somewhere along the way, the bed got too small, the boys grew over six foot four, and had other things to do, so we let it go. Now the boys are young men, they still remember those times so fondly. I as their mama smile deep inside so happy to have created this practice of Full Moon Nights.

Dacher Keltner, a renowned professor at Stanford University in *Born To Be Good*, shares:

> *Recent scientific studies are identifying the kinds of environments that cultivate compassion. This moral emotion is cultivated in environments where parents are responsive, and play and touch their children. So does an empathic style that prompts the children to reason about harm. So do chores, as well as the presence of grandparents. Making compassion a motif in dinnertime conversation and bedtime stories cultivates this all-important emotion.*

So drag out the mattress, switch off the lights, and play a little. Sleeping outside brings us an intimate connection with the outside world. It can connect us to the planets and stars. Animals that chat in the night are heard and spoken of. You are building compassion and a boxful of memories. Both of my boys to this day love sleeping outside. One just returned from snow camping. I like to think it started with our Full Moon Nights.

## Resources

### ADULT BOOKS

Thich Nhat Hanh. *A Handful of Quiet: Happiness in Four Pebbles*. Berkeley, CA: Plum Blossom Books, 2012.

Rick Hanson and Jan Hanson. *Mother Nurture: A Mother's Guide to Health in Body, Mind, and Intimate Relationships*. New York: Penguin Paperbacks, 2002.

Starhawk. *Circle Round: Raising Children in the Goddess Tradition*. New York: Bantam, 1998.

### CHILDREN'S BOOKS

Barbara Helen Berger. *Grandfather Twilight*. New York: Puffin Books, 1996.

Sam McBratney and Anita Jeram. *Guess How Much I Love You*. Somerville, MA: Candlewick, 2008.

Robert Munsch and Sheila McGraw. *Love You Forever*. Richmond Hill, ON: Firefly Books, 1995.

# Teachers' Guide

## Integrating the Practices and Lessons Seamlessly into the School Day

> *"To be a teacher means that we take our turn standing in our life as full as possible, so we might reflect what matters and be bright enough for those nearby to find their way. If practice can lead us here, we will not want for sanity or company."*—Mark Nepo

Always keep your parent group well informed. Invite them into the classroom on a casual basis or have a parent night and invite parents to participate in some relaxation practices. Let them know you are offering students strategies to calm their minds, focus their attention, and become more aware of themselves, others, and their environment.

## What Your Day Might Look Like as a Teacher Using the Awakening Joy Practices

### Create the Container

Invite children into the practices. The practices are a gift and an offering. If anyone does not want to partake, please honor his or her decision. Ask them to quietly sit and relax while allowing the other children to have a quiet space to practice.

### It's as Simple as Baking a Cake

It really is very simple. You are doing what you do so wonderfully already; now you are adding in an overlay that will reap benefits tenfold. Set a series of times for yourself and the children to center yourselves and self-regulate. No pressure; just practice over time.

The children will probably remind you if you miss the practices, as they come to love them. You will notice that you will miss the practices when the energy is very high and you are exhausted.

## The Structure of the Day Is Somewhat Like Baking a Cake

I chose the metaphor of baking a cake so if you get lost and forget the structure of a day it will be easy to find your way. You can copy the instructions below and clip them in your daybook, moving the outline from day to day. You may want to copy down the steps in your day plan to ensure that you practice the target areas. Once you feel confident in the structure of the container you might let it go and find that the steps become part of your day quite naturally. Until that time have pictures of delicious cakes around the room to trigger your memory and remind you it really is as easy as baking a cake.

1. Gather the students—Get the things you need to bake.
2. Read the emotions of the group—Read the recipe book.
3. Take a breath—Get settled and choose a recipe to focus on.
4. Set intention—Think of how wonderful it will turn out.
5. Choose a practice—Bake the cake.
6. Breathe in and appreciate the result in gratitude—Eat and enjoy.
7. Gratitude practice—Take the cake home and give a lovely extra piece to a friend.

Repeat day after day ... until it becomes natural and part of you.

## 1. Gather In

Five to ten minutes. (These minutes will reap innumerable benefits. This will help the children to let go of home, and make the transition to come into the room to the here and now.) Children can all sit together on the floor or stay at their desks. If I have a really squirmy group I tend to bring them to a circle on the floor. The older kids seem to prefer their desks. Once they are gathered

and you have read the emotions of the group (see below) you can choose a short practice.

## 2. Read the emotions of the group and choose one of the following short, quick practices

**Body weather:** In this practice I have the children check in with themselves and tell the group what weather conditions they are. If they had a fight with a sibling or could not find the clothes they wanted to wear, they might say they were thundershowers with lightning and pending rain. If they had the best morning, they might say they are sunny with rainbows. I find this an amazing practice, as often when I look at the children I am completely wrong about what is going on inside of them.

**If I were a color:** I would be _____ today. This practice allows the children to describe color and feelings. They might be yellow with spots of black to describe sunshine and some sad moments. Pairing color with feeling just gives them one more way to describe the climate inside of their bodies.

**If I were an animal:** I would be _____ today. This practice is self-explanatory yet the children love it. We talk about the different characteristics of various animals. Often times they say they are soft like a bunny and needing tenderness today. Many of my active children describe being in monkey mode and needing to play.

**Leave Behind:** One thing I am leaving behind today is _____ and one thing I am bringing in is _____ .

This allows the children to let go of what they might have been involved in before school. They verbally acknowledge to the group what is bothering them. If I notice it is a big issue I might come back to it later or speak privately to a child.

## 3. Take a breath

One to five minutes. These can be very short to regulate the brain and move children into learning mode.

**How to set it up:** I usually gather the younger children in the carpet space in a circle so we can see each other and acknowledge all the voices in the group. In the intermediate classrooms there is not generally the space to gather, so we sit at our desks. The first time we gather, I tell the children that what we are learning is science. We will be regulating our brains and emotions. I simply ask the children to be respectful of each other and either close their eyes or look at their hands. I often find children look around for the first few sessions to see what others are doing and then settle in after that. When I am guiding the practice, I start with my own eyes closed and then open them to see where to guide the class. If a child is having difficulties with settling, I might directly address him, mindfully saying, "Settle in, let your brain relax. Try to do your best to just let go of your thoughts.... You may be wondering when this will be over. I will guide you."

**What to expect:** After many, many years of guiding mindfulness sessions, I find the children take it very seriously and yet hold it lightly. Sometimes in large classes with behavior challenges, I have to ask a person to leave, as they are not holding the group intention for respect and quiet. I check in with the child later and we talk about what held them back or what was difficult that day. They are always invited back to start again. Generally, the children love this time so they will participate and not cause disruption. You will have to assess your own group. Just keep doing the practice and stay with it. Slowly over time, they will come to know what to expect and how to do it. I also do a practice called "Monkey Mind," which I modified for this book as "Puppy Meditation." I tell the children that when I was in Southeast Asia, many monkeys were often frantically running all over the place. The monkeys are like our minds bouncing all over, thought to thought. How do we calm the monkey? We get calm ourselves and settle our own breathing and invite the monkey to our lap. When the monkey feels safe it might settle. You can substitute a dog or cat for the monkey if you wish. The children, after the session, will describe their monkey. "Mine was very settled today!" "Mine was all over the place." Just focusing on the monkey itself calms the mind.

## 4. Set intention for the day

Setting an intention for the day allows students to mindfully connect with what is meaningful for them. It also guides the brain to look for an experience, seek it out, and bring gratitude. I ask the students to be fairly general with their

CHOOSE A PRACTICE

intentions. The intention might be, "I want to experience play today." "I want to experience quality time with my friends today." "I want to learn something new."

**Circle format:** Bring the whole group into a standing or sitting circle and begin. This can be a quick and easy way to share the whole class intention.

**Write it at the top of a page:** Get the intention in writing and it is magnified. Keeping a log of our intentions is a powerful way of seeing what is important to us in the world.

**Write in chalk on the cement:** Okay, we love being outside and we have access to lots of chalk and abundant rain. It is easy to write one day and it is washed away by the next.

**Tell a friend:** Loving to pair up, students can share their hearts with a friend. Check in at the end of the day and see if and how the intentions unfolded.

**Choose one of the larger practices:** Choose one of the larger practices in the book or expand on a current practice.

## 5. Choose a breathing practice

Three to five minutes. I do the central breathing practice for a few minutes. You might start with one minute and build up. I have had classes request longer periods of up to twenty minutes. The breathing practice is central; this is the main one you will come to know. Have the children simply find

their breath in their bodies. You might want to say: "Find your breath. See if you can feel the gentle rise and fall of your tummy. You may get lost in thoughts. That's okay. Just come back to your breath. Come back."

Or you can choose one of the following breathing practices.

**Stuffy breathing:** Children can bring in their favorite stuffy or you have a basket of stuffies ready in the classroom. They lie down or sit up with their stuffy on their tummy gently feeling the rise and fall of the animal as their breath moves through their bodies.

**Bunny breathing:** This is soft and gentle. I have the children imagine they are bunnies and breathe very slowly and softly through their noses feeling the air pass through their nostrils. They love this practice.

You might even draw little whiskers on them with an eyebrow pencil.

**Animal breathing:** This one can be tricky if they want to pick a large animal. I generally ask them to pick a quiet animal that does not want to be heard. How might they breathe? The children can share how they imagine the different ways the animals breathe.

**Mindful smelling:** Before doing this, check for allergies! This practice can be done inside or outside. The children focus on their sense of smell, totally taking in what they sense through their nostrils. They can close their eyes or put on a little blindfold before smelling. The kids might sniff certain items in the classroom like the pencil sharpener, compost bucket, or the crayon bin while trying to guess what each item is. I also set up an essential oil sniff. The children close their eyes and I wave a bottle of orange, spearmint, or lavender under their nostrils. I also have little tissues on their desks and put one drop on the tissue. They sit quietly and breathe. This slow breathing can deepen and extend the practice. If we choose to go outside we smell Mother Earth, the herbs in our school garden, or the air as each day it is different.

**Mindful seeing:** Pick a color, texture, or subject to focus on for this mindful experience. Again, I love to be outside every day for a few minutes so we put on our coats and go out to look. Another mindful seeing practice I gleaned from a workshop is to have students choose a rock from a pile you bring in. I gather rocks that are pretty much the same color and size. The kids then see if they can look very, very carefully at their own rock noticing any dents, scratches, or color differences. They then meet up with three other students and put the rocks into the center of the desks and try to find their own. After they can do that, I have them pair up with another group and try to find their rock in a group of eight. Finally, we put all the rocks of the entire classroom group into the center and try to find our rocks. This takes concentration, but the children can easily describe their rocks by this time and have been mindfully seeing for more than five minutes.

**Mindful listening:** This is one I fall back to very often, as there is always noise in the hallways and the surrounding areas of the school. I start by having the children try to hear the ticking of the clock in our room. The clock is pretty quiet, so they have to listen very hard. I then expand their awareness to take in the classroom itself. I ask that as best they can, they try not to make any noise so we can hear even further. I then ask them to expand out to the classrooms beside us and finally to the whole school. After sitting listening to the sounds of the school, I gently bring their attention back to their own breathing. Usually by this time the children are settled and ready to begin the next activity.

**Mindful tasting:** Have an extra bag of raisins or grapes at home? Mindful tasting is a wonderful way to slow down and become aware of what goes into our mouths.

This is what I say: Look at your item as if you have never seen it before. Smell your item. Put your item on your skin and feel it. Gently bring your item to your lips but don't eat it. Place your item in your mouth. Roll it around. Put it between your back molars. Now you can eat your item. Report back to the group.

**Attention to thoughts or labeling:** Just watching our own thoughts and labeling them as either a thought, feeling, memory, or worry, etc., helps to let them go without attaching to them. Have the children sit for one minute only and just watch their thoughts while coming back to their breath. Label gently and let go.

**Counting:** Counting the breath is a lovely way of slowing the mind. Breathe in one, breathe out one; breathe in two, breathe out two, and on you go.

## Mindful Movement:

**Yoga or stretching:** Have you seen the yoga cards that have the poses on them? Children can pick poses and practice one for the full mindfulness session or you can guide them in a series of poses. I have huge expectations for my yoga classes, as they can quickly get silly and out of control, thus throwing mindfulness out the window. I have led groups of over ninety at a time, but I suggest small groups for maximum effectiveness.

**Circle walking:** This is one of the practices I have adapted from *qi gong*. The children arrange themselves in a large circle, one behind another, with three chairs in the middle back to back. I put on some music and we begin walking in a circle. The idea is to give the person ahead enough space to walk and not to pass or touch them. Students need to be mindful, and walk behind the person in front. I set the pace and ask them to simply walk with their hands on their tummies. The energy of the circle builds as we go round and round. Generally, the circle will be about eight feet across. When someone gets tired or just wants to feel the circle energy, they can sit on one of the three chairs. They cannot race to the chairs but only walk mindfully when a chair is open. Set your times for about seven minutes and then change direction. At the end of the fourteen minutes ask the children how they felt while walking. My students absolutely love this, and ask to do it often.

**Guided journey:** There are many on the web and on my website (happinessandjoylessons.com) you can play. One that my students have loved, which you can read aloud (Magical Cave) is on page 59 in this book.

## 6. Breathe in and appreciate the result

At the end of the day, do a short central breathing practice. You have seen it before and you will see it again. Breathe, breathe, and breathe.

## 7. Gratitude practice

**Out the door:** One thing you liked about the day. This is one of my favorite parts of the day, as I am often surprised by what the children deem as their favorite parts of the day. It is amazing feedback and a great way to connect before they leave for the day.

If there has been any disconnect, you have a chance to check in before they board the busses or hop on their bikes. I simply ask:

"Tell me one thing you liked about the day."

**Pass the stone:** Name one thing you are grateful for. I have several special stones that we use for this practice. They are kept by my mindfulness bell and are used for this time exclusively. Children are also invited to bring a stone in and that special stone can be used that day and taken home. In this way they have their own "CHARGED" gratefulness stone.

**Sparkles:** See chapter eight on Loving Others for this special practice. It is absolutely the favorite of the week.

**Write it:** Write down one thing and share it with your family. I have a home see book that goes home each night for parents to see what has been happening in the classroom. It might include math sheets, spelling words, notes about the week or a little note from their child describing something they loved about their day. This pulls parents into the room who are unable to spend time with us and they feel connected and open to ask questions.

## Take it out to the world:

1. Share one thing with your parents, a friend, or your family.
2. Do one random act of kindness.
3. Breathe.
4. Do one thing mindfully and report back.

OUT TO THE WORLD

# Conclusion

THERE ISN'T ONE! How absolutely delightful this is when you really think about it.

There is no conclusion.

New moments spring up again and again and again, magically, and we meet them. We get to experience afresh the fullness of being human every day. No day or moment is ever the same. The question is, really, how do we meet these moments?

We get into our habitual activities, but we pause and remember. We can go through long periods of time and forget what really matters to us: being alive, in gratitude, sharing love. So we can remember what we treasure. We can become more aligned with our hearts.

Practice and strengthen your Awakening Joy muscles every day. Remember, nourishing yourself is nourishing your family or your classroom. When you fill yourself with well-being, it naturally spills over to the world around you. That is why we wrote this book with tandem practices for parents, teachers, and children. We want you to be well and happy! Peaceful and at ease! When you are at peace, your loved ones will benefit. As our wise friend Rosemary said at the age of ninety-five: Be radical and love yourself. We can take these words and give them a try. Wake up in the morning and ask yourself what act of self-love you can do today. Make it a game. Make it playful and joyful.

Pick a section in this book or work through it in stages. Keep returning to these foundational practices, and at those times when all else seems out of reach, simply take a moment to feel your body's sensations and breathe. This will start to become natural over time and the strength you'll gain from this practice will serve you when your battery is low.

When you are with your children, imagine looking through the lens of *Awakening Joy*. See each situation as an opportunity to practice. Ask yourself how you can bring compassion, mindfulness, and gratitude into your daily life and the lives of your children. For example, when you are at the grocery store and your child is getting agitated, you might ask them then to look for something, for example, purple objects that are purple. Each time they see a purple object, they can take a breath in for three counts and out for four.

After a while, such games will become part of your family's ongoing process of discovering the world in a different way. Your children will become pioneers of fresh ideas and ways of seeing. What an incredibly dynamic lens mindfulness is. What could really be better? There is never a *boring* moment, only new experiences to meet.

As parents, we can also slow down and just be present to what is happening. Be self-compassionate when you fall down. Cherish and celebrate yourself when you feel good.

Your mantra can be: *slow down, breathe, change lenses, and find self-compassion.* Write it on the fridge, write it on your mirror, and record it on your phone for those moments when it all seems too much. Then come back and do what you know works to center yourself again and begin afresh. There are no mistakes, just miss-takes, and then a chance to learn and try again.

These lessons are not written in stone in any way. They are fluid. Your child and your family are unique. You get to see what works on any given day. You watch over time to see the changes. When things are difficult, change your direction.

If you are a teacher in the classroom, start with adding one or two little practices in a day. Get the students involved and new ideas and lessons will arrive with each unique and special group that comes to you. Invite the students to design lessons based on the ten steps. What could be better than lessons on gratitude, serving others, and creating community?

To give you an idea why we didn't write a prescriptive book, we know after teaching countless groups that the exact same lesson, given on the exact same day to two different groups of children can land totally differently. We are dynamic beings. And if you are reading this book and are trying these practices, thank you: you are one of the lively human beings who is open to change.

We encourage you to dive in to develop your own ideas, to use our ideas as anchors when you need them, and most of all to have fun. Bring joy to your family and to your own heart. Share your ideas with others. As the principles of gratitude, kindness, and meeting difficult times with compassion awaken in our own hearts they effortlessly ripple out and grow into the consciousness of others. Nothing is ever put out into an abyss. You are the pioneers planting the seeds of the future. Trust yourself. Let go of striving to do more, and just be present. Take a breath, feel your body, notice the sounds and sensations that are right here, notice the alert inner presence in the background listening and watching, and step into your day ahead.

And with great gratitude, as much gratitude as there are stars in the night sky, we give thanks.

—James and Michele

# Acknowledgments

### James

First, I'd like to express my deep appreciation to Michele. She brilliantly turned the *Awakening Joy* material into lessons that transformed the principles into an embodied experience for children. And I also want to thank her for encouraging us to co-write this book as an offering that so many more can benefit from. What a pleasure it's been to work with this beautiful being who exudes such creativity and goodness! Thank you.

Deep bows to Michele's partner, Peter, for all the support he gave in tirelessly converting all of our material into the format that we needed.

I'm grateful to Rachel Neumann and the team at Parallax Press for enthusiastically embracing the project from the very beginning.

I want to acknowledge Shoshana Alexander, my coauthor on *Awakening Joy*, for helping create a book that touched Michele and encouraged so many to bring more joy into their lives. Shoshana's gifts transformed a book with good material into something special.

Thanks to my sons, Tony and Adam, for helping me experience the love of a parent and for being such inspiring expressions of good-heartedness.

Great gratitude to all the students I was fortunate enough to have in my classes at PS 122Q during my years as a schoolteacher so long ago. You helped bring out something good in me that I didn't know was there.

And finally, my deepest gratitude goes to my wife, Jane Baraz, who's been there through thick and thin as my support, best friend, and life partner for the past thirty-five years. I feel so incredibly blessed to share this journey with you. And it's good to know that, after all this time, I'm still crazy about you.

### Michele

I thank James for jumping in and writing with me and for his unending encouragement and depth of being. What a gift you have given me by sharing your presence. It has been pure joy.

Dr. Rick Hanson for encouraging me to write a book and for publishing my work. To Michele Keane for taking a chance on me. To Robert Gonzales and my '06 group, for sharing the art and practice of Living Compassion.

I offer Peter Francis, my partner, huge hugs for spending endless hours happily editing, encouraging me, and helping to polish the offering, while he could have been out kayaking or running up a mountain.

I would like to sparkle gratitude on my family, friends, colleagues, and my teachers who contributed to this book, to all those who provided support, talked things over, read, wrote, offered comments, allowed me to quote their remarks, take their pictures, and test out lessons and practices.

I thank the children in my classes who with wide-open hearts shared their beauty and authenticity. I thank their parents too!

I would like to thank the wonderful people at Parallax Press: Rachel, Terri, Jason, Terry, and Nancy, for their support in publishing this book.

A special thanks to the amazing teachers and educational assistants at my school who support me and share their own heartfelt teachings everyday. How lucky I am to work with all of you!

To my dear ones whom I call on regularly: Karen, Annie, Evelyne, Jill, Corrie, Monica, Rosemary, Sara Jane, Yoli, Patty, and Victoria. You are my lifelines.

I thank my parents, Dawn and Ralph, who died too young to see this book manifest. I feel your grace and love every day.

To my pup, Teddy Bear, who embodies joy. You bring so much to life just by being you!

To the Sacred Mystery, Grace, Spirit, the Divine.... Thanks for hearing me call.

To all those who bring goodness to the world through their teachings—thank you.

Mother Earth, you are magnificent.

To the boys' dad, Terry, for helping bring these incredible lads into being and for co-parenting all these years.

Finally, my greatest gratitude of all goes to my boys, Kieran and Jaden Lavery. Every day you awaken me to joy. I love you to the stars and back.

**PARALLAX**
**PRESS**

Parallax Press is a nonprofit publisher, founded and inspired by Zen Master Thich Nhat Hanh. We publish books on mindfulness in daily life and are committed to making these teachings accessible to everyone and preserving them for future generations. We do this work to alleviate suffering and contribute to a more just and joyful world.

For a copy of the catalog, please contact:
Parallax Press
P.O. Box 7355
Berkeley, CA 94707
parallax.org

## Related Titles from Parallax Press